THERE'S A
LIGHT
AT THE END OF YOUR TUNNEL

Unless otherwise indicated, all Scripture quotations are taken from the *New King James Version*® (*NKJV*). Copyright © 1982 by Thomas Nelson, Inc. Used by permission. All rights reserved.

Scripture quotations marked (*AMP*) are taken from the Amplified® Bible. Copyright © 1954, 1958, 1962, 1964, 1965, 1987 by The Lockman Foundation. Used by permission. (www.Lockman.org)

Scripture quotations marked (*MEV*) are taken from THE HOLY BIBLE, MODERN ENGLISH VERSION. Copyright© 2014 by Military Bible Association. Published and distributed by Charisma House.

Scripture quotations marked (*NLT*) are taken from the Holy Bible, *New Living Translation*, copyright © 1996, 2004, 2015 by Tyndale House Foundation. Used by permission of Tyndale House Publishers, Inc., Carol Stream, Illinois 60188. All rights reserved.

There's a Light at the End of Your Tunnel

ISBN: 978-1-7370596-1-5
Copyright © 2025 Michael F Clark
Michael Clark Ministries
PO Box 3131
Broken Arrow, OK 74013
Michaelclarkministries.org

Editor: Roni Bagby
Cover and text design: Lisa Moore

Printed in the United States of America. All rights reserved. No portion of this book may be reproduced or transmitted in any form or by any means — electronic, mechanical, photocopy, recording, scanning, or other — except for brief quotations in critical reviews or articles, without the prior written permission of the Publisher.

THERE'S A
LIGHT
AT THE END OF YOUR TUNNEL

Michael F. Clark

DEDICATION

This book is dedicated to every person who is looking for more in life than what life is currently handing to you. I am just like you, and I know what an impact learning to trust God has made in my life. There is more for each of us if we are willing to have hope and hold on to that hope through the hard times.

I talk to people every week who are struggling to receive the blessings God has for them, and I have written this book to help each person see God's character more clearly and recognize the love He has for each of us. Within the pages of this book, I've endeavored to address common issues that I've found people struggling with, and it's my hope that you will find your answer and move from a place where you are struggling and worn out to a place where you are winning and strong.

I am convinced that God is loving, compassionate, merciful and trustworthy. What He desires to hand you is far above whatever circumstances life will ever hand you. Reach for Him and His results. If you stick to it, you will not be disappointed.

Blessings,

Michael F. Clark

CONTENTS

Foreword ix

Acknowledgments xi

Introduction 1

Chapter 1 – There's a Light at the End of Your Tunnel 9

Chapter 2 – How I Came To Find Myself
in the Tunnel of Cancer 21

Chapter 3 – Satan's Lies vs. God's Love .35

Chapter 4 – Focus On What Can See You Through 45

Chapter 5 – Know Who Your Enemy Is and His Tactics 63

Chapter 6 – God Can Help You Even When
Your Enemy Says He Can't .83

Chapter 7 – God Is Willing and Able To Move
in Your Situation 97

Chapter 8 – Understanding Biblical Hope 115

Chapter 9 – Remember You Are Walking in a Miracle 137

Chapter 10 – The Key To Resisting the Devil 163

Chapter 11 – Seagulls and Bad Thoughts 183

Chapter 12 – Jesus' Pattern for Resisting the Devil 197

Chapter 13 – Trusting God When Things Aren't Going
as You Expected 211

Chapter 14 – Strengthening Your Faith To Receive
God's Results 227

Resource: Come Down to the Brook – Topical Scriptures
To Stand On 249

FOREWORD

First, I want to say it is an honor and privilege for me to write this foreword for Mike Clark's new book *There's a Light at the End of Your Tunnel*. I have known Mike for many years, and he has faithfully served as a man of God in our ministry. Not only do I know him as an author, but as a fellow worker and friend in the Kingdom of God. Before I ever speak about his book, I want to express how much I respect him and state that he is among the greatest gifts that God ever sent to our ministry.

As I read Mike's book, I kept feeling the compassion and heart of Jesus toward anyone who has ever been through a difficult time. To be honest, this book *oozes* with a pastoral heart. In it, he transparently refers to difficult moments in his own life. I can personally testify that he faced those moments bravely, he stayed in faith, and embraced the victory that belongs to every believer. Knowing his background and what he has faced made me appreciate this book even more. I promise this is not a book based on theory, but on life experience that has been steadily and victoriously walked out.

While in the midst of any potentially life-shattering ordeal, one is exposed to pounding thoughts, many of which are hurled at the mind from the enemy, and the person under attack must choose either to be rendered inoperative because of those thoughts — or to align himself or herself with the truth of God's Word about the situation. I saw Mike firmly align himself with God's Word and to remain aligned regardless of what doctors said or how he felt. Believe me when I say he has the authority to address this subject and show others the way to align themselves appropriately amidst the trials of life.

In this book, Mike adeptly makes the case that God is willing and able to move your mountains. Against all odds, Mike saw God move a massive mountain in his own life. He states, "One of the hardest things to deal with when you're facing hard times is the struggle that can happen between what you want to believe and what your mind is telling you is believable. It is a place where, in your mind, the pieces don't seem to add up. You can conceive that good things are happening in your situation or be convinced that something beyond the natural can't or won't happen for you."

Mike adds, "Scriptural answers to this ongoing war each of us deal with are presented to help you not only survive during a trial, but to thrive and ultimately make it to the other side of what you are going through — intact and with purpose."

Many people go to pieces when they come under attack and cannot see light at the end of the tunnel. *But there is a light at the end of the tunnel!* And not only does this book ooze with compassion, it is packed with powerful, heart-centered, life-changing principles that will help you identify wrong thinking so that, as Mike says, you can make it to the other side "intact and with purpose."

He also states, "It's my great desire that you can take what you have learned in the pages of this book and make them part of who you are and how you go about life. I know as I've learned them in my own life, they have been instrumental in my making it to the other side of many a 'tunnel' situation, some longer and darker than others. The light at the end of your tunnel is assured when your trust is placed in Jesus. He will meet you where you are to take you to what He has for you, and you will see His salvation."

This book is so good that it took me off guard, and I know that you will feel the same. If you know someone who's facing a challenge, *this is the book you need to give that person.* God will use it to walk many from where they are into the wonderful future that He has planned and prepared for them. This book is like an instrument tooled to help anyone in trouble see that there is light at the end of the tunnel. Make sure you read it all the way to the end, as every page is important.

Rick Renner
Minister, author, broadcaster
Moscow, Russia

ACKNOWLEDGMENTS

I would like to thank Veronica Bagby and Carmela Skierski for their input on my original draft. Ladies, your feedback helped me greatly in organizing the material that became this book, and I am grateful for your time, care, and honesty.

I would also like to thank Kalea Ellison and Pam Grosse for their feedback and encouragement as I worked to complete my final draft. Your belief in me and this material have impacted me greatly, and I am honored to have such treasured friends.

I would like to thank Dr. Craig Johnson, Dr. Scott Cole, and Mackie Sutton APRN-CNP. You each played a pivotal role in guiding me through my battle with cancer, and I can't thank you enough for your kindness, understanding, and medical expertise in caring for me.

I would like to thank my family at RENNER Ministries who walked by my side every day of my battle with cancer. Each of you encouraged me to stay strong, held me up in your prayers, and took care of my family when I was unable to.

I would like to thank Andrell Corbin and Trula Roberson. Thank you for being true sisters to me. Your love and encouragement mean more than even I, a writer, can adequately express.

I also want to acknowledge the late Erlita Renner for her unending kindness, love, and encouragement. Erlita reminded me what a mother's care looks like, and I am blessed to have had such a godly woman in my life.

To my wife, Rebecca, thank you for loving me every day and liking me on most of them. You patiently handle my writing habits, the daily thoughts I want to share, and the latest item I'm mulling over. Your prayers have been a source of strength, as has your love.

Lastly, to my father, Emory Clark, thank you for teaching me how to seek after God and to love His Word. I am alive today because of what you instilled in me by your words and the example you lived out before me. I love you, Dad.

Michael F. Clark

INTRODUCTION

For years I've watched difficult situations bring heartache, chaos, and hopelessness to those around me, and at times I've even encountered these myself. When you are going through hard times, it can seem like the walls are closing in around you and there is nowhere to turn. That's why I set out to write this book — to assure you that there is hope, and it is real. If you are looking for hope in your situation or in someone else's, I think you'll discover your answer is found in the One who gives true hope — Jesus.

In the following pages, I am going to talk about hope, where it comes from, and how you can grab hold of that hope and ride it to the other side of whatever you are going through. Seeing you come out of your challenging situation intact and with hope is my greatest desire in sharing my story. I believe the principles that helped me walk through my battle with cancer and receive God's amazing results in my life will encourage and empower you to do the same. I'm not a unicorn — I'm a testimony to the goodness and faithfulness of God, just as you can be. If you have the courage to stand up and fight for your hope and your future, you can see the impossible become a reality in your life. I have experienced this transformation myself on multiple occasions; I've seen it happen in the lives of family, friends, and even strangers; and it can be your experience as well.

Do yourself a favor. Instead of asking the question, "Why would this happen to me?" and resigning yourself to whatever might come next, change your perspective and say, "Why not me?"

THERE'S A LIGHT AT THE END OF YOUR TUNNEL

Don't disqualify yourself from the goodness that God intends for your life just because you don't see it as possible. God loves you and wants to be more to you than you realize. He is looking at you, and from His perspective He is saying, "Why not you? If you trust me, all things are possible."

Walking through hard times isn't easy, but it can be done — and not just so you survive but in a way that you thrive. I dealt with several of my own challenges before cancer ever reared its ugly head in my life, but cancer was the first one that had me staring death in the face. Over the years, I have learned many important lessons in my life that have helped me get through some difficult times, and several of those same concepts proved to be vitally important in facing cancer and overcoming it. Winning my battle required me to take an active role in resisting what cancer was doing to my body, and denying its existence was not going to make it go away. I realized quickly that I had to march onto the battlefield and fight if I was going to beat cancer and keep pursuing my dreams.

We all have a choice to make when life throws us adverse situations and circumstances — we can defend ourselves, or we can allow ourselves to be controlled by our enemy. You can be sure there is no neutral ground that your enemy will recognize or respect. You aren't a target of chance. You have been selected to assault by an enemy who desires to dominate every facet of your life until he has taken it from you. Everything is fair game to him.

COME OUT TO THE BACKYARD AND LEARN TO DEFEND YOURSELF

When I was young, I suffered from the undesirable trifecta of being small, skinny, and red-headed. I'm talking *red-* (almost orange in the sunlight) headed. This was long before being a

Introduction

"ginger" was considered a desirable thing. Being small and skinny made me a target for bullies, but my red hair made me a *preferred* target.

When I entered middle school, my older brother thought it was important that I learn how to defend myself. He came by our house one day and took me outside to our backyard. He was in the United States Army and was one of my heroes. Normally when my brother came home, he would bring me trinkets from his service — old dog tags, sew-on badges, and old ration kits — and our mom would shake her head as she watched me open up those rations and take a few bites before I realized Army rations were made for sustenance and not for flavor. That level of realism wasn't what I had expected from playing with my G.I. Joe and his kung-fu grip. It was a wake-up call to another life I hadn't experienced.

I can still remember what my brother told me that day as we stood in the backyard:

Mike, you're small and skinny, so you are going to get picked on. If someone gets ahold of you, you won't last long. You can't take much damage. You are quick though, so you will get in a couple of good hits before they take you down. I'm going to show you how to defend yourself.

My brother went on to show me how to throw a punch and how to use my bony elbows to my advantage. He warned me against grappling and allowing my opponent to take me to the ground. That followed with a demonstration and lecture on not letting my opponent take repeated shots at me without defending myself. We had been raised to not start fights and to be kind to people, but Dad had never really covered what to do when someone else started a fight and could care less about being kind. I really hadn't thought much about being picked on physically until my brother brought it up. He acquainted me with the reality that bullies existed and that they tend to pick on those smaller than themselves. He then pointed out that my trifecta of target status would sooner or later put me in someone's crosshairs. He finished with these words of wisdom:

> Most bullies don't want to fight if it means they take damage. Aim for the nose. If they see their own blood, most will stop. The ones that won't will get madder and look to take it out on you. Get in as many good hits as you can. Even if you lose, it will make others think twice before messing with you. *If you don't fight back, you'll become a perpetual target.*

As I went through school I wasn't involved in many fights. I took my brother's advice and did my best to stay out of those situations. There were a few times when I had to defend myself, but I heeded my brother's words and made the best of what defense I could put up. In doing so, I didn't become a perpetual target.

You or someone you know may be going through a very difficult time right now. Maybe life seems to be bullying you, picking on you, and taking away your peace, your strength, and with it, your hope. Life is a collection of our experiences, and it is defined by how you respond to the circumstances and situations you face day to day. You can't point your finger at life and tell it to stop being mean and to leave you alone. Yet the situations, circumstances, and actions of people that oppose you all have a root in a true adversary, and it is vitally important that you recognize who he is.

THE KEY TO UNDERSTANDING WHAT YOU'RE FACING

Often we get hit by something in life, and we react to *what* hit us, instead of *who* was behind the hit. This reminds me of old movies

Introduction

I've watched in which there was an evil boss who had a group of henchmen at his disposal. Fighting to bring justice to the land, the good guys in the story would fight valiantly against wave after wave of evil henchmen, but until the boss was dealt with, the henchmen wouldn't stop coming — bringing chaos and destruction with them. The movies that end well always have the hero confronting the evil boss and eventually winning. It's from this analogy that we learn an important principle — when the *who* behind the dastardly deeds is recognized and confronted, things change.

In the same way, you have to recognize who is ultimately behind the hard times you are facing so that you can have a proper perspective of:

- Who *isn't* behind your problems.
- Who *not* to blame.
- Who to look to for help.
- How to honestly evaluate your situation.
- How to decide on a course of action.
- How to maintain that course even when things don't change quickly or seem to get worse.

I didn't understand the answers to these questions earlier in my life, and some of my results showed it. I was doing my best, but it led to middling results. When cancer did hit, I was so thankful I had grown enough to approach that challenge with an understanding of how to face it. All the way through my fight, I continued to grow, and I am still growing to this day.

In the following pages, I'm going to share about my walk through some very difficult times and how learning to trust God got me through them. From dealing with fear after losing my mother in a car wreck when I was 12 years old to watching my young daughter ill in the hospital and seeing nothing change, God met me where I was at to take me to a higher place in Him. These and other situations prepared me for a life-or-death bout with cancer and trusting God to see His faithfulness once again in my life. I'll share the details of that battle — the thoughts I dealt with, the physical challenges I faced, and what I held on to that got me through. I want to be clear that I am no hero. What I did was trust in God throughout my ordeal. I looked to Jesus every day as I trusted Him to heal my body. I believed that by Jesus' stripes healing was available to me and I would live (*see* Isaiah 53:5). When the surgeon opened me up in March of 2011 expecting to find a cancerous tumor to remove, he found the goodness and faithfulness of God in my body in that tumor's place. Contrary to the early days when the tumor was large and the cancer was expected to travel throughout my body, no cancer spread, no cancer grew, and ultimately, there was no cancerous tumor to remove. I want you to experience God's goodness in your life, just as I've had it in mine. As of this writing, it has been 13 years since my cancer diagnosis. I have been declared cancer free, and I am continuing to fight my enemy when he tries his bullying tactics in my life. He won't stop trying, and you and I don't have to stop resisting him.

Jesus told us that in this world we would face trials. Every hero of faith in the Bible walked through life facing hardships, doubts, and failures, but what they did was continue to trust God to help them make it through those hard times. God gave each of them His promises to hold on to, and even if they had moments of weakness, doubt, or despair, they corrected their approach by looking to God and trusting Him to lead them through. The devil will use every trick and maneuver at his disposal to keep you from reaching the destination God has for you, and he will rob you of every blessing God has intended for you — but you have a choice in the matter.

Dive into this book and come to the backyard with me so that we can talk about who your enemy is. Allow me to share from my own fights and teach you how you can defend yourself when he comes to bully you — I'll even show you how you can keep from becoming a perpetual target. When he comes to harass you, you can fight back, and when you fight back, *leave a mark!* Your victory is just that — the bloody nose or black eye he wears from his unsuccessful encounter with you.

God's desire for you is to walk through life with a hope that is grounded in His love for you. He has created you for a purpose that He is invested in, and as you trust in Him, you will see Him do amazing things. No matter how dark the situation may seem, He is the Light that overcomes the darkness, and your hope in Him is the *light* at the end of your tunnel.

CHAPTER 1

There Is a Light at the End of Your Tunnel

LIFE WILL SHOW you that events happen that will take you by surprise. A bad report from the doctor, a fractured relationship, financial difficulties — these problems and others can take you to a dark place if you have no way to process them, especially when there is no hope for a good outcome. As the pressure mounts, it can seem like the walls are closing in, and as much as you would like to turn around and leave, you find there is no actual turning back. Turning backward isn't an option based in reality. You can't get to the other side of your challenges in life when you stand at the beginning and never move forward under your own power. In most cases, your circumstances will push you along whether you want to move or not, and they will control the direction in which you are going. Thankfully, you don't have to be swept along by your situation to a place of hopelessness. You can have a say in how you go forward and where you end up.

I have faced many challenges in life, some larger than others. While each had its own difficulties, none came at me the way a cancer diagnosis did in the fall of 2010. I had gone in for a routine colonoscopy and woke up from the procedure with a new cancer diagnosis and appointments with an oncologist and a surgeon. My life was changed in an instant with the news of the tumor, and I was confronted with the possible end of my life. The initial response I received from the doctors was not encouraging.

With that diagnosis, I was standing at the mouth of a dark tunnel. Its walls narrowed in and nothing but blackness stood before me. This was a serious, life-or-death situation, and it felt like a conveyor belt appeared under my feet pulling me into this tunnel whether I wanted to move forward or not.

You may have experienced something in life that felt this way. Perhaps you are going through something like this now. Your head may feel like it is spinning from all the news you are receiving and the numerous opinions of well-meaning people. I know that feeling well, as I quickly found myself surrounded by several doctors after I received my diagnosis. One doctor was talking to me about chemotherapy. Another about radiation treatment. Another doctor wanted to talk about the multiple surgeries that could be involved. Last but not least, there was the chemo port that needed to be scheduled for installation that week. I finally had to look at them all and tell them that I needed to take the weekend to wrap my head around everything they were telling me. Thankfully, one of the surgeons heard what I was saying and told me he understood. He advised the other doctors to let me take the weekend to get a handle on all they were asking me to process.

It was during that weekend that I did a lot of soul searching and prepared myself for what I was heading into. Like an old U.S. Navy frigate, I spent that weekend working to get my bearings, to batten down the hatches, and to prepare to sail into the storm I was facing.

Facing your storm is a decision, and sailing through it is a process. It is the same with the tunnel you are facing. You must look into it and make a determination to walk through it to the other side. A tunnel can be defined as:

> *An underground passageway dug through the surrounding soil, earth, or rock and enclosed except for an entrance and exit, commonly at each end.*[1]

A tunnel has an *entrance* and an *exit*. A cave has an entrance but not necessarily an exit. As you look down the opening in front of you, you must decide if you are going *through* a tunnel or not, or your approach may end up leading you to descend into a cave with no exit. This so important to grasp. Just as a ship's captain expects to sail until he comes out of a storm, you must look at your trial as a tunnel — something with an *exit* at the end. Your expectation has to be toward that exit and what is beyond it. The captain of the ship is looking forward to calm seas and sunlight on the other side of the storm. You should be looking for the light at the end of your tunnel, and the life you will have beyond it. Don't just pray you will survive. Look toward the hope of thriving once you've come out of your tunnel. Your survival has a purpose beyond just staying alive. God has so much more for you!

> **Your survival has a purpose beyond just staying alive. God has so much more for you!**

The first time I had to stand up for myself I was not confident. Honestly, I was scared that I was going to get the snot knocked out of me. Yet as I stood there with my classmates gathered around anticipating some playground entertainment, I knew that if I ran away things would only be worse. I also had the realization that if I ran away, my antagonist might very well chase after me and make me pay for causing him to make an extra effort. I made the decision to stand there and did as my brother had taught me. When my foe moved in to strike, I threw a couple of weak punches that landed with little damage, but they caught him by surprise. He hadn't expected me to put up much of a defense, and my response caused him to reevaluate his decision. He did and apparently decided that thumping on me still sounded appealing. He then proceeded to grab me and throw me to the ground. When he grabbed me and tossed me to the ground, I grabbed him and held on for dear life.

I had decided if my enemy couldn't draw back his arms to pummel me, I might have a chance at the fight ending without a bloody nose, busted lip, or black eye. I probably looked like a flailing octopus hanging on to him for my life, but after a couple of minutes of having me in various forms of a headlock, he was ready to end the fight. Since I had been in the headlock, I technically was the loser — but I had accomplished what I had set out to do. Other than a few scratches and bruises from the grappling, I had survived without any substantial damage. I had also made a statement: Mike Clark would defend himself, even if it was awkward and less than awe inspiring.

Looking back, I realize standing there that day on the playground was like standing at the mouth of a cave. I could have chosen to run, but my problem would not have disappeared. Likewise, you can choose to stand there and wait for what may seem inevitable or even to run away, or you can also choose to be an active participant in the outcome of your situation and confront what you are facing.

There are testimonies of people who have chosen to face their problem head on and who have watched God miraculously deliver them then and there. God definitely still heals and delivers today, just as He did throughout the Bible, yet not everyone experiences that instant change in their situation. So many of the heroes of faith in the Bible went through their own tunnel experiences and came out the other side. They trusted God through their tunnels to come out of the other side in victory. *They didn't focus on the darkness in the tunnel. They focused on the light at the end of it and experienced God's results in their lives.*

These biblical heroes were each faced with circumstances that seemed improbable or impossible, but they did not allow how the situation looked to dictate how they would see their final outcome. They did not allow what was happening to them to overshadow *who* was with them — *who* they had placed their trust in. As they faced their trials, they were not oblivious to the challenges they faced or the doubts that came against their hope. They each made a decision to have hope in something more than what seemed to be the normally accepted outcome. They decided to truly place their trust in God, not merely to give trusting Him a try. Then they continued to trust in Him and the hope they had through Him. They kept their focus on Him throughout the ups and downs, fighting off doubts and fears as they pressed toward the light they knew awaited them on the other side of their trial.

The example in the Bible that had the most impact on my understanding of this came from a most interesting person — Sarah, the wife of Abraham. One day I was searching for a simple answer on what trusting God looked like, and I found it in Hebrews 11:11, which describes how Sarah came to her own place of trusting God in the middle of a hopeless situation:

> *By faith Sarah herself also received strength to conceive seed, and she bore a child when she was past the age, because she judged Him faithful who had promised.*

Sarah had hoped to conceive a child in what had been her barren reproductive system (one that had failed her throughout her life). She had desired to conceive a child, to carry that child, and to give birth and have a family with her husband Abram. This dream had eluded her for her entire life, and when God said she would conceive and bear a child in her old age, she laughed at the idea (*see* Genesis 18:12). Yet along the way she began to reflect on God's goodness and faithfulness to her and Abraham, and she made the decision to trust God to be who He said He would be and do what He said He would do in her life, even if physically it made no sense.

Sarah came to a place where she saw past the limitations of her and Abraham's bodies and began to see the limitless possibilities found in God. She began to see herself pregnant and being a mother, experiencing God's results in her life — the results she had always hoped for. That's what biblical hope does — it sees past your limitations, or the world's limitations, and envisions what is possible with God. It takes what was once a deep, dark place and brings light to it, a bright light shining at the end of whatever tunnel is involved. The light of God's hope provides not only illumination, but also a future. This light doesn't stay only at the end of your situation; it extends into the bright future that is ahead of you because it is found in God.

> **That's what biblical hope does — it sees past your limitations, or the world's limitations, and envisions what is possible with God.**

As for Sarah, her hope and trust in God not only ended her life of barren disappointment, it yielded much more! God gave her the experience she had longed for her whole life because she trusted Him. We read about this beautiful result in Genesis 21:1-7:

> *And the Lord visited Sarah as He had said, and the Lord did for Sarah as He had spoken. For Sarah conceived and bore*

Abraham a son in his old age, at the set time of which God had spoken to him. And Abraham called the name of his son who was born to him—whom Sarah bore to him—Isaac. Then Abraham circumcised his son Isaac when he was eight days old, as God had commanded him. Now Abraham was one hundred years old when his son Isaac was born to him. And Sarah said, "God has made me laugh, and all who hear will laugh with me." She also said, "Who would have said to Abraham that Sarah would nurse children? For I have borne him a son in his old age."

Sarah conceived a child, carried him to term, and gave birth to him. Where she had once laughed at the idea of becoming pregnant at an old age and after being barren her whole life, now she laughed as she held her child in her arms. (God has a way of taking our original hopeless response and turning it into joy when we trust Him.) Not only did God give Sarah the ability to have a child with Abraham, He also granted her the desire of her heart — to be a mother. I can just imagine her holding her baby boy to her breast and nursing him, hugging him close to her heart and looking down upon the little miracle baby, understanding that her trust in God's Word had brought about what nature and reason said was impossible.

When I was going through my bout with cancer, I experienced so many hard days. On those days, I would think back to the example of Sarah and how she "judged Him faithful who had promised" (*see* Hebrews 11:11). I understood that her faith, her trust, was in God. She looked at Him and made the decision in her heart that she could trust Him and His word. She didn't jump through hoops to make it happen — she trusted the person of God. It wasn't a formula that brought her a baby; it was a relationship.

THERE'S A LIGHT AT THE END OF YOUR TUNNEL

Early on in my journey, the analogy of a tunnel and a light at the end of it came to signify to me what I was facing and what I was hoping for. I knew I had to face cancer and fight through the battleground to get to the other side. My hope was in God's goodness and His faithfulness, in the healing that Jesus' sacrifice had purchased for me, and in the love God had for me. I read about these things throughout His Word and determined to place my trust in them.

During this time, I was reminded of a song by the Christian band Third Day called "Tunnel" that resonated with my situation and my approach to dealing with it. It quickly became my theme song during this time, and I would often sing the chorus to myself when one of those hard days weighed on me, and it encouraged me to remember there was a light at the end of my tunnel and to keep holding on.

I chose to keep holding on:

Holding on to hope.

Holding on to God.

Holding on to His Word.

Holding on to who I am in Christ.

So I did. I stayed in my Bible. I stayed in prayer. I continued to seek out resources to strengthen my faith. I placed the whole of my trust in the love that God had for me. I placed the whole of my trust in Jesus, who came and died for my sins to bring me back into fellowship with God. I trusted in the finished work of the Cross, the redemption that Jesus gave his life for, and the healing that the stripes He bore on His back purchased for me. I held fast to His goodness, His love, and His faithfulness.

I did seven weeks of chemotherapy and 28 radiation treatments — at the same time. The chemotherapy regimen I was prescribed involved having a pump attached to a tube push the chemo drugs into the port in my shoulder 24 hours a day. The pump was removed for two hours each Monday when I would go see my oncologist and do blood work and any other treatment drips they felt were needed while I was there. At the end of my visit, the refilled chemo pump was hooked back up to the needle in my chest and I was sent home. To make things lighter around the house for my children, I dubbed the chemo pump my "Gameboy." It went everywhere with me, much like my son's actual Gameboy did with him.

I was scheduled for six weeks of chemo, but after five weeks of treatment, I was so ill they sent me home without the Gameboy or treatment for week six. I was so far gone there was a question of whether I would make it back the next week to take my final chemo treatment. That week I understood what it really felt like to be dying. It was very surreal, but I knew that I was not going to die. I believed God was faithful, and I was convinced in my heart that I was indeed going to see His goodness in the land of the living. Although, from the outside my chances didn't look good.

I made it through week six and arrived back that next Monday morning for my last round of chemo. I was weak but still cracking jokes and working to rub off my hope on whoever I could. I wasn't a dead man walking. I wasn't a sick man trying not to die. In my mind and in my heart, I was a well man fighting off the sickness that was trying to kill me, and I had placed my trust and hope in God.

I finished my chemotherapy and soon after finished the last of my radiation treatments. My body had gone through almost every side effect they had listed, along with others that no one could either explain or take responsibility for. Some years later when I came in for a follow-up visit, the Nurse Practitioner that walked with us through our journey told my wife and I that I was the story she told to patients when they talked about the side effects and suffering they were going through from their own treatment. She told us I had been one of, if not the, worst cases of side effects she had seen. To say it was a brutal time would be an understatement — and God saw me through it all, all the way to the other side.

What was that other side? you might be wondering. The initial imaging of the rectal tumor when it was found in early November of 2010 was around 6 cm. Imaging later that month measured it at 5.5 cm and showed it had grown around and encompassed an area of lymph nodes. Then, after all the treatment was complete and time was given for it to have effect, by mid-February of 2011 the tumor had shrunk from 5.5 cm to 3 cm. My surgery to remove the tumor was scheduled for Monday, March 21, 2011. The expectation of the medical staff was that I would have a permanent colostomy performed. I was still expecting them to find a miracle had happened and that there would be no cancer and no need for a colostomy.

My surgeon Dr. Johnson used the DaVinci robotic surgical system to perform my procedure. It lasted over four hours. When he came out from surgery, he smiled and told my wife, "You got your miracle!" The tumor was no longer there, and the surgical work he performed did not include a permanent colostomy. A biopsy of the lymph nodes showed no trace of cancer.

At the time of this writing Rebecca and I have been married almost 31 years, and we have five grandchildren. I am a living testimony of seeing the goodness of God in the land of the living. God is faithful, and His Word is true.

Jesus is real, He loves you, and He's given His all to give you a life of purpose and freedom. His help is there for the asking. Just as He has saw me through my hard times, He will see you through yours as well.

> **Jesus is real, He loves you, and He's given His all to give you a life of purpose and freedom.**

Much of the material in this book has been gleaned from teachings I had from earlier days that I took out to help me during this fight with cancer, and there are others that I learned during and after. I still live by them today and face each trial strengthened by them. Each is an important part of facing trials and trusting God to be who He said He would be and do what He said He would do. That phrase will be repeated throughout this book because God spoke it to my heart in those early days of fighting cancer, and it became my focus — the simple approach of trusting in Him.

In the following chapters, I am going to share with you from my fight with cancer, and how God walked me through it one step at a time. I faced fear, doubt, depression, hopelessness, uncertainty, and several other feelings and conditions. It was hard but not impossible. Things that I had learned in the years leading up to this time in my life served me well in fighting each battle, and I was grounded in my expectancy of God's faithfulness in the fight I was in. Let me be clear — I did have hard days where I was shaken. I am not a faith rockstar. I am simply a man who made the decision to trust God and expect Him to be who He said He would be to me and to do what He said He would do for me. He did the work; I did the trusting.

THERE'S A LIGHT AT THE END OF YOUR TUNNEL

You can do the same and see God move in your situation. He is the light at the end of your tunnel, and He will be your Guide all the way through it.

CHAPTER 2

How I Came To Find Myself in the Tunnel of Cancer

FOR THE BETTER part of 2010, I had planned on having a colonoscopy. No, I didn't raise my hand and run to the front to volunteer. The thought of having a colonoscopy had come to me early in the year, and after discussing it and my family history with my doctor, he thought it might be a prudent thing to do. I had other older family members who had polyps found during their exams, so it made sense to be proactive and make sure all was well. I had begun making plans to schedule the procedure when, in May, a tornado came through our neighborhood and damaged our house. I moved my plans for the colonoscopy to July and went about getting our house repaired. As July came, another wrench flew into my plans. My wife's grandmother passed away, and I had to miss my scheduled colonoscopy as we attended her funeral in another state. August came, and I began to notice blood in my stools. It had become a noticeable occurrence, and I was concerned I might have hemorrhoids. I had another visit with my doctor, and he agreed to treat me for hemorrhoids and reschedule the colonoscopy again. With the office schedule being busy, I finally was able to get the procedure scheduled for early November.

I was not looking forward to the colonoscopy and all that came with it. I had heard horror stories about the colon prep you had to drink the day before the procedure and how it tested a person's gag reflex to the highest levels. Soon that day came for me, and I found out firsthand how true the stories had been. If you've had the displeasure of drinking and eventually gagging on that nasty liquid, you know exactly what I'm talking about. If you haven't experienced it yet, may God's grace be with you when it is your time. It can be alluded to but must be experienced firsthand to truly understand its effect as it assaults the nose, the mouth, and the rest of your digestive system. It was the most unpleasant substance I had ever tasted.

Thankfully, I survived the colon prep and the internal gymnastics it put me through. The next morning, I got up early and my wife took me to the clinic for my procedure. Little did I know the day would be full of surprises.

Everything had been normal from check-in. I'd donned the backless gown and had done my best to wrap it around myself and preserve what modesty I could while I was still coherent, and the nurses had prepared me and taken me to the procedure room. As I lay there on the table waiting for the doctor to come in and begin the procedure, I took in my surroundings and noticed something out of place across the room. There on the other side of the room was a utility cart, a tool chest if you may. To my surprise, I recognized it as such because with its red paint and black trim it stood out from the rest of the bland, off-white furnishings. As I squinted to see more clearly, I made out the nice shiny "Craftsman" logo on the front, just like the ones I had looked at when I was in the hardware section of Sears.

By then I was a bit woozy from the medicine they had given me, so I asked the nurse if I was seeing things or if there really was a Craftsman tool chest in the room with me. She laughed as she commented on my observation and verified it was indeed one just like in the Sears hardware section. She said they were much cheaper than the off-white ones from the medical supply company but served the same purpose and were a cost-saving measure. I must admit, after hearing this I had a fleeting thought of what else from Sears might be in the room and then the anesthesia kicked in and I was out.

I don't remember anything from the next two hours. What I later learned is that shortly after beginning the procedure Dr. Morris found a large mass in my rectum, just above the sphincter. From his experience, it looked to be cancer. He lengthened my anesthesia, biopsied the tissue for review and then went about informing us of what he had found.

I want to pause here for a moment to point out that life-changing events happen in real time, with little to no warning. Your day starts out on one track, only to be turned upside down in a matter of moments. One comfort I can offer is that what you have fortified yourself with during the times before your crisis will ground and sustain you during those moments after the news comes to you. What happened to my wife is an example of how a commitment to be grounded can be what keeps you from being paralyzed and unable to move, think, or cope.

While I was recovering from the anesthesia, Dr. Morris met with my wife Rebecca and broke the news of his findings to her. She was shocked, scared, and heartbroken. We had four children at home that we would have to tell. For all she knew she was on her way to being a widow and raising four children on her own. She had walked in thinking she would take me home loopy from the anesthesia and have me sleep it off. Now she was blown away with so many different thoughts, including whether she was taking me home to eventually die. To this day my heart goes out to her when I think of what she must have gone through while I was lying there asleep. I wasn't there to comfort her or be strong for her. She had to face it alone.

Eventually I began to wake up and get dressed, and Dr. Morris shared the news with me. I remember nothing of this, as apparently, I listened intently and then laid back down and went back to sleep. Soon I woke again, and Dr. Morris and my wife shared the news with me — again. Rebecca said I asked intelligent questions and seemed to understand what I was being told only to lie back down and fall back asleep again!

Several minutes later we repeated the entire scene. Dr. Morris and Rebecca once again explained the situation to me. This time I remained awake, in shock and somewhat woozy. I was coherent enough that the news had finally begun to sink in.

Rebecca had absorbed the dreadful news not once, twice, or even three times. She had gone through the explanation *four times* in the span of three hours. It was like getting hit by a Mack truck and then being backed over time after time. How she held things together that day is a testimony to how she had grounded herself in God during the better times. When the storm of life hit, she held fast to her trust in God. It anchored her. There's no doubt that in that doctor's office her mind was racing and her heart was breaking — but she held it together for us both. She was the hero.

As my wife and I left the office, we were given appointments with an oncologist and a surgeon. That was my first inclination of how bad the doctor thought the mass he had found might be. From his experience, he deemed it was bad enough to already have me scheduled to meet with an oncologist and a surgeon. As we drove home, we talked about how we would tell our kids.

We arrived home, both drained by the day's events, and after going to our bedroom, I fell asleep once again! I woke a short time after, and Rebecca had to go through the whole explanation of the day's events again. She then showed me the pictures Dr. Morris had taken during the examination to explain what was found and what we were facing. I am so thankful that she didn't strangle me and get things over with that night! In the middle of the heart-wrenching news and my repeated bouts of drowsiness, she remained patient with me and showed compassion.

After some time, we called our three older children into the bedroom and broke the news to them. We showed them the pictures that Dr. Morris had taken of the tumor and did our best to tell them not to worry and everything was going to be alright. That was what they needed to hear from us. We needed to hear it too because we were still shell-shocked by the news. Eventually we had them go back out of the room and looked at each other for several moments. I looked into Rebecca's eyes and realized I had no answers for her. I felt like I was failing her, but at that moment I was not at a place where I could give her anything but hold her. I was still a bit groggy, and slowly but surely, I was coming to grips with what this diagnosis might really mean for us.

For her part, Rebecca had reached the end of holding it together. She needed time to sort things out and have a good cry. What she had been subjected to for the day was overwhelming, and she needed the time to let things out. After we sat together for a time holding on to each other for dear life, I left her to process and went to do the same. Our future had changed in a few hours into one of chaos and uncertainty, and we each needed to regroup. Have you ever experienced an event like this that shook your world? How do you approach it?

LESSON 1: TAKE TIME AND ASK QUESTIONS

I sat on the bed and looked over the pictures of the tumor. It looked malevolent, and as my daughter had said, it was "in my butt." *Yes,* I thought to myself, *Dad had a cancerous tumor in his butt, and he was trying to wrap his head around that news.*

When you go through something difficult, it is so important to pause for a moment and allow yourself time to wrap your head around things. Many mistakes are made or compounded because of rash thinking or acting, but you can avoid this by taking time to assess what it is you are facing. When you do this, you must do it *honestly*. Doing so will require you to look at your situation and to be willing to acknowledge where you may be in the wrong. You might be the cause of your mess, and if so, you will have to own up to it so that you can move forward to address it properly. The truth can be painful, but it has the power to set you free.

Later that evening after the kids were in bed, I went into our bathroom and closed the door. I sat on the toilet and put my head in my hands, still in shock and near tears. I had woken up that morning with my whole life ahead of me, and later that day I was faced with the possibility that my life might, instead, be measured in weeks or months — not years. I sat there for quite some time, my mind racing, my heart aching, wondering what my next step might be.

As I sat there overwhelmed, I remembered that my situation wasn't the end for me — not that night. I was standing at the entrance to my latest tunnel, and I knew I would have to face it if I wanted a chance to come out the other side.

I tend to look at things analytically, so I began to process the horrible news.

I had what they believed to be a cancerous tumor.

It was in my rectum.

It had all the indicators of being malignant.

I had never thought that in my life I would have to deal with cancer. It was nowhere on my radar. The thought was foreign to me, yet there I was staring at the wall and toilet paper roll realizing that the "Big C" was now going to figure into my conversations.

Why? wasn't the first question that crossed my mind. That first question was, *How?*

How did this happen?

How was I going to handle this?

How will this affect me and my family?

I didn't have a solid answer for *how*, and I knew it was not the time to begin asking *why*, so my next question, which was actually the most important, was — *who*.

Who was behind this?

Understanding *who* is so very important, as it impacts the answers to many other questions, including *How?* and in time *Why?*

LESSON 2: ASSIGN THE BLAME WHERE IT BELONGS — AND LEAVE IT THERE

As I sat in the bathroom with thoughts racing through my head, I reminded myself that the cancer I was dealing with did not come from God, and I was not going to place the blame on Him. I decided then and there that God was the answer to my problem, not the cause of it. He wasn't the author of the cancer — He was my Healer.

I remembered in John 10:10 (*MEV*) where Jesus spoke of the difference between Himself and Satan:

The thief does not come, except to steal and kill and destroy. I came that they may have life, and that they may have it more abundantly.

If an event or circumstance in your life steals, kills, or destroys, its author is Satan.

> **If an event or circumstance in your life steals, kills, or destroys, its author is Satan.**

I had a cancerous tumor, a tumor that if given free rein would steal my peace, kill my body, and destroy my future. All these outcomes pointed to a distinct author — Satan. This cancer wasn't going to produce health in my body or expand my life and my future, therefore, it could not be from God.

If you are facing a difficult circumstance right now, as time passes it will be tempting to blame God for your situation, especially if it is prolonged. It is tempting because the enemy is working behind the scenes to have your circumstances bring God's goodness into question. This is how he operates and a principal way he works. He tries to convince you to question God's goodness and His faithfulness, and the longer you have to wait for an answer or for breakthrough, the easier it will be to question what you once believed, but remember, one of your anchor points during any storm of thoughts you face is this: *God is not the author of your problem.*

The devil looks for any opportunity to step into a life and wreak havoc for his pleasure. Stealing, killing, and destroying aren't merely his job description — they are his passion. He is consumed by the desire to challenge God at every turn and seeks to do so through the lives of God's creation. He seeks to mock God as he takes out his anger and hubris on people, those whom God created in His own image.

While Satan blinds the eyes of some so that they do not acknowledge God, he also sets his sights on those who do acknowledge God. He seeks to manipulate their lives and surroundings to take them from a place of worshiping God and trusting Him to a place of falling away from God and turning their back on Him. Don't look at your trials in a vacuum, as if you are the only person who is afflicted, and don't blame God for what your enemy is bringing into your life for his own nefarious purposes.

This is a point that you will need to become settled on as you face your battle: **God is not the cause of your problem; He is your solution to it!** When bad things happen in your life, don't fall into the trap of blaming God. You may be like Job and, through no actions of your own, you might be facing a very difficult situation. Or perhaps, you have made bad choices that have gotten you to the place you find yourself. In either case, God isn't the place where blame for your situation rests. *He is your answer to it.*

Jesus was very clear in John 10:10 as to what motive and actions He takes as opposed to those that Satan takes:

The thief does not come except to steal, and to kill, and to destroy. I have come that they may have life, and that they may have it more abundantly.

Whatever comes into your life that steals, kills, or destroys did not originate from God. Period. Don't assign it to Him, because He is not its author. Jesus said He came to do the opposite — to give *life*, a life more abundantly or to the fullest.

Jesus spoke of this in Matthew 7:8-11:

For everyone who asks receives, and he who seeks finds, and to him who knocks it will be opened. Or what man is there among you who, if his son asks for bread, will give him a stone? Or if he asks for a fish, will he give him a serpent? If you then, being evil, know how to give good gifts to your children, how much more will your Father who is in heaven give good things to those who ask Him!

God does not give evil in place of good. James, a leader in the Early Church, pointedly explained this in James 1:13:

Let no one say when he is tempted, "I am tempted by God"; for God cannot be tempted by evil, nor does He Himself tempt anyone.

James was the half-bother of Jesus and the pastor of the church in the city of Jerusalem. At the time he wrote this verse, the persecution of Jesus' followers had increased and many were forced to flee to other cities or countries. Some remained in Jerusalem, though, and were subjected to ridicule, suspicion, loss of their livelihoods, and other hardships that negatively impacted their lives. Many believers were trying to make sense of the calamities they were facing and where God fit into the equation. As they began to see their lives deteriorating, they assumed that God must be involved in some way. From this place they had begun to question God's goodness and faithfulness, asking whether God could have caused their situation.

Upon hearing this, James strongly responded, beginning his letter to the church with, "Let no one say…." This statement was James' way of emphatically saying that no one should think or say, "I am tempted by God." When he is in a place of temptation — in a place where he begins to think or act against God's Word and His ways — God did not instigate it or cause it to occur. James went on to explain that claiming God is the cause of any temptation or problem we face is flatly wrong because, as verse 13 says, "...God cannot be tempted by evil, nor does He Himself tempt anyone."

This same lesson applies to you and me. When you are facing hard times, God is not bringing them on you in order to see you do wrongly. He is not seeking to subtract from your life — that is what Satan does. God's desire is to add to your life. James pointed this out in verse 16:

Do not be deceived, my beloved brethren.

James warned his readers not to be deceived. How were they being deceived? They were looking at their tough circumstances and hard situations and thinking that God might have been involved in their problem. Their faith was fluctuating and unstable because they were looking to God one minute to be the answer to their problem but then, when the next negative thought or circumstance hit, they began to doubt His goodness and faithfulness in their lives. Satan was working to cause them to doubt God's character and to question what He had said.

James in effect was telling the church, "Don't allow yourselves to be deceived into doubting God's love for you or His goodness and faithfulness to do all He has promised. It is *absolutely wrong* for you to say, 'God is the cause of these horrible things in my life.' God has nothing to do with evil and is not originating evil events into your life. It is not His character." James went on to explain why in verse 17:

Every good gift and every perfect gift is from above, and comes down from the Father of lights, with whom there is no variation or shadow of turning.

Every good and perfect gift. God gives things that are good and perfect for us — things that add to our lives and bring us further along in our walk with Him. That is the standard you are to hold up to what you are going through to and evaluate it by, asking yourself, *Is this circumstance subtracting from my life and my walk with God or adding to it?* In my case, when I sat that night in our bathroom trying to wrap my head around the news I had received and the coming events that would follow, I had to make a decision — what perspective was I going to use to view my situation?

I'm so thankful that I understood Jesus was (and is) the Good Shepherd and He came to give me life — a life of fullness!

I'm so thankful I knew that if I, being a sinful man, know how to give good gifts to my children, how much more my Father who is in Heaven will give good things to those who ask Him! (*See* Matthew 7:11.)

I am so thankful that I was settled in the fact that every good gift and every perfect gift is from above and comes down from the Father of lights, with whom there is no variation or shadow of turning! God never changes (*see* Malachi 3:6). His light does not change like the phases of the moon; He remains steady and bright like the sun. God is *always* good.

As I faced this overwhelming situation, I had a template, a standard of *Who God is* and *how He goes about things*, that I could take this news of cancer and compare it to. Cancer was going to drain my body, my finances, and my life. It was already subtracting from my health and my peace, and now it was attacking my family. None of those things were good or were ever going to add to my life; therefore, their origin had not come from God. It was coming from the one who comes to steal, kill, and destroy.

My enemy had been identified and so had the source of my hope and my answer. You can do the same with your situation. Look at it and ask yourself the same questions about what you are dealing with and who is behind it. Settle this issue in your heart — God is *for* you and desires to bring you out of what you are facing so you are more than a conqueror (*see* Romans 8:37).

> **God is a good God, and His greatest desire is to have you walk closely with Him.**

God is a good God, and His greatest desire is to have you walk closely with Him. He is slow to anger and patient because He desires that no one should perish under judgement, as He draws no pleasure from their demise (*see* Ezekiel 18:23; 33:11) He desires that everyone should come to repentance and walk in fellowship with Him. That is why He sent Jesus. Jesus came to give us life, an abundant life we can live to the fullest. That is your answer when the enemy comes to entice you to blame God for what you are going through. If he can get you to blame God, he knows you will be unable to receive the answer that God has for you — your light at the end of the tunnel.

I'm so thankful that I remembered God's goodness when I found out that I was dealing with cancer. You may need to ask yourself this question and then seek God about the answer if you don't already know what it is:

Do I have need of repentance in my life for disobedience that was the cause of my trial?

God didn't cause the situation you're going through, but you may need to do some soul searching to make sure that you are not dealing with the natural consequences of bad decisions or behavior. We have an enemy who seeks to attack us at every turn, and without doing our part to repent and get right with God, we can't receive the answers and revelation He wants to give us. I knew God wasn't giving me evil — in this case a cancerous tumor. I knew that I was fighting sickness and that my enemy was using it to try and steal, kill, and destroy in my life. I also knew that Jesus came to give me life, and life to the fullest. He wasn't the cause of my situation — He was my solution to it.

Whatever hard time you are going through, God is not the author of it. Settle that in your heart and then move forward with the assurance that you are not alone. Anchor your trust in God's goodness, that Jesus is your Good Shepherd and that He is totally invested in seeing your through what difficulties you're facing. He is with you every step of the way. He is your light at the end of the tunnel as well as your guiding light, leading your every step through it.

CHAPTER 3
Satan's Lies vs. God's Love

IT'S EASY TO get caught up in your circumstances. We've all had it happen to us at one time or another. As human beings, none of us is immune from the twists and turns of life. If you took the time to sit down and write down the different things you've been through, you could probably make a good list, but you are still here and able to make that list. Life isn't over. No matter how much your circumstances may try to convince you otherwise, you are still here and there is hope for you. It's that hope that the devil wants so badly to steal from you, and he will try to come from many angles to convince you to give up and give in to his designs on your life. Those designs are not for your good.

The effects of your battles with the devil may take place in the physical realm, but your actual battles occur in the spiritual realm. Jesus understood this. He knew that His spiritual position determined His earthly authority. He understood that who He was to God and what God said about Him were the true measure of His ability to walk through life victoriously. The devil understands this as well and will do all He can to hide that information from you or to get you to doubt it. He knows it is your key to victory.

Ideally, Satan would prefer that you had never heard the good news the God loves you and sent Jesus to pay the price for your sin. He does not want you to know that God desires to be involved in your life at a deep and intimate level. Satan knows that if you are oblivious to who God is, what He did, and who He wants to be in your life — you can never see the hope that is found in Him.

Because of this, Satan's number one approach in trying to deceive you is to question what God has said and convince you to do so was well.

You may be familiar with the first detailed account of this found in the book of Genesis. God created the world and all that is in it, and He created Adam in His own image, breathing His own breath into him and placing him in the special place He made for him — a garden in Eden. There were many wonderful things in Eden, including a tree which God warned Adam to have nothing to do with.

> *The Lord God placed the man in the Garden of Eden to tend and watch over it. But the* Lord *God warned him, "You may freely eat the fruit of every tree in the garden — except the tree of the knowledge of good and evil. If you eat its fruit, you are sure to die."*
> — Genesis 2:15-17 (*NLT*)

Adam's helpmate Eve received this instruction as well, but in a deceptive plan, the devil in the guise of the serpent came to the woman and began his clever attack:

> *The serpent was the shrewdest of all the wild animals the* Lord *God had made. One day he asked the woman, "Did God really say you must not eat the fruit from any of the trees in the garden?"*
> — Genesis 3:1 (*NLT*)

Do you notice the approach that was taken? The devil did not use an outright challenge to what God had said. Instead, he posed his challenge as a question. Challenging statements often elicit a strong defense, meaning they often open the door for an argument to be presented, but the devil did not want Eve to recognize his attack on God's character and resist, so he used this subtle approach instead.

Think about how this works in your own life. If someone tells you that your favorite singer or sports team is bad, you probably will quickly come to the defense to refute the statement. Yet if that same person poses their statement in the form of a question, you are engaged at a different level. It can, instead, provide an opening where they can present an argument with hopes of gaining concessions or changing your mind. Let me illustrate:

If I said, "Bob Dylan isn't that great of an artist."

As a Dylan fan, you may go ballistic or at least become irritated and defend Bob's career and impact on music. You might feel the need to defend his artistry and your choice of finding his music appealing. However, if I used this other questioning approach, the result might be different:

"I know many people say Bob Dylan is a great singer, but to me his voice is nasally and he mumbles. Sometimes I can't tell what he is saying. Have you noticed that?"

When a differing opinion is presented as a question, you may not initially agree with the premise, but you are more apt to consider the argument being posed and allow a discussion to happen. You are then engaged in a discussion which is meant to change your perspective and possibly convert you over to the questioner's position. Because it wasn't an outright assault on your musical hero, you likely hear the statement with a more open mind.

This is the tactic Satan used on Eve as he approached her in the Garden. He posed a question that misstated what God's intention was in order to draw her into a place for his argument. She listened to his question and then responded:

> "Of course we may eat fruit from the trees in the garden," the woman replied. "It's only the fruit from the tree in the middle of the garden that we are not allowed to eat. God said, 'You must not eat it or even touch it; if you do, you will die.'"
> — Genesis 3:2-3 (*NLT*)

The woman replied to his question with a true, valid answer. She even stated exactly what God had instructed her and Adam to do. It was at that time that the devil saw his opening and made his accusation:

> "You won't die!" the serpent replied to the woman. "God knows that your eyes will be opened as soon as you eat it, and you will be like God, knowing both good and evil."
> — Genesis 3:4-5 (*NLT*)

Know this — Satan will always bring into question what God has said, but his full intent is to bring into question God's character and motives. His intense hatred for God is never satisfied, and since he can't be like God, he seeks to bring God down to his level with his accusations.

> **Know this — Satan will always bring into question what God has said, but his full intent is to bring into question God's character and motives.**

Satan took Eve's response and then wove it into his own narrative — a form of character assassination against God — in his reply. This is his consistent mode of attack and deception that we find throughout the Bible, and he is still using it today. Paul made mention of being aware of this in Second Corinthians 2:11:

Lest Satan should take advantage of us; for we are not ignorant of his devices.

When the apostle Paul wrote this to the church in Corinth, he was encouraging them to handle the restoration of one of their members in a gracious way, to strengthen the man by sharing their love for him. By doing so, they would acknowledge the man's truly repentant heart and actions and not add continued hardship that would cause that brother to fall again. Paul knew a sense of rejection would cause the man to possibly fall away from God for good, so he directed the church to behave accordingly.

Paul followed up his instruction with this verse, stating that this situation was one Satan would like to use for his own advantage. Paul's warning to the church reminded them not to be ignorant of how Satan operates. They had seen enough and learned enough of Satan's ways to understand that he will seek to influence people to think wrongly about a situation with the aim of bringing reproach on the church and causing the man who had repented to fall away again to the point of abandoning his faith. They were to understand that the devil's ultimate aim is to destroy their trust in God.

When you are going through hard times, the devil is intent on not only making you question what God has said, but also what His motives are and His faithfulness to you. Satan wants you to see yourself in a cave. He will tell you God doesn't exist or that He doesn't care about what you are going through. He will try to convince you that you aren't worthy of God's love or His touch. He will tell you that you have no hope when he knows fully well that God is your hope. Satan will lie to you at every turn, just as he did to Eve.

God knew that the Tree of the Knowledge of Good and Evil contained something that was detrimental to Adam and Eve. His directive wasn't given to Adam and Eve to withhold something beneficial from them; it was given out of His great love for them in order to protect them. In their relationship with God, they truly had a knowledge of GOOD. Every facet of God was full of goodness and radiated that goodness on them. God had forbidden them from eating from that tree because in doing so they would also "know," or have an intimate relation with, evil.

This knowing wasn't a head full of information. The word used for "know" in the original language is the same one used later to describe Adam "knowing," or having intimate relations, with his wife Eve. It infers being joined to the core at a very deep level. God knew that the day Adam and Eve joined themselves to evil, they could no longer be in His presence. They would pass from eternal life with Him to a place of spiritual death — a place of separation from His presence. That separation would cause them to no longer be able to abide in His presence and would also bring about their eventual physical death.

Using this tactic, Satan entered in and presented his argument that God was actually being selfish, withholding what Satan suggested was a wonderful knowledge from them. He told Eve that God was forbidding them from eating of the Tree of the Knowledge of Good and Evil to keep them from being like God, but think about that for a moment. Who in the Bible up to this point best exemplified one who had known good and evil? Was it God? No — He has no place for evil. It was Satan!

We read in Ezekiel 28:14 that Lucifer had been the anointed Cherub in God's presence. He lived and basked in God's goodness, yet he was filled with pride and eventually rebelled against God, casting aside God's ways and desiring to be like God while pursuing his own desires. This change was a total transformation, as all that was of God that had been in Lucifer departed when he "took of" evil. In his own way, he had reasoned to himself that the glory of God that radiated upon him when he was in God's presence belonged to him as well. He viewed himself as an equal to God, and in his pride, he shared his thoughts and motivation with other angels of Heaven and caused a number of them to join him in his rebellion against God and His ways. In doing so, he embraced the knowledge of evil — of embracing that which is contrary to God's ways — and he was cast out of Heaven (*see* Isaiah 14:12; Luke 10:8).

> **Satan wasn't encouraging Eve to take of the Tree to be like God — he was tricking her into taking of the Tree to be like him!**

When Satan approached Eve with his argument, he was not merely trying to change her mind. He was attempting to lure her into his realm — the realm of the knowledge of evil — as he was the original partaker of both good and evil.

Satan wasn't encouraging Eve to take of the Tree to be like God — he was tricking her into taking of the Tree to be like him! He was enticing her and deceiving her to act in a way that would cause her to take on his nature, a nature of sin and rebellion against God, that would ultimately put her in bondage to him. Sadly, his argument persuaded her:

> *The woman was convinced. She saw that the tree was beautiful and its fruit looked delicious, and she wanted the wisdom it would give her. So she took some of the fruit and ate it. Then she gave some to her husband, who was with her, and he ate it, too.*
>
> — Genesis 3:6 (*NLT*)

Notice that the woman was "convinced." The devil had proposed thoughts and arguments to her that changed her mindset and caused her to act on it. Eve accepted Satan's misrepresentation about God and went against God's directive in order to gain what the devil had convinced her was being withheld from her. She then persuaded Adam to join her and eat from the Tree as well.

When I was diagnosed with cancer, it was up to me to choose how I would look at my situation and where God was in it. What I was "convinced" of would be what I would eventually act on or not. It was vitally important that what I was convinced of and would act upon was based on what God had to say.

So how could I make sure I wouldn't be swayed by the opinions of others or the lies that Satan was sure to tempt me to believe? I had to dedicate myself to reading my Bible and spending time in prayer. I had to talk to God from my heart and listen for Him to speak back to me through His Word. The devil will show up often and do what he can to get you away from God's Word because he knows it is your answer to your problem and the boundary he must respect in your life. He is the one seeking the opportunity to shake you to your core and steal God's blessings from your life. If you let him, he will invade your thoughts and your life to have his way.

The renowned Nineteenth Century evangelist Charles Spurgeon described this battle for the soul of man, in which Satan seeks to take each person he can along with him into spiritual death:

Consider how precious a soul must be, when both God and the devil are after it. You never heard that the devil was after a kingdom, did you? No, he is not so foolish; he knows it would not be worth his winning; he is never after that; but he is always after souls. You never heard that God was seeking after a crown, did you! No, he thinketh little of dominions; but he is after souls every day; his Holy Spirit is seeking his children; and Christ came to save souls.[2]

The Bible is full of scriptures speaking of God's love for you and me and the lengths He has gone to show that love. Those scriptures are there to make it perfectly clear how valuable you and I are to God, and that is a knowledge that Satan wants to hide from you at any cost. God has been very deliberate in not only loving you and showing you that love, but also in documenting His love for you so that you can go back to it over and over to keep yourself strong in remembering and understanding how deeply and completely He cares for you. Below are some beautiful examples of God's love for you and me:

The more you read the Bible and meditate on what it says, the more you will come to understand God — His love, His ways, and His desires for you.

> *But God demonstrates His own love toward us, in that while we were still sinners, Christ died for us.*
> — Romans 5:8

> *For God so loved the world that He gave His only begotten Son, that whoever believes in Him should not perish but have everlasting life.*
> — John 3:16

> *But God, who is rich in mercy, because of His great love with which He loved us, even when we were dead in trespasses, made us alive together with Christ (by grace you have been saved....*
> — Ephesians 2:4-5

THERE'S A LIGHT AT THE END OF YOUR TUNNEL

God showed how much he loved us by sending his one and only Son into the world so that we might have eternal life through him. This is real love—not that we loved God, but that he loved us and sent his Son as a sacrifice to take away our sins.
— 1 John 4:9-10 (*NLT*)

The more you read the Bible and meditate on what it says, the more you will come to understand God — His love, His ways, and His desires for you. You'll understand his character — who He is, what He does, and most importantly, what He does not do. It's with this understanding that you can see through the mischaracterizations and lies that the devil will use to try and bring you along in his way of thinking and realm of control. In the following chapters, you will find a breakdown of the devil's tactics and learn not only how to defend yourself against them, but also how to overcome them and be victorious.

It's God's desire for you to know His love, walk in His blessings, and experience His goodness in your life. There is a light at the end of your tunnel, and He will walk with you every step of the way as you trust in Him.

CHAPTER 4

Focus On What Can See You Through

WHEN I WAS diagnosed with cancer, I had many appointments scheduled out for me in a short amount of time. To this day the one that stands out to me is distinctive, not for what the doctor said to me that day, but because of the atmosphere I walked into when I arrived.

My first appointment with my oncologist was in the early part of the morning. The uncertainty and dread of what my wife and I might be told had us both a bit apprehensive, and we had tried to prepare ourselves as best we could. As we opened the door to the clinic office to go inside, we found the room nearly full of people. We made our way to the front desk to check in for the appointment, and once I had checked in, we found seats to sit in while we waited for my name to be called.

As I looked around the waiting room full of people, I was struck by the solemnness and silence that was in the room. As I surveyed the faces of those around me, I found almost all of them shared a commonality — sullen faces that were devoid of smiles and eyes dull from the weight of what they were dealing with. Each of those precious people were suffering from some type of serious physical ailment, and now I was sharing the same room and while walking through a similar experience. I had never been in a room that seemed so devoid of hope.

I leaned over to my wife and asked if she was seeing the same things I was seeing, or if I was projecting what I was processing onto the group of people we were with. She assured me that she was seeing the same thing I was — a room full of people weighed down by the diagnoses they had been given.

As I looked at their faces, I realized that I was carrying in my heart what seemed to be missing from that room — hope. I had hope, found in Jesus, for my situation, and I believed that I would come out of this battle with cancer alive and well. I knew God was faithful, and He would be my strength through this difficult time. As I took time to look at each person individually, my heart went out to them for the gravity of what they must be facing. There were so many layers of impact to what each of the people around me were dealing with, and at that time, I could only imagine what all was really involved.

Looking around the room, I made a commitment to myself that throughout this cancer journey I would rub off my hope on anyone who was near me, anyone open to the message and willing to listen. I wouldn't push my hope on others, but as conversation would lead, I decided I would intentionally share with others here that hope existed, that there was hope for them in their situation, and that the true hope I had found in Jesus could be theirs as well.

In prioritizing my decision to share this hope with others, my focus changed from *what* I was going through and *why* it was happening to me, to *who* my hope was found in. I hoped that as I conversed with those around me, it would encourage them to do the same.

Keeping that focus was how I stayed strong during my battle with cancer. I didn't allow "why" to be my focus. I focused on "who" was with me — the One who could see me through the hard times and bring me to the other side. I kept my joy in the midst of the horrible effects of my treatment because my focus was on Jesus, the One who took me through that battle to the health and the future He had for me on the other side.

I shared this hope with the nurses who treated me. I would sit in the chemotherapy treatment room and share my hope with the other patients near me too, and in doing so, I saw the atmosphere in those rooms change as hope entered in and dispelled the dread. Eyes would light up and people would lean forward in their chairs to hear how God was good in the middle of hard times. His faithfulness and love became their focus for that brief time, and their spirits were lifted as people saw past their circumstances into the possibility of something more awaiting them at the end of their cancer journey, more than death or merely surviving. It was amazing to see the power of hope at work.

HOPE AND MR. JONES

The most impactful example of focusing on hope was during my sessions of radiation treatment. I met Mr. Jones early into my cancer treatment. We had our radiation treatments scheduled one right after the other — I would go first, then Mr. Jones. With this scheduling, we would see each other multiple times a week in the radiation treatment center waiting room as we each waited for our appointment time to come. Mr. Jones was a pleasant man with a warm smile. While some people in the room would come and keep to themselves, Mr. Jones was comfortable engaging in casual conversation. It would help pass the time. All of us in that waiting room knew what we were there for, and over time, some of us who saw each other regularly would begin to share how were holding up from our treatment regimens and would support each other's fight with cancer. Seeing each other regularly, Mr. Jones and I struck up a friendship. We got to the point where we would often joke about me leaving enough radiation in the machine after my treatment for him to get his "nuking" in too.

When I first met Mr. Jones, he was very depressed. His health was poor, as he had cancer and had to use an oxygen tank to get around. Sitting next to him, I was thankful that besides the cancerous tumor I was fighting with, I was in good health. I wasn't lugging around an oxygen tank, my weight was good, and my blood pressure was normal. I seemed to be the picture of health — with a 5.5 cm tumor in my rectum. The cancer could have easily sent me into depression, but early on I had decided not to focus on what the treatment was doing to me or what the cancer was doing to me. Instead, I chose to think about how I was going to make it to the other side of this journey and keep on living. I had things to do, people to see, and a destiny to fulfill. Most of all, I had trust in Jesus that He was with me every step of the way.

During those first days of getting to know Mr. Jones, I noticed that there was little talk from him of a future. His thoughts were dominated by the plight he was in and the negative outcome that seemed to await him. It broke my heart to see this big, warm fella pretty much resolved to his life devolving into nothing. I saw something there that gave me insight into where he and so many other people find themselves. He saw no future for himself. He had no *hope*.

AN AVENUE TO THE HEART

Each day I sat a few of feet away from Mr. Jones and with the answer he was looking for. I expected to see God's goodness in my body. That was my hope, the trust I had placed in the fact that Jesus was my light and my salvation; He was the strength of my life. So the question became, *How do I share my hope with Mr. Jones?* I could've gone into a fine scriptural dissertation for him. I could teach and preach and pray. Yet I had gotten to know him well enough to understand that in doing so, I would probably lose him. Instead, I prayed and asked the Holy Spirit to show me a way to share with Mr. Jones that his future wasn't already over and that he could have hope. There could be a light at the end of his tunnel.

The next time we met for treatment, Mr. Jones and I began to talk, and he told me about visiting with his granddaughter over the weekend. I noticed a light in his eyes when he spoke about her, and I realized that she was my way in to sharing my hope with him. Over the next few days of treatments, I made sure to bring his granddaughter up in conversation, and each time he would smile, telling me more about her and how much she meant to him. I would talk about my expectations for life after cancer and mention my hope for him to enjoy getting to spend time with his granddaughter and see her grow.

Before long Mr. Jones was starting the conversations about life after cancer. He was no longer the depressed man I had met. He would come in smiling and joking. We would talk about how we were handling our treatments and how our families were doing. It was during those times that I had the opportunity to share with him about my hope and where it came from. He was open and receptive, and we had good conversations.

During the later days of my treatment, I arrived one morning to see Mr. Jones had made it in before me in. I noticed something different about him. He smiled when I asked what had changed, and he informed me that he wasn't using an oxygen tank any longer! I was seeing firsthand how hope had been working in him. *God is so good!*

'KEEP THE FAITH'

On my last day of treatment, Mr. Jones and I talked about our days together in that little waiting room. We reminisced about how things started and how far each of us had come in our journeys. It was such a great relief to be finishing my radiation treatments, but it was a bit bittersweet to say goodbye to Mr. Jones. As I walked back for my last treatment, I looked to him and let him know I wouldn't use all the radiation up and would leave some for him, to which I got a big smile and a hearty laugh.

When I finished my treatment and walked back to the waiting room Mr. Jones met me at the door. We laughed a bit, hugged, and said our goodbyes. Then as I began to leave, he looked at me and said, "Mike, you keep the faith." That made every one of those 28 treatment days with Mr. Jones worth it. When the radiation burns would make things almost intolerable, I would think back to Mr. Jones and his encouragement: "keep the faith." I was in awe of the change that hope had produced in him.

The depressed man I met was transformed by hope. Hope is such a powerful thing. When hope exists, a person can see a future that belongs to him. He can look beyond his circumstances and believe that better things can happen. Faith can rise up and motivate that same person not to settle for things as they are, but to instead aspire to more, to expect something better. The key for Mr. Jones was his granddaughter. How precious the Holy Spirit was to show me that and allow me to be used to bring hope to that dear man. I don't know what all God was doing in that man's heart, but I am blessed to have been a part of it.

Mr. Jones' focus changed from *what* and *why* to **who**, and it made all the difference.

DON'T GET CAUGHT UP IN 'WHY?'

When something challenging in life happens it is nearly inevitable to ask the question, "Why?" Wanting to understand the reason behind the events that have shaken your world is a natural response. It has happened to me, and I'm almost certain it has happened to you.

Sometimes having an idea of why something has happened can make it feel as if you have a bit of control in an otherwise out of control situation. That elusive quest for *why* something has happened has a place in the process of understanding what is going on, but it's important to realize that you may not know or understand the why until much later. It may even be after your ordeal is over that you receive your answer. You may very well enter the tunnel asking why and walk through that tunnel to the light at the other end without an answer to that question. That answer may indeed come later.

I know what it's like to have the "whys" screaming in your ear. Each day they were waiting for me. The night I came home with the news I had cancer was full of several of those "why" moments. With each test result, a new "why" came to pose its own new question.

"How could this be?"

"Why was this happening to me?"

I think back to the day my PET scan results came in, and they confirmed the size and location of the cancerous tumor. I had been doing everything I knew to do, trusting God to heal me of cancer, and here was a scan report telling me that the tumor was there and I was headed for some very nasty treatment.

"Why isn't this working?" I would ask.

"Why didn't I get healed?"

My encouragement to you is don't allow yourself to become fixated on "why."

"Why did this happen to me?"

"Why am I having to go through this?"

"Why didn't God do something about this?"

I admit, it was hard to deal with. Yet that was one of the keys to getting to the other side of my tunnel — I had to deal with the "why" factor of my fight. "Why" becomes a bully who will push you into a cycle of questioning and doubting, draining your energy and your resolve, keeping you confused. I had to face it head-on to make sure it would not overtake me and cause me to miss out on the miracle I was trusting God for.

Getting caught up in "why" is like playing pin the tail on the donkey. You are blind to the full scope of the facts, you're spun round and round with questions, and then you're pushed in a direction to somehow put your finger on the exact answer to "why."

A few years ago, there was a leak behind the toilet in one of the bathrooms at my house. My daughter came running into the living room and announced that water was coming out from behind the toilet and was quickly pooling on the tile floor. We soon had towels on the floor to soak up the water while we tried to figure out what was going on.

I didn't stand looking at the toilet while the water on the floor slowly started to rise, wringing my hands and asking:

"Why is this happening? How could this be happening to me, especially now?"

I looked at the wall behind the toilet. I knew that water shouldn't be coming from back there. I stooped down to look and found a leaking hose to be the culprit. A few twists to the water shut off valve in the wall, and the leak was stopped. The cleanup had just begun, but after replacing the hose and taking care of the water on the floor, we were back in business.

After getting everything back in working order, I investigated **why** the hose had begun to leak. The hose was old, and the fitting had corroded to the point that it began to leak. It wasn't visible unless you looked closely, and it gave no indication of having an issue until the day it failed.

You may be asking what fixing leaking toilets has to do with getting through what you are facing. The illustration has a point — focus your

Chasing after *why* will cloud your focus and steal your energy.

attention and energy on the problem you are facing and its solution. Know what is right and then evaluate what you are facing with that as your baseline. Only after that are you in the proper position to begin asking *why*.

It is the same approach you must take when you're facing the trials of life, whether it be in your relationships, your finances, your health, or your thoughts. Chasing after *why* will cloud your focus and steal your energy. Your success is found in "who" will give you hope and strengthen you as you face and overcome the situation you are dealing with.

DEALING WITH THE BLINDSIDING EVENTS OF LIFE

Over the years I've been known as a proactive person. By nature I'm a planner and builder. I love to think up knew ideas and how to make them work. In business it works very well, yet I've learned that in everyday life there is so much that I have little control over. Life happens during my planning, and as good as I have been at times in being proactive — life has no regard for my skills or plans. Life is a series of events and situations that are fluid.

You might be wondering what events in my life took me off-guard while I was doing life. Here are just a few of these unexpected events I'm referring to:

- I lost my mother in a car wreck when I was 12 years old. How do you prepare for that?

- The company I was building a career in had a huge financial scandal and went bankrupt. How do you prepare for that?

- I was a healthy man in my early forties when they informed me that I had an aggressive cancer eating away at my body. How do you prepare for that?

These situations weren't of my creation, and I had no control over them. Over time I've learned that you can't prepare for the trials of life from a natural standpoint. There are too many tangents to ever successfully account for. Eventually you will face a situation that has you reacting — and with it comes pressure, uncertainty, despair, and a slippery slope to hopelessness — but that doesn't mean all hope is lost.

When the trials of life blindside you, you have a choice in how you deal with them. You can blame others around you or even God. You can become defiant and angry. You can wilt and allow the situation and its effects to consume you. You can also choose to look to the One who is the answer to your problems and hold on to Him until the clouds clear and you see the sunshine again — until you see the light at the end of your tunnel. This last approach requires you to *actively trust* God before, in the midst of, and all the way through the mess you are dealing with.

When I was in the first month of dealing with cancer, my doctors spent time asking me about my eating habits, social habits, etc., to try and determine what the root cause of the cancer I was dealing with might be. They found that my diet was not out of line; I wasn't a smoker or in environments that exposed me to secondhand smoke. I hadn't worked in an industry that exposed me to cancer-causing agents. I even did a genetic test for markers that could show a predisposition to cancer, and it was negative. There were no indicators that I had been doing something overt that caused the nasty tumor to be in my body.

I wasn't getting an easy answer to the question: "Why did I have cancer?"

The night that I came home from the colonoscopy and locked myself in the bathroom and sat there stunned for quite a few minutes, the questions "WHY?" and "HOW?" screamed loud in all caps as I tried to wrap my head around the news. I eventually remembered what I had been taught years before, that there are events in life that we experience that are direct results of our disobedience to the Word of God, so I asked myself, *Had I been so callous to something that I had opened myself up for this?* I also knew that the devil wants to kill, steal, and destroy in my life at every opportunity (*see* John 10:10), so then I asked, "Could this be the case?" I didn't readily recall an area that I had consistently thumbed my nose at God, but I needed to know the answer so that I could repent and make things right if I did.

(God is very patient in bringing the effects of judgment to our lives, but they do eventually show up if we refuse to acknowledge them and make the needed corrections.)

As I sat there on my porcelain throne, I humbled myself and came before the Throne of my loving and merciful Heavenly Father and asked Him if the cancer was a result of my disobedience or if it was an attack of the enemy. I knew according to James 1:5 that I could come and ask for wisdom and God would give it to me, and He did. He spoke to my heart by His Spirit as He so often has — in terms I could understand. To this day I can still hear His words to me:

"Son, you have a lot of things to work on, but this is an attack of the enemy."

That one phrase calmed my spirit and my mind. From then on, I knew that I was being bullied and had an enemy to deal with, and I knew how to go about it. I still had much to learn, but I wasn't going into this fight with my arms at my sides and full of fear. I had been learning from God's Word how to defend myself, and I wasn't going down without a fight. I was going to trust in God and His Word and do my own damage to the enemy's plans.

Had my disobedience been the root cause of the cancer, I would have needed to ask God to show me what my disobedience was. I would have needed to acknowledge it as exactly that — disobedience to God. Then I would have needed to stop doing whatever it was and ask for His forgiveness. Repentance isn't just saying you are sorry; it is recognizing the error you've made as sin, saying you are sorry, and deciding not to do it any longer. It is when you make a change of direction and turn from it. Anything else is just an act of remorse and an apology at best.

I had several subsequent opportunities to ask God for a full disclosure of what caused my situation and all the underlying details, but He didn't give me a grand dissertation. He didn't even give me a short overview. There was a time when I would have been frustrated with what I could have perceived as God's lack of candidness, but over the years, I had learned to trust Him even when I didn't have all the details.

WHAT I LEARNED FROM 3-DIMENSIONAL CHESS

You will have to get to this place as well. What helped me in this came from a time earlier in my life when I was complaining to myself (and God) about how a situation wasn't lining up the way I thought it should. As I sat there in my by-invitation-only pity party, a picture came into my mind of a chess board with the pieces on it, and I heard this in my heart:

"This is the board you are playing on...."

Then in my mind came an old scene from Star Trek. Captain Kirk and Spock were sitting at a table playing a version of three-dimensional chess that had multiple levels and boards, one above another. Then I heard this in my heart:

"This this is the board I play on. You see on one level. I am making moves on multiple levels with multiple pieces."

I then understood that there was so much more involved than I what I saw or knew, and that there were so many other pieces in

> **Your life isn't a game to God — and He always has your best interests in His mind.**

play than just mine. God was telling me what He knew was pertinent to me and for me to know at that time — *but I needed to put my focus on the One who held all the pieces and desired not to lose one of them.*

Your life isn't a game to God — and He always has your best interests in His mind. There are, however, many people intertwined in your life, and He is taking all that into consideration as the events of your life unfold. There are no pawns to God — you are of great value to Him.

While I was preparing to deal with the cancer and make decisions on how to approach it from a medical perspective, I was spending time with God, and He encouraged me one day by speaking this to my heart:

"Trust Me to be who I said I would be to you and to do what I said I would do for you."

With that encouragement He was calling me to see Him as my true answer — as personal as one can get. Amid a situation I didn't see coming, that I had no control over, and that had the potential to derail everything in my life, He was calling me to *actively* trust Him. We need to live every day of our lives trusting Him to be true and faithful. It's the only approach for a child of God to have. Jesus is the answer to every one of our problems. In fact, that became one of my mantras during my battle with cancer — "God is not the cause of my problem; He is the solution to it!"

You will need to make this your position and mantra as well. Do not blame God for a situation you have gotten yourself into or one that has seemingly come out of nowhere. God is not the author of it, but He is your way out.

YOU CAN SEE GOD'S GOODNESS IN THE LAND OF THE LIVING

During my battle with cancer, I spent quite a bit of time reading in the book of Psalms. In it I saw in David a man whose life was not one that went easily. Even though God had chosen him and Samuel had anointed him as the next king of Israel, David had a variety of trials come to his life. The king he had faithfully served turned against him and pursued him throughout the kingdom to catch him and take his life. Even after King Saul's death, David had to fight others to obtain the kingdom he had been ordained for and acknowledged to receive. There was no smooth ascension to his God ordained position. It was a tedious, perilous journey that was overwhelming at times, but the book of Psalms gives us a window into how David handled these calamities and persecution. This is the man that God spoke of and said:

> *He raised up David to be their king, of whom He testified, saying, "I have found David the son of Jesse, a man after My own heart, who will fulfill My entire will."*
> — Acts 13:22

As I read in the book of Psalms to draw strength for my battle, I found a key to staying strong and winning my fight in Psalm 27. In the time it describes, David had been accused of wrongdoing. He had enemies all around him who sought to kill him, but in the midst of this, he made this statement in verse 13:

> *I would have lost heart, unless I had believed that I would see the goodness of the Lord In the land of the living.*

David would have lost hope, lost his confidence in his situation, if he hadn't believed that he would see God's goodness in the land of the living. He believed he would see God's goodness in his situation while he was still alive. He wasn't focusing on "why?" He was intently looking to the "Who" that could sustain and save him.

I can remember reading this during my difficult time and how it resonated with me. I needed to see God's goodness in the land of the living. Some people were telling me that I would be healed when I made it to Heaven, but I wanted to see His goodness while I was still alive! So, what would that goodness look like for me? To be cancer free!

What would that goodness look like to you?

- To be healed of your sickness?
- To have your marriage restored?
- To see your child break free from addiction to drugs?
- To have your financial situation stabilized and productive?
- To be free from pornography?
- To have a sound mind free of fear and confusion?

It could be one or more of these things or something different. The fact is, you want to see this happen while you are still alive to enjoy it. David said he was confident that he would see God's goodness in his situation while he was still alive to enjoy it. He was confident in God's faithfulness and the promise He had made about his future. What made David so confident that he would see God move in his situation? And how can you look to God in your situation and find confidence that you will see His goodness? We find the answer in verse 1, as David states:

The Lord is my light and my salvation; whom will I fear? The Lord is the strength of my life; of whom will I be afraid?

This was who God was to David — God was his light, the illuminator of the darkness around him. David looked to God to reveal to him his surroundings. He did not rely only on his senses. He looked to God as his salvation — the answer to his problems! God was the one to whom he looked to save him from his trials. He looked to God as his strength in life. When situations occurred that would weaken his confidence, his resolve, and his peace — he would look to God to be his strength.

David took inventory of these things and said, "Hey, with God as my Revealer, my Savior, and my Strength — why am I afraid? Who is bigger than God, that I should be afraid of them?"

Then David went on to list some of what he had been dealing with in verses 2 and 3:

When the wicked came against me to eat up my flesh, my enemies and foes, they stumbled and fell. Though an army may encamp against me, my heart shall not fear; though war may rise against me, in this I will be confident.

Although the wicked came against David to eat his flesh, they stumbled and fell; although an army encamped around him and war rose against him, he remained confident that the Lord was his Revealer, his Savior, and his Strength. He expected to see God deliver him because he had placed his trust in God. David was actively trusting God, and he was confident in God's care for him. You can be confident as well. In the middle of your mess, your tunnel, you can look forward with an expectation that there is a light at the end. Just as David saw the Lord as his light and salvation, you can too.

THERE'S A LIGHT AT THE END OF YOUR TUNNEL

Imagine David standing in his own tunnel while his enemies made accusations against him and the king's forces hunted for him throughout the countryside. To stay a step ahead of his pursuers, David was sleeping in caves to stay hidden, moving from place to place to keep from being cornered and caught. From the looks of his situation, things were not good at all, but he did not focus on the darkness around him. He did not allow his focus to stay on the bad that could happen if his enemies won. In reading Psalm 27, you will find that David focused on who his light was and what that light would do for him.

Remember this?

"Trust Me to be who I said I would be to you and to do what I said I would do for you."

That was what David was doing when he said in verse 13: "I would have lost heart, unless I had believed that I would see the goodness of the Lord In the land of the living."

Let's put them together:

I would have lost my strength and my resolve to see this through and win had I not believed I would see the results of God's goodness happen in my life, because I am trusting Him to be who He said He would be to me and to do what He said He would do for me.

This is a key to fighting your fight. It is your light as you go through your tunnel, intent on making to the other side. Even if things don't look good today, it doesn't change who God is to you or what He said He would do for you. He is faithful. That was David's declaration; that was my declaration. Let it be yours too.

God is *faithful*.

CHAPTER 5

Knowing Your Enemy and His Tactics

IN HIS WORLD-renowned treatise *The Art of War*, famed General Sun Tzu lays out key points of wisdom with regard to facing and overcoming your enemy. One of the pearls of wisdom he shares is the following:

> If you know the enemy and know yourself, you need not fear the result of a hundred battles. If you know yourself but not the enemy, for every victory gained you will also suffer defeat. If you know neither the enemy nor yourself, you will succumb in every battle.[3]

It's vitally important to know your enemy — who he is and how he goes about things. In the previous chapter, we touched on this, and it bears repeating it again here. We have an enemy whose desire for our lives is destruction. He is the author and orchestrator of the evil in the world that we live in — and you must understand that he is not a spectator in those things. He and his minions are very active participants in the evil that plagues the earth and its inhabitants.

As a reminder, Jesus had this to say about the difference between Himself and Satan:

> *The thief does not come, except to steal and kill and destroy. I came that they may have life, and that they may have it more abundantly.*
>
> — John 10:10 (*MEV*)

If it steals, kills, or destroys in life, its author is Satan. In First Peter 5:8, we are given a description of Satan's disposition and approach to you and I:

> *Be sober, be vigilant; because your adversary the devil walks about like a roaring lion, seeking whom he may devour.*

He walks about like a roaring lion, seeking whom he may devour. He is not causally lying around waiting for some unsuspecting soul to come near him and be pounced on. Satan still roams today, actively looking for those whom he might attack to steal from, destroy, or kill. He wants to cause you suffering in life for his own pleasure and also to draw you to a place of blaming God and turning your back on Him.

Knowing who your real enemy is and the ways in which he attacks will put you on the path to resisting and defeating his attacks in your life. Satan will always try to convince you that what you are facing is bigger than God's ability to overcome it, but knowing the tactics he uses in attempting to deceive and attack you will help you best answer his accusations, repel his attacks, and obtain your victory. You can defend yourself and counter his attacks with your own according to God's Word, which is the true authority on what is possible and who you are in God's eyes.

THAT SATAN, HE'S A BULLY

Bullies and their behavior have existed throughout the history of mankind, as the behavior is rooted in a desire to establish superiority and influence at the expense of others. Many of us probably experienced our first bully at school. It was likely a person who was looking to establish superiority and influence at your expense, and by making themselves look better than you, they were able to secure a higher opinion than you in the minds of others and in your mind as well.

When a bully tries to assert dominance over someone, it can happen in a variety of ways. It could be through a physical confrontation where the bully starts and wins a fight. It could be through demeaning comments he made about you to other people you know or to you directly. The bully does whatever he can to make you look and feel weak, out of touch, and undesirable to be around. He moves to diminish or eliminate your status, your influence, and results in the world he seeks to control.

Knowing what we do about Satan and his intentions, we can firmly say he is the Original Bully, and it is his constant mode of operation to seek how to make you look and feel weak, out of touch, and undesirable to be around. He moves to diminish or eliminate your status, influence, and results in the world that he seeks to control. Thankfully, we also know that bullies are not all powerful and that they must be dealt with, as their appetite for power is never satisfied. Realizing that they can be confronted and defeated and then understanding how to act on that belief will change your life.

JUST BECAUSE YOU ARE BIGGER DOESN'T MEAN YOU ARE INVINCIBLE

In First Samuel 17, we read of arguably the most well-known bully in history. Goliath of Gath was a physical giant who was a champion of the Philistine army. His stature is described in verses 4-7:

And a champion went out from the camp of the Philistines, named Goliath, from Gath, whose height was six cubits and a span. He had a bronze helmet on his head, and he was armed with a coat of mail, and the weight of the coat was five thousand shekels of bronze. And he had bronze armor on his legs and a bronze javelin between his shoulders. Now the staff of his spear was like a weaver's beam, and his iron spearhead weighed six hundred shekels; and a shield-bearer went before him.

The cubit was an ancient measurement known to be taken from the length of a man's arm, from the tip of his elbow to the tip of his middle finger, which was typically found to be between 20 and 22 inches.[4] A span was measured by the distance from the extremity of the thumb to that of the little finger, when stretched apart; approximately nine inches. According to scholars, this would have made Goliath between nine and ten feet tall, more than four feet taller than the average man. Goliath towered over all those around him, and he thrived on his stature and the power it gave him.

Along with his height, the description of Goliath's armor and weaponry shows that he was a very strong man whose body matched his height with a fully muscled physique. Scholars estimate that the weight of his armor was at least 150 lb. He was a mountain of a man whose physical match was not to be found in Israel.

The Philistines did not expect the army of Israel to have a match for Goliath, and they desired to take the army of Israel with as few casualties to their own troops as possible. What better way than to send Goliath out as their champion to take on whoever Israel would send in a single one-on-one fight — that meant the winner's army would be declared victorious while the loser would be obligated to surrender. With the show of strength that Goliath provided, the Philistines assumed the armies of Israel would be in fear and give in to their demands, increasing their influence and rule in the region. Goliath strode out into the middle of the battlefield and shouted:

> "...Why have you come out to line up for battle? Am I not a Philistine, and you the servants of Saul? Choose a man for yourselves, and let him come down to me. If he is able to fight with me and kill me, then we will be your servants. But if I prevail against him and kill him, then you shall be our servants and serve us." And the Philistine said, "I defy the armies of Israel this day; give me a man, that we may fight together."
> — 1 Samuel 17:8-10

Bullies always have something to say — some speech or threat given to praise own their power and abilities while demeaning their opponent. It is a classic form of psychological warfare, and often it is effective in achieving its desired effects. We see that the Philistines sent out their champion, who by all outward standards outclassed what the opposing army had to offer, and then they attempted to dictate the battle on grounds they choose according to rules that heavily weighed in their favor. This is how your enemy works, seeking to control all aspects of your actions and dictate your outcome. In doing so, he effectively ensures his own advantage and causes you to lose what confidence you have.

Notice in verse 11 that the Philistine army's tactics were effective:

> When Saul and all Israel heard these words of the Philistine, they were dismayed and greatly afraid.

Does this sound like how you have felt? Have your circumstances seemed to come to the forefront to make themselves known each day, just like Goliath did? Do they look to draw your attention as they cry out to you, challenging your confidence? Maybe they look so big, so insurmountable, that you're tempted to believe that you have to face them all by yourself. It might feel as if one-on-one combat, winner takes all, is your only option, but the truth is, you don't have to face your circumstances alone.

Each day King Saul and his army listened to Goliath's boasting, they were paralyzed with fear and dismay. They feared what would happen if they confronted Goliath in single combat and were distraught that they had no alternative to his challenge. They were looking for an answer in their own ranks, among themselves, and could not find it. That may be where you have often found yourself, in that same place looking to the right and to the left to see if there was someone who had the answer to what you were dealing with. However, when you do that, you can lose sight of who else is with you — the One who truly loves and cares for you — God Himself.

While Saul and the army of Israel looked among themselves and endured Goliath's mockery each day, God was watching. Let me assure you, too, that in the midst of whatever you are facing, God is not sitting by uninterested in your plight or oblivious to the affront being made to His love for you and His desire to move in your situation. When Saul and his army were not putting their trust in God to deliver Israel, God inserted a young man He knew would trust in Him — David, the son of Jesse.

David had three brothers who were serving in Saul's army, and his father gave him supplies for them and sent him to where the armies of Israel were encamped. When David arrived where the army was stationed, he found something peculiar to him. Each day the Israelites and the Philistine army had been marching out and forming up for battle opposite of each other, but all they did was shout at each other without actually engaging in battle, and this day began no differently:

> *And David left his supplies in the hand of the supply keeper, ran to the army, and came and greeted his brothers. Then as he talked with them, there was the champion, the Philistine of Gath, Goliath by name, coming up from the armies of the Philistines; and he spoke according to the same words. So David heard them.*
> — 1 Samuel 17:22-23

Just as he had done the previous 40 days, Goliath strode out to the field between the armies and issued his challenge, berating the armies and the God of Israel. Standing there, David heard Goliath's words firsthand, listening to the booming voice of the giant who took delight in boasting of his own strength and insulting his opponent and their God. Then, just as they had for the last 40 days, the armies of Israel listened, doubted in themselves and their God, became afraid, and fled.

> *And all the men of Israel, when they saw the man, fled from him and were dreadfully afraid.*
> — 1 Samuel 17:24

Yet when David witnessed these events, instead of being moved in fear and wanting to run away from the situation, he asked an interesting question:

> *...For who is this uncircumcised Philistine, that he should defy the armies of the living God?*

David asked, "Who is this uncircumcised Philistine?" He wasn't concerned with how big Goliath was or how well armored and fit for battle he was. David saw him as an uncircumcised Philistine — a pagan with no covenant with the Living God. Who did he think he was to be speaking in such a way about the God of Israel and to daily defy His armies? David's indignation was for Goliath's disregard for God and His people. In contrast, when the armies of Israel heard the words of Goliath, they looked at their inability to deal with him and looked *no further* than themselves. They surely had prayed to God to help them, but they had lost sight of who God was in their situation. He was the one that being maligned. He was also their answer in facing Goliath, but they had not seen Him as such. Verses 31 and 32 continue:

> *Now when the words which David spoke were heard, they reported them to Saul; and he sent for him. Then David said to Saul, "Let no man's heart fail because of him; your servant will go and fight with this Philistine."*

David's words were reported to King Saul, and the king promptly sent for him. When David arrived, he sought to assure King Saul that God was indeed watching the situation and that He desired to move on their behalf. He then volunteers to go face Goliath in combat. From this passage, there is no indication that any of the soldiers, including the king, had offered to go face Goliath. They saw it as certain death, followed by the enslavement of Israel to the Philistines. They saw no light at the end of the tunnel they were facing, and they were groping for a way out. Instead, David saw an end to Goliath and his threats and a quick resolution to the Philistine army's attack against Israel. He looked at an outcome where God was involved and moving on behalf of His people. In the darkness surrounding them, David looked forward and saw light!

Verse 33 goes on to tell us:

> *And Saul said to David, "You are not able to go against this Philistine to fight with him; for you are a youth, and he a man of war from his youth."*

As Saul looked at David, he saw a young man who was much smaller than Goliath and unskilled in the ways of war. It is important to understand that how you see yourself and what you draw your conclusion from will help form the basis of your answer to your problems. David realized that Goliath was much larger and stronger than him, adorned in shining armor and armed with a huge sword and spear — but David saw himself as armed with something that Goliath could not compete against — the presence of Almighty God! In David's reply to King Saul, we see that the reason for his confidence was based on how God had been with him and saw him through dangerous times. David testified that he was going to face Goliath fully expecting God to deliver him from Goliath's hand. He expected to kill Goliath and return from the battle alive and well because he wasn't facing the giant alone in his own strength. He wasn't going out the battlefield relying on other's experiences for his trust in God. He was relying on who God was to *him*.

> *But David said to Saul, "Your servant used to keep his father's sheep, and when a lion or a bear came and took a lamb out of the flock, I went out after it and struck it, and delivered the lamb from its mouth; and when it arose against me, I caught it by its beard, and struck and killed it. Your servant has killed both lion and bear; and this uncircumcised Philistine will be like one of them, seeing he has defied the armies of the living God." Moreover David said, "The Lord, who delivered me from the paw of the lion and from the paw of the bear, He will deliver me from the hand of this Philistine...."*
>
> — 1 Samuel 17:34-37

While David was watching over his father's sheep, he battled with dangerous animals to protect the flocks he was given responsibility over. He engaged the lion and the bear *directly and* rescued the lamb from their mouths. He faced the enemies who came to steal from him and tried to kill him, trusting God to be with him.

> *"And when it arose against me, I caught it by its beard, and struck and killed it."*

David struck the wild beast, and in turn it let go of his lamb. Then the beast rose up to attack him, and he "caught it by its beard, and struck and killed it." You can't get any closer to your enemy than looking into his and taking hold of him with your hands, yet David challenged the fangs and the claws to take back what he knew was rightfully his. He defeated his enemy and rescued his lamb. It wasn't a simple recounting of the incidents with the wild animals, it was spoken from a place of deep conviction. David trusted the Lord to be with him then, and he was trusting Him to be with him now.

David's confidence in God was the powerful weapon he carried.

Looking out across the plain to where Goliath came daily to taunt Israel, David expected his battle with Goliath to be no different than facing the lion or the bear. To David, he was going to rescue another lamb from the mouth of a beast, and again, he was expecting God to be with Him. David's confidence in God was the powerful weapon he carried. After hearing David confidently share his story and testify of his trust in God, Saul was inspired to look beyond his fear of the giant and agreed to send out David as Israel's champion against Goliath, saying:

"Go, and the Lord be with you!" (v. 37).

What would it take for you to agree to allow an untrained shepherd to face the enemy in combat that would decide the fate of your kingdom and its people? This champion from the flocks isn't even properly trained, armed, or armored according to common military standards, and he stands before you with a staff and a sling, content to do battle with his shepherding tools. Yet it was what King Saul heard in David's words and what he saw that every other man in his army lacked:

Trust in God.

It was this trust in God that inspired Saul and gave him hope. Saul himself did not have this level of trust, but he recognized it in David. It was because of this trust that King Saul looked at David and told him: "Go, and the Lord be with you!"

IT'S MORE IMPORTANT TO KNOW WHOSE SIDE YOU ARE ON THAN WHO IS ON YOURS

When you are facing a trial, it can seem insurmountable. A survey of your allies and supplies at your disposal may appear to be severely lacking for the battle you face. Saul and his armies looked at each other for a suitable answer to their Goliath problem and found nothing and no one they could put their trust in. Because of this they spent day after day preparing to make war, lining up in battle formation and saying the right things, only to tremble in fear and retreat when Goliath confidently strode out onto the battlefield and began to berate them and their God. The soldiers of the armies of Israel and their king went back to their camp and waited another day for someone to come to their aid. That day finally came in the form of a young shepherd who was confident — not in his own abilities — but in the power and strength of his God.

Just as David was, it is so important that you be settled on where the Lord is in your situation. When you are facing a daunting trial, not knowing this can cause you to go through the motions day after day, week after week, just as the armies of Israel did. You can get up in the morning and confess that God is your deliverer, then march out and line up for battle. You can raise your voice and talk about how things are going to be better, yet when the situation doesn't quickly resolve or the circumstances remain or get worse, you hang your head in disappointment and run away from the battle in fear. *It's not working*, becomes the thought you focus on, instead of *He is working!* Remember, your enemy is after your resolve. God *is* working, and while you may not see the results overnight, you can rest assured that He has not left your side and is indeed at work on your behalf.

King Saul and his armies knew they were representing the kingdom of Israel, but they had lost sight of *who* the kingdom of Israel was to be representing. Goliath mocked them and more importantly, he mocked the God of Israel. The Israelites may have experienced indignation at this mocking, but they did not act on it. It was as if they had lost sight of the fact that the God of Israel that Goliath mocked had parted the Red Sea. They seemed to have forgotten that God had delivered them from Egypt and had been with them as they subdued the land He had promised them. There were so many great things had God done for his chosen people, so many great things He had done to defend His name — and now Saul and His soldiers did not trust in Him to deal with Goliath. Have you found yourself at this place where you've lost sight of God's goodness in your life?

When David first heard Goliath mocking the armies of Israel and God, he was appalled, saying: "…Who is this uncircumcised Philistine, that he should defy the armies of the living God?" (v. 26).

The God of Israel was very much alive to David, and He saw Goliath in the light of who God was, not in the light of who the king or the soldiers around him were. David wasn't looking to see who was on his side — *he understood that he was on God's side.* God had chosen Israel as his own nation and had made a covenant with them. He was their God, and they were His people. They belonged to Him, and He watched over them and provided for them — just like a shepherd would his flock.

David did not let the circumstances around him dictate how he saw God.

David did not let the circumstances around him dictate how he saw God. He did not let them shape his thinking of what God was able to do in the situation. He looked to God as faithful and able to do what others thought was improbable or impossible. To him, God was infinitely bigger than Goliath or anything else he would face. With God on his side, he understood that the bigger the enemy, the harder the fall.

And now with Goliath standing in the middle of the Valley of Elah, boasting of his strength and his might, David didn't see a giant of a man who was skilled in battle and able to defeat anyone whom Israel would bring out to meet him. Instead, he saw a small man in comparison to David's big God.

Does the problem you deal with act like Goliath in your life? Does it constantly try to get your attention and make you feel inadequate to face it and overcome it? Does is stand in defiance of what you know God has said about your life? Does it bully your thoughts and bring despair and fear? That sounds like a Goliath to me.

I can remember those type of thoughts coming to convince me that cancer was free to roam my body and destroy as it went. The tumor was malignant and had encroached on lymph nodes. I had to make the choice to not see cancer as bigger than the God who loved me, saved me, and was healing me. I was reminded of how David faced his own giant. By looking at how David faced Goliath and battled with him, you can learn how to fight your own giant as well.

After accepting David's offer to meet Goliath in battle, Saul attempted to prepare him:

So Saul clothed David with his armor, and he put a bronze helmet on his head; he also clothed him with a coat of mail. David fastened his sword to his armor and tried to walk, for he had not tested them. And David said to Saul, "I cannot walk with these, for I have not tested them." So David took them off.
— 1 Samuel 17:38-39

Saul was acting in good faith to prepare David for battle, giving him armor and sword to fight with, as David had none of his own. As he outfitted himself in the armor and sword, David tried to walk to learn how well he could move encumbered by them. He quickly found that he was unable to move freely in them, as he had not "tested" or "proved" them. He had not learned how to effectively operate with them, so he did a hard thing — but the correct thing — he took them off.

It wasn't that what King Saul offered was bad to use, but David was wise enough to understand that *he* wasn't ready for them. He chose to face his enemy using what he was currently settled in and confident with. Later in life David did use armor and a sword, but at this particular time, he was not yet acquainted with them and able to use them effectively.

As you face trials, be wise like David and careful to not let others push their personal experiences and understandings on you. You must grow in your trust of God and face your enemy with what you have peace with. That is where your faith will operate. Notice King Saul did not force David to wear his armor or take his sword when David was unsure of it. Be open to Godly counsel, seeking to grow in God and in your trust in Him, and allow Him to instruct you as to how He would have you handle your situation, even using people to speak encouragement into your life. In doing so, be careful not to grab everything presented to you without prayerful considering it. Use God's Word as your guide.

Seek God about where He is in your situation and what your part is in it. That is where your success will be found. There is a simplicity in trusting God to be who He said He would be and doing what He said He would do. First Samuel 17:40 tells us:

Then he took his staff in his hand; and he chose for himself five smooth stones from the brook, and put them in a shepherd's bag, in a pouch which he had, and his sling was in his hand. And he drew near to the Philistine.

As a teen, I had wondered: *Why did David pick up five smooth stones when he went to face Goliath?* Being the inquisitive type, I sought an answer. There was practical significance in choosing smooth stones, as the slinger would need smooth projectiles for the most aerodynamic and accurate missile to fire against his enemy. Rough stones with edges would not exit the sling in a reliable manner and wouldn't be predictable in their flight toward a target. Stones taken from a brook would be well worn by the passing water, making them ideal for this situation.

David gathered those stones into a pouch and kept them with him until the time that they were needed. He didn't merely grab the first five stones he found. He took time to study the stones he would be using to ensure that he had held them, tested them with his fingers, and became acquainted with their feel. In a sense he came to know those stones.

You can do the same with God's Word, taking His promises and placing them in your heart and mind. It's only when they have been taken into yourself and handled that you gain the familiarity with them that will allow you to use them properly. You are then prepared to draw them out as needed and use them effectively.

As David came out into the valley and moved toward Goliath, the giant began to come toward him as well. When Goliath came close enough to see David, he couldn't believe his eyes:

> *And when the Philistine looked about and saw David, he disdained him; for he was only a youth, ruddy and good-looking. So the Philistine said to David, "Am I a dog, that you come to me with sticks?" And the Philistine cursed David by his gods. And the Philistine said to David, "Come to me, and I will give your flesh to the birds of the air and the beasts of the field!"*
>
> — 1 Samuel 17:42-44

When you come to face your trial, you may very well meet resistance. Your enemy has no desire to back down and leave, and he will do all he can to cause you to back down. He will call you names and tell you the many ways and degrees of pain he plans to inflict on you. He will try to convince you that you have no hope of winning.

That's when you need to remember whose side you are on.

When the enemy tells you that there is no hope, remember whose side you are on.

If you are on God's side, then He inherently is with you.

David remembered whose side he was on, and answered Goliath:

Then David said to the Philistine, "You come to me with a sword, with a spear, and with a javelin. But I come to you in the name of the Lord of hosts, the God of the armies of Israel, whom you have defied."
— 1 Samuel 17:45

Where Goliath came to battle with a sword, a spear, and a javelin — David came with a most potent weapon — he came in the name of the Lord of Hosts, the God of the armies of Israel.

"This day the Lord will deliver you into my hand, and I will strike you and take your head from you. And this day I will give the carcasses of the camp of the Philistines to the birds of the air and the wild beasts of the earth, that all the earth may know that there is a God in Israel."
— 1 Samuel 17:46

David said, "This day the Lord will deliver you into my hand… that all the earth may know that there is a God in Israel." He understood that Goliath's daily affront to the armies of Israel was a show of defiance toward the God of Israel. Hearing of Goliath's berating of the Israelites and their God, other nations would begin to wonder if the God of Israel was no longer with them or able to defend them and fight for them. The defeat of Goliath and the Philistine army by a young shepherd would send a definite message to the surrounding region. The God of Israel was alive and well, and He was not tolerant of those who disparaged and defied Him.

It would also serve as a reminder to the people of Israel that their own ability to save themselves was inadequate; God's ability to move on their behalf, however, was not. He had rescued them again and again over their nation's history, and He had not suddenly become powerless against this latest threat. David spoke the following to be heard not only by Goliath and the Philistine army, but by King Saul and the armies of Israel:

> *"Then all this assembly shall know that the LORD does not save with sword and spear; for the battle is the LORD's, and He will give you into our hands."*
> — 1 Samuel 17:47

When you are a child of God, He has a personal interest in your life and well-being. You are a precious part of his family — so precious He gave His Son Jesus to redeem you and bring you back into fellowship with Him. What you are going through is not a set of events He sees from far away. He is not detached from the anxiety and fear that come against you as you face your trial. He is, as we read in Psalm 46:1, our refuge and strength, a very present help in trouble.

> **When you are a child of God, He has a personal interest in your life and well-being.**

That is how you need to see Him in what you are going through. That is how David viewed Him when he faced the lion and the bear. When David saw Goliath and heard his threats to the armies of Israel and his mocking of God, he saw God as his very present help in time of trouble. The time of trouble was there at that moment, and David looked to God to be the answer to the trouble he and the nation of Israel were facing. He knew that the battle with the Philistines belonged to the Lord, and he knew that he was on the Lord's side. David's expectation was that God would be with Him and help him defend Israel. He did not shrink back from the battle he was facing. He didn't whine about the conditions he would have to fight his battle in. He placed his trust in God to be with him and moved forward to face the giant head on.

> *So it was, when the Philistine arose and came and drew near to meet David, that David hurried and ran toward the army to meet the Philistine. Then David put his hand in his bag and took out a stone; and he slung it and struck the Philistine in his forehead, so that the stone sank into his forehead, and he fell on his face to the earth. So David prevailed over the Philistine with a sling and a stone, and struck the Philistine and killed him. But there was no sword in the hand of David. Therefore David ran and stood over the Philistine, took his sword and drew it out of its sheath and killed him, and cut off his head with it.*
> — 1 Samuel 17:48-51

David used an improbable approach to gain what seemed to be an impossible victory. With no armor and only a sling, David defeated a man who was well equipped and expertly trained — a giant of a man whose strength far exceeded that of David. David would quickly have been defeated had he faced Goliath on Goliath's terms. David understood this, and instead faced Goliath in a way that kept him out of Goliath's reach while inflicting lethal damage where Goliath did not expect it.

David aimed his stone where all of Goliath's thoughts and words were originating from — his forehead, and more specifically, his brain. Once the stone sunk into Goliath's forehead, it shut down his ability to respond. With that, Goliath, the giant of a man, fell to earth with a loud thud! David then moved in close and ended the giant's life and the terror he had been projecting over the armies of Israel with Goliath's own sword. Goliath's threats and mocking would no longer be heard, and his menacing presence was lying on the ground in the form of a headless corpse, lifeless and devoid of any ability to do further harm. The God of Israel was bigger than any challenge they were facing. His is just as big and able to overcome any situation you may be facing. Follow David's example and trust Him to be *your* very present help in time of trouble.

CHAPTER 6

God Can Help You Even When Your Enemy Says He Can't

ANOTHER LIE THAT Satan uses to drain your hope and cause you to see no good outcome to your situation is to try and convince you that there is no one that can help you. As you look at your situation, he will bring thoughts to magnify the gravity of the situation you are facing from a negative point of view, minimizing the possibility of any good outcome. His design is to draw your attention to other situations similar to what you are facing and those who have faced them and lost.

Uncle Bob who tried but just couldn't shake his addictions.

Cousin Sue who had one failed relationship after another.

Brother John a good, church-going man who lost a long bout with cancer.

Your good friend Elizabeth whose loss of a loved one in a tragic accident left her fighting depression for the rest of her life.

I remember going through this, as my diagnosis brought back the memory from many years ago of a dear friend of my father who was diagnosed with cancer. Danny was a fine man who loved the Lord and lived a life of integrity. I had developed an affinity for him for his kindness and playfulness that he had shown toward me. We prayed for him as a family and as a church, but over a period of time, we watched his health deteriorate until he one day passed from this life. It was one of the first experiences I remember in which I understood what tragic situation was happening and what we were praying for.

Those first few days after learning I was dealing with cancer, thoughts of Danny and his experience would come to me. I would remember how good of a man he was, how much he had been prayed for, and that he didn't get better and eventually died. Was that to be my outcome as well?

I don't know why Danny wasn't healed. I was young and didn't know the whole situation and little about the things of God that I know now. Staring at the pictures of the tumor I was dealing with, those thoughts tried to draw me into accepting other's experiences in hard times as my own impending outcome. The Holy Spirit reminded me that others' experiences were not my own and did not have to be. Instead, I could choose to hold fast to Jesus and trust Him to be who He said He would be and do what He said He would do. There was light for me in the darkness.

There are examples of battles that were not won. There may be some battles that were not even fought that come to your mind as well. They are sent by the enemy to convince you that disappointment is all that awaits you. These thoughts seek to convince you that you have no advocate who can help you, that your situation is lost, and that it is best for you to give up now and go along with the outcome.

I'm telling you now that your situation is not lost, and you *do* have an advocate who can and does want to help you. No situation is too far gone for God, and He is listening for your voice to call out to Him. We find an excellent example of this in Second Kings 18 where King Hezekiah did not let stories of other's negative experiences dictate how he viewed what God could do in his own situation:

> *Now it came to pass in the third year of Hoshea the son of Elah, king of Israel, that Hezekiah the son of Ahaz, king of Judah, began to reign. He was twenty-five years old when he became king, and he reigned twenty-nine years in Jerusalem. His mother's name was Abi the daughter of Zechariah. And he did what was right in the sight of the* Lord, *according to all that his father David had done.*
>
> *He removed the high places and broke the sacred pillars, cut down the wooden image and broke in pieces the bronze serpent that Moses had made; for until those days the children of Israel burned incense to it, and called it Nehushtan. He trusted in the* Lord *God of Israel, so that after him was none like him among all the kings of Judah, nor who were before him. For he held fast to the* Lord; *he did not depart from following Him, but kept His commandments, which the* Lord *had commanded Moses. The* Lord *was with him; he prospered wherever he went.*
>
> — 2 Kings 18:1-7

King Hezekiah was the son of King Ahaz, who had not lived according to God's ways and had worshiped other gods during his reign. He had continued to take the people of Judah along a path of disobedience to God and did not walk in God's favor. Yet when Hezekiah became king of Judah, he sought after God's ways and enacted reforms to stop the worship of other gods and to honor and worship the one true God, the God of Abraham, Isaac, and Jacob.

We read in verse 3 that King Hezekiah "did what was right in the sight of the Lord." We are also told that the Lord was with him, and he prospered wherever he went. Why does it say this about King Hezekiah? Our key is in verses 5 and 6:

> *He trusted in the* Lord *God of Israel, so that after him was none like him among all the kings of Judah, nor who were before him. For he held fast to the* Lord*; he did not depart from following Him, but kept His commandments, which the* Lord *had commanded Moses.*

King Hezekiah held fast to the Lord. Even when things did not look good, he kept his grip on who God was to him — who He said He would be to His people and what He said He would do for His people. King Hezekiah placed his trust in God and then held onto the One he trusted and faced a foe that threatened his existence and that of his kingdom.

During King Hezekiah's reign, the king of Assyria sought to take the kingdom of Judah by force, as his father had in previous years subjugated many of the surrounding kingdoms. King Hezekiah resisted, and the king of Assyria Sennacherib marched on Judah.

> *And in the fourteenth year of King Hezekiah, Sennacherib king of Assyria came up against all the fortified cities of Judah and took them.*
> — 2 Kings 18:13

Setting his eyes on the capital city, Sennacherib sent emissaries to Jerusalem to convince them to surrender to him and give up their resistance. They brought the following message to King Hezekiah and the people of Jerusalem:

> *Then the king of Assyria sent the Tartan, the Rabsaris, and the Rabshakeh from Lachish, with a great army against Jerusalem, to King Hezekiah. And they went up and came to Jerusalem.... Then the Rabshakeh said to them, "Say now to Hezekiah, 'Thus says the great king, the king of Assyria: "What confidence is this in which you trust? You speak of having plans and power for*

> war; but they are mere words. And in whom do you trust, that you rebel against me? Now look! You are trusting in the staff of this broken reed, Egypt, on which if a man leans, it will go into his hand and pierce it. So is Pharaoh king of Egypt to all who trust in him. But if you say to me, 'We trust in the Lord our God,' is it not He whose high places and whose altars Hezekiah has taken away, and said to Judah and Jerusalem, 'You shall worship before this altar in Jerusalem'?" Now therefore, I urge you, give a pledge to my master the king of Assyria, and I will give you two thousand horses — if you are able on your part to put riders on them! How then will you repel one captain of the least of my master's servants, and put your trust in Egypt for chariots and horsemen? Have I now come up without the Lord against this place to destroy it? The Lord said to me, 'Go up against this land, and destroy it.'"
>
> — 2 Kings 18:17-25

When you are facing a daunting situation, your enemy, the devil, uses the same tactic. In fact, he is the author of it. He will always bring into question God's character, words, and ability, and seek to get you to forsake God and His promises.

Sennacherib challenged King Hezekiah's trust in God by effectively saying, "Why should your god help you when you took down his places of worship and restricted it to the once place you decided? You've robbed him of his worship, and because of that he has instructed me to come against this place and destroy it."

They went on to address the people of Jerusalem, saying:

> "...Hear the word of the great king, the king of Assyria! Thus says the king: 'Do not let Hezekiah deceive you, for he shall not be able to deliver you from his hand; nor let Hezekiah make you trust in the Lord, saying, "The Lord will surely deliver us; this

> *city shall not be given into the hand of the king of Assyria...." But do not listen to Hezekiah, lest he persuade you, saying, "The Lord will deliver us." Has any of the gods of the nations at all delivered its land from the hand of the king of Assyria? Where are the gods of Hamath and Arpad? Where are the gods of Sepharvaim and Hena and Ivah? Indeed, have they delivered Samaria from my hand? Who among all the gods of the lands have delivered their countries from my hand, that the Lord should deliver Jerusalem from my hand?"*
> — 2 Kings 18:28-34

Your circumstances will often challenge you to reason and justify why you should have any hope — especially hope in God to help you. Thoughts will try to convince you that you don't qualify for God's help and that what you are going through is actually God's judgement against you. People might also speak these things to you as they grasp for a reason to give for what you are going through. It's so important that you take these things not only with a grain of salt but also hold them up like a photo negative against the light of God's Word to see the true picture of what is there. Just as Judah's outcome was not relegated to what had happened to the other nations that Assyria had conquered, your outcome is not relegated to what others have or haven't experienced.

When King Hezekiah held up Sennacherib's challenge against what God had said, he knew that it was wrong. He had honored God with his actions, as he had followed the commands that God had given Moses concerning worshiping Him. He was aware of the plight of the other nations around him, but he did not let their outcomes be the measurement of who God was to him. Instead of looking at his circumstances and hopelessly giving in to Sennacherib's demands, Hezekiah turned to God.

And so it was, when King Hezekiah heard it, that he tore his clothes, covered himself with sackcloth, and went into the house of the Lord. Then he sent Eliakim, who was over the household, Shebna the scribe, and the elders of the priests, covered with sackcloth, to Isaiah the prophet, the son of Amoz. And they said to him, "Thus says Hezekiah: 'This day is a day of trouble, and rebuke, and blasphemy; for the children have come to birth, but there is no strength to bring them forth. It may be that the Lord your God will hear all the words of the Rabshakeh, whom his master the king of Assyria has sent to reproach the living God, and will rebuke the words which the Lord your God has heard. Therefore lift up your prayer for the remnant that is left."

So the servants of King Hezekiah came to Isaiah. And Isaiah said to them, "Thus you shall say to your master, 'Thus says the Lord: "Do not be afraid of the words which you have heard, with which the servants of the king of Assyria have blasphemed Me. Surely I will send a spirit upon him, and he shall hear a rumor and return to his own land; and I will cause him to fall by the sword in his own land."'"

— 2 Kings 19:1-7

When King Hezekiah heard the boastings of Sennacherib, he went into the house of the Lord. He didn't go to his own house and sulk. He didn't go look for friends to talk with about how unfair things in his life were going. He went to find God and talk to Him about what he was facing. This is so important to understand — going to God with an open and

Going to God with an open and honest heart opens the door for His grace to strengthen you and do amazing things.

honest heart opens the door for His grace to strengthen you and do amazing things.

I want you to notice something about what King Hezekiah has to say in Second Kings 19:4:

It may be that the Lord your God will hear all the words of the Rabshakeh, whom his master the king of Assyria has sent to reproach the living God, and will rebuke the words which the Lord your God has heard.

King Hezekiah understood that what he was facing was not just a dire situation for him, but the act of defiance that Sennacherib had made was also a reproach to God Himself. Just as David understood Goliath's threats were an affront to who God was, King Hezekiah understood that Sennacherib's threats were a direct assault on God's character and His Holiness. In both cases, their enemy was making threats to them, mocking who they were to God, and who God was to them.

It's likely the same in the situation you may be facing. You might be facing a trial that threatens to cut you off from the future God has for you, but if you trust Him, He can move in what may seem to be impossible circumstances to bring you through to the other side of what you are facing — not as a ragged survivor, but as an intact victor. Ultimately, God has a plan for your life that involves you walking in relationship with Him, and He is the One who can see it through.

Trusting in God and holding fast to what he had spoken by the prophet Isaiah, King Hezekiah did not give in to Sennacherib's demands. Realizing this, Sennacherib dispatched his emissaries once again to Jerusalem to issue more threats. Notice that when the threats, the thoughts, that come against you don't shake your resolve and cause you to give in, they do not automatically cease.

Your enemy does not give up easily and will be persistent in an attempt to change your focus and frame of mind. He will cause a new round of challenges to test your resolve. We see this in Sennacherib's next set of threats:

> *...So he again sent messengers to Hezekiah, saying, "Thus you shall speak to Hezekiah king of Judah, saying: 'Do not let your God in whom you trust deceive you, saying, "Jerusalem shall not be given into the hand of the king of Assyria." Look! You have heard what the kings of Assyria have done to all lands by utterly destroying them; and shall you be delivered? Have the gods of the nations delivered those whom my fathers have destroyed, Gozan and Haran and Rezeph, and the people of Eden who were in Telassar? Where is the king of Hamath, the king of Arpad, and the king of the city of Sepharvaim, Hena, and Ivah?'"*
>
> — 2 Kings 19:9-13

When I first learned of the cancer diagnosis I was facing, thoughts came to my mind just like those Assyrian emissaries who rode up to the city walls of Jerusalem. Those thoughts shouted out and said the same type of things about my situation:

"Don't be deceived about trusting God in this. He can save your soul and give you peace, but healing your body of cancer is a different situation. Don't you remember what happened to Danny? He was a good man, and he didn't get healed. What about all those other people you've prayed for who died? You can pray that God will help you deal with your situation, give you some peace and maybe keep you alive for a while, but to have the tumor go away and be cancer free with what you have is really going to have to be a miracle. Those only happen when God decides to do it for other people. They call them miracles because they almost never happen!"

I'm so thankful that when those thoughts came, I didn't see my situation the way that they portrayed it. This wasn't a spiritual version of Willy Wonka where I was hoping to somehow get a golden ticket. They weren't spinning a jewel encrusted wheel in heaven to see if it stopped on my name and I got that week's miracle. That isn't the way God does things. God responds to our faith, our trust in Him. God is relational at the core, and He was watching and listening to what I was going through, just as He was watching King Hezekiah's situation — and yours.

King Hezekiah received Sennacherib threats and did what he knew best to do — he took them before God:

And Hezekiah received the letter from the hand of the messengers, and read it; and Hezekiah went up to the house of the Lord, and spread it before the Lord. Then Hezekiah prayed before the Lord, and said: "O Lord God of Israel, the One who dwells between the cherubim, You are God, You alone, of all the kingdoms of the earth. You have made heaven and earth. Incline Your ear, O Lord, and hear; open Your eyes, O Lord, and see; and hear the words of Sennacherib, which he has sent to reproach the living God. Truly, Lord, the kings of Assyria have laid waste the nations and their lands, and have cast their gods into the fire; for they were not gods, but the work of men's hands—wood and stone. Therefore they destroyed them. Now therefore, O Lord our God, I pray, save us from his hand, that all the kingdoms of the earth may know that You are the Lord God, You alone."

— 2 Kings 19:14-19

Hezekiah spread the threats and accusations of his enemy before the Lord. He laid what he was dealing with before the Lord in its detail and then he laid out his heart before the Lord in prayer. That is our pattern to follow — we are to go to God with what we are dealing with, lay it before Him, and open our heart before Him.

Just as His ancestor King David had done so many times, as we read in the book of Psalms, King Hezekiah presented his situation to God and then began to speak of who God was and present his request for God's hand to move in his situation.

You can say the same thing about your situation: "God, You are He who sits on His throne in Heaven, and You alone are the one, true God. Everything is subject to Your Word. I trust You to have open eyes and ears to my plight, which is beyond my power to deal with. It threatens my well-being and threatens Your plan for my life. I know that what I am facing has destroyed others, but what happened to others is not what has to be my outcome. I choose to trust in Your goodness and Your faithfulness. Your Word is true, and You watch over it to perform it. I ask You to move in my situation and save me, not only for my relief, but that I may testify of your goodness and faithfulness to everyone I meet, so that they may know that You are God and You move on behalf of those who trust in You."

After King Hezekiah's prayer, we read in Second Kings 19:20 that the prophet Isaiah sent word to the king saying, "…Thus says the Lord God of Israel: 'Because you have prayed to Me against Sennacherib king of Assyria, I have heard.'" Because Hezekiah went to God and "spread it before the Lord," God heard him. God then pronounced a prophetic judgement through the prophet Isaiah against Sennacherib and his kingdom, assuring King Hezekiah that God was moving in the situation. He finished with the following:

"Therefore thus says the Lord *concerning the king of Assyria:*

> *'He shall not come into this city,*
> *Nor shoot an arrow there,*
> *Nor come before it with shield,*
> *Nor build a siege mound against it.*
> *By the way that he came,*
> *By the same shall he return;*
> *And he shall not come into this city,'*
> *Says the* Lord.
> *'For I will defend this city, to save it*
> *For My own sake and for My servant David's sake.'"*
>
> — 2 Kings 19:32-34

This was a victory beyond the scope of what king Hezekiah could hope to achieve, even with allies who might go with him into battle. This would require the hand of God to accomplish. And hearing this, Hezekiah placed his trust in what God had to say about his situation. I had to do the same, and so must you if you want to see God's results. The light at the end of the tunnel was defined for King Hezekiah — God Himself would defend the city and save it. When God is involved, His results show up. So what happened to Sennacherib and his army?

Second Kings 19:35-37 tells us:

> *And it came to pass on a certain night that the angel of the* Lord *went out, and killed in the camp of the Assyrians one hundred and eighty-five thousand; and when people arose early in the morning, there were the corpses — all dead. So Sennacherib king of Assyria departed and went away, returned home, and remained at Nineveh. Now it came to pass, as he was worshiping in the temple of Nisroch his god, that his sons Adrammelech and Sharezer struck him down with the sword; and they escaped into the land of Ararat. Then Esarhaddon his son reigned in his place.*

Sennacherib's army was decimated in a single night. The force that had been threatening to overwhelm and destroy Jerusalem and King Hezekiah was miraculously dealt with. Not a single Assyrian assaulted the city's gates. Not an arrow was shot. The mighty Sennacherib, conquering Assyrian king, went back home by the way he came — and was later murdered by the sword in his own land, just as God had said.

> By knowing the devil's tactics, you can resist him and stand strong to see God move in your life.

My friend, the devil will try to convince you that God isn't able to move in your situation and help you, but I want to assure you that He certainly can. By knowing the devil's tactics — the ways he often comes against you to have his way with your life and steal from you what God would do in it — you can resist him and stand strong to see God move in your life.

As you continue to read the following pages, you will find scriptural, rubber meets the road approaches to help you stand your ground, stay strong in the middle of your trial, and come to the other side to enjoy the good things God has for you there. The tunnel you may find yourself in does indeed have a light at the other end of it. David and King Hezekiah trusted in God to get them to it, and so can you.

CHAPTER 7

God Is Willing and Able To Move in Your Situation

ONE OF THE hardest things to deal with when you are facing hard times is the struggle that can happen between what you want to believe and what your mind is telling you is believable. It is a place where, in your mind, the pieces don't seem to add up. You can be confused about what you can conceive of happening in your situation or convinced that something beyond the natural can't or won't happen for you.

For years I struggled with thinking I had to have everything perfectly in place before I went to God with my needs. I studied and worked to educate myself on what the Bible had to say and how it applied to my life — that is very scriptural and necessary (*see* 2 Timothy 2:15). You should have a high regard for what God has to say, as it will serve as the guide for your life and the key to success and peace.

My issue came from believing in my heart that God's Word was true and that He was able to do everything He said He would but still trying to figure out how it would or should work. I found my mind and my spirit were at odds with each other at times, and I struggled internally to see how God could honor my faith while my mind still had questions.

Does this sound familiar to you? You want to trust in God's power to move supernaturally in your life, but you have problems wrapping your head around it. This is a place that the devil loves to exploit. He will use this place of confusion to convince you that:

- God *can't* move in your life because you are struggling mentally with the thought of Him moving supernaturally in your life.
- God *won't* move in your life because you are struggling mentally with the thought of Him moving supernaturally in your life.

Over years of ministry, I have encountered numerous people fighting with these thoughts — where they believe in God, His Word, and His power yet their inner struggle to line up things mentally was causing them to question, not God's ability to move in their lives, but His *desire* to.

DOES GOD REALLY WANT TO MOVE IN YOUR LIFE?

In Matthew chapter 8, we find a man suffering from leprosy — a foul and horrible disease that infects the skin and other tissues, often causing a slow rot of flesh that results in the loss of fingers, toes, ears, and nose and eventually leads to death. This gruesome disease made the infected person an outcast of society in biblical times, and according to Mosaic Law, they were also ritually unclean.

Lepers were required to stay away from the regular population, and in cases where they did come into contact with non-lepers, they were to keep a distance and announce themselves by crying out "Unclean!" when they were near others (*see* Leviticus 13). This was the condition of the man in Matthew 8 who approached Jesus looking for something that no doctor could provide. There was no natural remedy for leprosy, yet the man desired more than to slowly suffer until his death. He had a hope, to see himself as a man cleansed of leprosy and returned into society.

> *A man with leprosy came and knelt in front of Jesus, begging to be healed. "If you are willing, you can heal me and make me clean," he said. Moved with compassion, Jesus reached out and touched him. "I am willing," he said. "Be healed!" Instantly the leprosy disappeared, and the man was healed.*
> — Mark 1:40-42 (*NLT*)

Jesus had been ministering with healing and miracles throughout the region of Galilee. A man suffering from leprosy heard about these wonderful events, and at some point, he came to the conclusion that this Jesus had the power to cleanse him of the disease that was plaguing him. With this in mind, he set off to find where Jesus was, and when he arrived at that place, he made his way toward Him. The leper knew his presence in the area was unwanted. He knew that the other religious leaders wanted nothing to do with him, yet he had heard a message that gave him hope for his situation. This spark of hope had him doing all he could to be in front of the person whom he believed had the power to change his life.

As he approached Jesus, he dropped to his knees as a sign of respect and contrition. He was convinced that this Man could help him, and he wanted to approach him with humility. From this position, he spoke with the faith that he had, even though there was still one concern that resided in his mind:

> *…If you are willing, you can heal me and make me clean.…*
> — Mark 1:40 (*NLT*)

The leper was ready to trust in Jesus and His power to change his condition, but he didn't know if this Man who performed miracles for others would be willing to look past his status as an outcast, his uncleanness, or any other issue that had sidelined him in the minds of others. His presence there and his bold approach to this Man of miracles had him laying all he was bare with the hope that he would be cleansed.

As the leper waited for Jesus' reaction, he noticed that Jesus didn't recoil at his leprosy, even though touching him would have made Jesus ritually unclean and exposed Him to the disease. Instead, we are told that Jesus was "moved with compassion" (v. 41). Jesus was moved deeply by the love of God that was within him, and He desired to act on and through that love. You can equate biblical compassion as this — the love of God in action. God's love isn't passive. It is active and moves — and that is just what Jesus did.

> ...*Jesus reached out and touched him.* "I am willing," *he said.* "Be healed!" *Instantly the leprosy disappeared, and the man was healed.*
> — Mark 1:41-42 (*NLT*)

Imagine for a moment that you are that leper kneeling before Jesus and asking Him to make you clean. You are hoping that He is willing to hear your plea and say something to cleanse your body, yet His first response is to reach out toward you with His hand. To touch you would make Him ritually unclean — it would expose Him to leprosy. It would cause those around Him to shun Him and avoid contact with Him, lest they become unclean as well. Yet you see His arm stretching toward you and then His hand touches you. Not a word was said by Him up to this moment when He reached out toward you and touched you — you are an unclean leper asking for the seemingly impossible. Then you hear Him say to the depths of your soul:

"I am willing. Be healed!"

As those words resonate in you, you understand that His desire is to see you cleansed and whole. In that moment, your body miraculously no longer has a trace

God defines Himself by His Word, and your answers are found there.

of the horrible disease you had knelt with moments before. You came to Jesus with a need and the hope that His power could meet that need. What you needed to know was that He cared for you and was willing to meet you where you were to move in your life as only He could. He was *willing*....

Willing to listen when others wouldn't.

Willing to be near to you when others fled from you.

Willing to meet you where you were.

Willing to touch you in the condition you were in.

Willing to move with compassion — God's love in action — to cleanse you and change your life.

The books of Matthew, Mark, Luke, and John are full of instances of Jesus being willing to act. We don't read about Jesus being unwilling. Jesus desires to move on your behalf and change your life. Look at God's Word. God defines Himself by His Word, and your answers are found there.

I've heard it said, "Faith comes where the will of God is known." The leper's encounter with Jesus highlights this truth. Whatever you may be going through, I encourage you to study your Bible to find God's will and notice what He reveals about it throughout scripture. Study the life of Jesus, and you will see God represented through Him, our earthly example (*see* John 14:8-11).

When your thoughts come to tell you that God doesn't want to move in your life, remember the leper who came to Jesus convinced of His power but unsure of His willingness to touch his life. He saw his life changed because he found that Jesus was indeed willing, and He is still willing today to move in your situation.

WHEN YOUR HEAD AND YOUR HEART DIFFER

As mentioned earlier, there are times when your heart says "yes" to God's willingness to move in your life and His ability to do so, but your mind isn't so sure. Thoughts about what others have to say, situations you know of that didn't work out, and the fact that by all natural standards this obstacle is insurmountable pull you to and fro.

The devil will work to convince you that you don't have things together and that your faith is inadequate. He will lead you down paths with formulas to follow, hoops to jump through, and endless conditions to meet. He wants to put you in a performance-based faith, where you must dot your i's and cross your t's in order for God to move in your life. However, performance-based faith is a lie from the pit of hell.

We are not saved by our own works.

> *For by grace you have been saved through faith, and that not of yourselves; it is the gift of God, not of works, lest anyone should boast.*
> — Ephesians 2:8-9

We do not receive the benefits of salvation and the promises of God through works. This is so important to understand, because the enemy will use this line to get you to focus on what you should be doing to make things change. God may indeed require you to make changes in your attitude, commitment to Him, etc., but your hope is based and settled IN HIM, not something you are doing. Jesus gave us peace (*see* John 16:33), but Satan will send you on a spiritual scavenger hunt with no solution if you let him.

So what does Jesus think when your heart trusts but your head isn't quite there? How do you bridge the gap, and what does that look like? In Mark chapter 9, we find a man who fits our scenario — a man who was looking for an answer from God but also had some issues believing. Does this sound familiar to you?

Mark 9:14-27 tells us:

And when He came to the disciples, He saw a great multitude around them, and scribes disputing with them. Immediately, when they saw Him, all the people were greatly amazed, and running to Him, greeted Him. And He asked the scribes, "What are you discussing with them?"

Then one of the crowd answered and said, "Teacher, I brought You my son, who has a mute spirit. And wherever it seizes him, it throws him down; he foams at the mouth, gnashes his teeth, and becomes rigid. So I spoke to Your disciples, that they should cast it out, but they could not."

He answered him and said, "O faithless generation, how long shall I be with you? How long shall I bear with you? Bring him to Me." Then they brought him to Him. And when he saw Him, immediately the spirit convulsed him, and he fell on the ground and wallowed, foaming at the mouth.

So He asked his father, "How long has this been happening to him?"

And he said, "From childhood. And often he has thrown him both into the fire and into the water to destroy him. But if You can do anything, have compassion on us and help us."

Jesus said to him, "If you can believe, all things are possible to him who believes."

Immediately the father of the child cried out and said with tears, "Lord, I believe; help my unbelief!"

When Jesus saw that the people came running together, He rebuked the unclean spirit, saying to it, "Deaf and dumb spirit, I command you, come out of him and enter him no more!" Then the spirit cried out, convulsed him greatly, and came out of him. And he became as one dead, so that many said, "He is dead." But Jesus took him by the hand and lifted him up, and he arose.

Jesus, Peter, and John came down from an amazing experience — Jesus' transfiguration on a mountain and found the rest of disciples with a group of religious scribes questioning and disputing with them. A large crowd gathered around and witnessed the commotion. As Jesus approached, the crowd recognized Him and ran to greet Him. As Jesus walked up to His disciples and the scribes, He asked the scribes: *"What are you discussing with them?"*

It was apparent that the scribes had taken an opportunity to confront Jesus' disciples on matters that He was more interested in addressing Himself. The scribes had proven themselves persistent, however, following after Him and questioning His teachings, often attempting to create situations that they could use to accuse Him of violating a religious law. With Jesus standing before them, now questioning them, the scribes were silent. No one readily spoke up. Then a man from the crowd answered, saying:

...Teacher, I brought You my son, who has a mute spirit. And wherever it seizes him, it throws him down; he foams at the mouth, gnashes his teeth, and becomes rigid. So I spoke to Your disciples, that they should cast it out, but they could not.
— Mark 9:17-18

This man had come looking for Jesus, apparently having previously heard of His ability to heal the sick and deliver those oppressed by evil spirits. He was desperately seeking an answer to the suffering his son had been enduring and brought the child to where he thought he would find Jesus. Finding some of Jesus' disciples, he presented his son to them, asking them to deliver him from the suffering. The disciples had attempted to cast the spirit out of the child but had been unsuccessful. It was probably at this time that the scribes seized the opportunity of the disciples' failure to remove the spirit to confront and belittle them in the eyes of the crowd.

Jesus answered the man, saying: "...Oh faithless generation, how long shall I be with you? How long shall I bear with you? Bring him to Me." (v. 19).

For many years I read that statement and saw it as Jesus being upset, frustrated, and agitated with the man, His disciples, the scribes, the crowd, and ultimately — me. It was as if He was saying: "Really guys? Really? You just don't get it do you? How long do I have to stay with you. How long do I have to teach you, how long do I have to hold your hand and spoon feed you because you are helpless without me? You are faithless, helpless, and close to worthless to Me. Alright, bring the child to me since you are incapable of doing anything on your own. Sheesh!"

If you see Jesus as a brooding figure, you will read the Bible and see things through that lens as well. Jesus did take the religious leaders of the day to task at times, and He was very straight with them — but it is important to remember that he was not against the religious leaders as a whole. The Bible tells us that there were Pharisees who believed in Him, and He even met with Nicodemus, a high-ranking Pharisee, personally to share the Gospel with him (*see* John 3). What Jesus was against was their misrepresentation of who God was and what His ways were. He pulled no punches when confronting this. In John chapter 14, Jesus spoke plainly to His disciples that He had been sent to show them the Father and to say and do what the Father instructed Him. It was when the religious leaders misrepresented God that Jesus stepped in to show the Father as He desired to be known.

When He spoke to His disciples sternly, it was not to berate them, but to take them to a higher place in Him and in their understanding. He was kind to them and to the people, showing love and compassion too. Jesus came to pay the price for their sin and the sin of mankind and bring them into a place of relationship and fellowship with God. His mission was born of love, served with love, and completed in love. In First Corinthians chapter 13, we are even told that love never fails. Jesus was the principal believer in that statement, and He walked it out each day of His time on the earth.

With that in mind, let's look at what Jesus said again:

"...Oh faithless generation, how long shall I be with you? How long shall I bear with you? Bring him to Me."
— Mark 9:19

Read it again understanding that Jesus' love for this man, his son, and the people standing around watching — His disciples, the scribes, and the other bystanders — was immense. This wasn't a brooding Man, frustrated and agitated, lashing out. This was the

Man who was destined for death on the Cross for each of them lamenting about where they were spiritually and concerned for where they would be once He was no longer with them physically to deliver them from the effects of sin and satanic oppression. They needed to grow in the things of God to learn how to walk in victory. This was not frustrated aggravation; it was pointed concern.

When the boy was brought to Jesus, we are told that *immediately* the spirit convulsed the boy, and he fell on the ground and wallowed, foaming at the mouth. This is a lesson to learn and understand. When the enemy is afflicting you in a situation and you take the situation to Jesus, the enemy will attempt to shake your resolve by causing the situation to flare up, possibly making it worse than ever before. This is done to make the case look as rough or rougher than ever before and to shake your confidence in there being hope for a better outcome.

This is possibly what the disciples experienced when the child was first brought to them by the boy's father. They did what they knew to do from what Jesus had taught them and then the spirit acted out in such a fierce manner that it shook their faith and resolve.

Have you experienced this before? Maybe you had a problem and decided to take it to God for His help and then the problem became agitated right away. It may have even seemed worse than ever before. Perhaps you saw what was happening and began to wonder if you'd made a mistake, *Is this too big for God? Is it too late for God?* That is how the devil works. He doesn't give up because you've decided to give God a try. He doesn't give up when you begin to pray and speak what the Bible has to say about your situation. He applies pressure to see if he can knock you off your place of faith or get you to back down. And it often works. That's why he continues to operate in this way — but I've got good news!

Jesus isn't moved by things looking worse than before or the devil acting up. Jesus isn't waiting for you to have it all figured out. He is looking for you to trust in HIM.

We see this unfold in the following verses, as Jesus met this desperate father where he was in his faith and did the amazing with that faith. In verses 21 and 22, Jesus asked the boy's father:

So He asked his father, "How long has this been happening to him?"

And he said, "From childhood. And often he has thrown him both into the fire and into the water to destroy him. But if You can do anything, have compassion on us and help us."

The boy's father had watched his son suffer since he was a child. He watched year after year as the boy was unable to speak and prone to being thrown into fits that could cause him great harm. He had lost hope of an answer to help his son and then had heard of a Man who had done amazing things in the lives of the people who had come to Him. This Man had healed the sick, caused the lame to walk, and opened the eyes of the blind to see. Those oppressed by evil spirits had even been set free. This Man had raised the dead and fed the multitudes with a few loaves and fishes. This father's love for his son had brought him to that place, in that crowd, where he hoped for an answer and a miracle for his son.

Jesus's disciples had been unable to help the boy, and now at Jesus's feet this father's son was convulsing in another of those fits he had watched so many times before. It was just like another day waking up with cancer for me, another morning spent trying to breath normal as I moved from room to room. It was just like another afternoon of someone crying over a relationship on the rocks or an evening pouring over bills that there wasn't enough money to pay. With all of that strain, stress, and weariness going on, this father laid his problem at the feet of Jesus, looked at Him, and asked:

> *...If You can do anything, have compassion on us and help us.*
> — Mark 9:22

The father asked the question — "If you can do anything...." Is that the question you find yourself asking Jesus? "If you can do anything.... If you can do anything with my situation, please do. I'm struggling, and now I'm here with you and things are still going crazy. I don't have any answers, and I'm worn down by it all."

Notice what the father said, *"Have compassion on us and help us."* Jesus had just told him he was part of a faithless generation, and instead of arguing the point or being hurt and walking away, the father looked to Jesus and asked Him to have compassion and help if He could. Jesus hadn't browbeat him moments before, He had addressed where the man's heart was. Now the man was responding to that and asking a question that if you will be honest with yourself, you have probably asked as well.

Maybe you are not experiencing the results you were looking for, and you are confused about why you're still in the situation you're in, wondering, *Can You do anything? Am I disqualified from your intervention because I'm floundering? Can you work in my life when I don't have everything figured out?*

Notice how Jesus replied to the boy's father, and it is His reply to you as well:

> *Jesus said to him, "If you can believe, all things are possible to him who believes."*
> — Mark 9:23

The father had asked a question — "Can you do anything for my child in this situation?" Jesus replied to him, in effect, that He could do anything if the man believed He could. It's so very important for you to see the simplicity and beauty of this answer.

"Jesus, can You do anything for my boy?"

"Yes, I can do anything if you can believe I am able to do it."

It was in that moment that the boy's father understood it wasn't about how much he knew, if he had things figured out, if he had followed after Jesus long enough, or if he had gone through some subscribed formula to get his miracle. It was truly about if he believed in the core of himself that Jesus was able to do anything that was needed. It was about believing Jesus was who He said He was and would do what He said He would do. And in that moment, the boy's father replied:

"…Lord, I believe; *help my unbelief!*" (v. 24).

This is where we often find ourselves. We believe that Jesus is able, but when we see the external effects of our situation, we are shaken. It isn't adding up, and we begin to wonder if the problem is that we aren't doing something right. Is there another prayer to say, another thing to do? Have we jumped through all the necessary hoops?

Trusting in Jesus isn't about hoops. It's not about verbal gymnastics. It's not a formula to follow. It's about looking to him, just as the boy's father did, and believing in your heart that Jesus is who He said He was and that He is able to do the amazing in your situation — and, more than that, He *desires* to. Just as He said to leper, "I am willing." Just as He said to the boy's father, "If you can believe in me, all things are possible." Jesus is saying the same things to you today.

The boy's father professed his trust in Jesus and then confessed that he still had an area in his understanding that he needed help with. I believe it's safe to say we are all in that place, where our situation as it sits is beyond what we in our minds see as having much hope. The circumstances around us bombard our peace, just as the boy laying at their feet convulsing was speaking against everything the boy's father was hoping for. Here Jesus was, asking him to trust Him, while at their feet the ruckus was going on.

I can remember lying in my bed several weeks into cancer treatment. My body was growing weaker by the day, and all sorts of ailments were presenting in my body. I was physically suffering on many levels, with the pain and side-effects taking a toll on me. I was slowly dying, yet I was holding fast to my trust in God to be who He said He would be to me and do what He said He would do for me. I was daily believing Him and asking Him to help where unbelief was trying to make its way from my head into my heart. The symptoms were doing what the evil spirit did to the boy in Mark 9, acting out and displaying themselves in an attempt to draw my focus away from Jesus — the answer to my situation — and onto the effects of my situation. Does this sound familiar to you? The circumstances may be different for you, but the progression could be much the same. Keep believing, trusting in God's love for you, and ask Him to help you with the thoughts that would draw you away from that trust — ask Him to *help your unbelief.*

When you trust and believe that Jesus is willing and able to move in your situation and that He is looking to your heart and not your head for that belief, you will see Him move in wonderful ways. As the boy's father stood before Jesus, His answer called the father to the place where his desire for his son to be healed was possible. Jesus was calling him to believe in His love and ability to do the miraculous, not to understand or reason it out. That is what

Jesus is asking you to do as well. We read of that same miraculous in verses 25-27:

> When Jesus saw that the people came running together, He rebuked the unclean spirit, saying to it, "Deaf and dumb spirit, I command you, come out of him and enter him no more!" Then the spirit cried out, convulsed him greatly, and came out of him. And he became as one dead, so that many said, "He is dead." But Jesus took him by the hand and lifted him up, and he arose.

> **When you stand on God's Word with expectation, you are confident for a desired outcome.**

Notice that the evil spirit acted out in the same way when Jesus commanded it to leave as it had before when confronted by the disciples — displaying the issues that had afflicted the boy and waiting for those ministering to the boy to be taken aback and shaken. This time, it did not find doubt as it had before and left the boy. Jesus' expectation was for the spirit to be cast out, and in the face of faith, the evil spirit was forced to leave.

It's important to point out that Jesus was not only looking for results but expecting them as well. When you stand on God's Word with expectation, you are confident for a desired outcome. When those changes don't immediately appear, you are unmoved because your focus is on what is on the other side of them not what is happening at the moment.

The disciples who had attempted to cast out the evil spirit stood watching Jesus talk with the boy's father, and as He ministered to the father and the boy they were in awe. Of the many questions that swirled in their minds from the series of events, they approached Jesus afterwards and asked this question:

> *And when He had come into the house, His disciples asked Him privately, "Why could we not cast it out?" So He said to them, "This kind only comes out by prayer and fasting."*

To fight off the confusion and doubt that can come when the enemy resists your stand of faith and throws up circumstances that are contrary to what you are hoping and standing for, you must spend time talking to God, strengthening your trust in Him. You must focus yourself on Him and what He says about your situation. This biblical example was not about Jesus giving us a formula about how to cast out a mute spirit. It was His counsel to His disciples about why they were unable to cast out the evil spirit from the boy.

His answer to the disciples could have simply been, "Fellas, you have to be Me to cast this kind out," but that is not what Jesus said to them. He did not cite a special ability that only He had. Instead, He cited the *approach* that is necessary to position oneself and enforce God's authority and will upon an attack of the enemy. Jesus understood that it was His relationship with God that was the source of His authority. He also knows that you need to have a deep revelation of it as well to function in the authority and results that God desires for your life.

When I faced cancer, I focused my efforts on fighting it from the physical side, but even more importantly the spiritual side. I strengthened myself by seeking God for who He was in my life, remembering He was, and is, the answer to everything I was dealing with. I spent time talking with Him about what I was going through and how I was feeling and asked Him to help me stay strong in my trust in Him. I was real and genuine with Him, because I knew He wasn't looking for me to follow a formula to please Him, He was asking me to press into Him and trust Him in a deeper way. When I did, He was right there waiting for me, ready to take me through the journey to the other side and His results. I believed, and He helped me shore up any area where my circumstances had tried to take me to a place of doubting that He was faithful and would take care of me. God's will was to heal me, and He was fully able to do that which He has promised.

CHAPTER 8
Understanding Biblical Hope

HOPE. IT'S A word that is often misunderstood. We hear people say, "I hope so," or "I hope it turns out that way," and we probably don't give it a second thought. "Hope" and "wish" have become interchangeable words in everyday conversation, but they definitely carry different connotations in their meanings. Many times the word hope is used in conversation, but it is really only expressing what someone *wishes*, and there is a big difference between a *hope* and a *wish*.

In common English usage, we find the following definitions:

Hope: to desire with expectation of obtainment or fulfillment; to expect with confidence.[5]

Wish: to have a desire for something, such as something unattainable.[6]

What is the difference between these two statements?

- I *hope* I can improve my guitar playing.
- I *wish* I could improve my guitar playing.

Remember that hope expresses something that the speaker believes is possible. The first sentence above means that I want to improve my guitar playing, and I think it is possible. I not only like the idea of my guitar playing getting better, I see it as a distinct possibility of attaining it. Another way of expressing the thought would be to say, "It's my hope that my guitar playing improves."

A wish, on the other hand, expresses something that the speaker believes is not possible right now. The second sentence above means that I want to improve my guitar playing, but I don't have confidence that it is possible. It is something that I would like to see happen, but I am not placing any expectation on seeing it come to pass. Another way of expressing the thought would be to say, "it would be nice if my guitar playing improved."

Granted, to some people this may seem like merely verbal semantics, but that is only true in casual conversation. When we apply this understanding to the issues of life, it has a huge impact. Wishing yearns for something, while hope anticipates it. Wishing says "Wouldn't it be nice *if*...," while hope says, "It will be nice *when*...."

Too often we have an idea of how we would like to see a situation turn out, recognize it as the desirable outcome, and then wait to see how close the actual results come. There is no expectation, only a desire. This is the essence of *wishing* for the sickness to be gone, the bills to be paid, the relationship to be restored.

Hope on the other hand, sees the desirable outcome and has an expectation that those results will be the ones that are experienced. Where a wish is based on a desire, hope is based on a belief that something or someone is able to help bring your desired result to fruition. Hope can lift your heart, your head, and your hands. It helps you fix your eyes on something else than your problem — to see yourself experiencing the healed body, the paid bills, and the restored relationship.

You can wish at any time with little thought or effort. However, hope doesn't always come all at once. There are many people, myself included, who start out with a wish, a desired result, but eventually come to a place of hoping. It's so important not to browbeat yourself over needing help to get from a place of wishing to a place of hope. Wishing at least puts your thoughts toward seeing a possibility exists. The key is to gain hope and know that the possibility not only exists, but that it can be yours. Your goal is to find a place where hope has a foundation and can stay solid until it is realized.

> **Your goal is to find a place where hope has a foundation and can stay solid until it is realized.**

That's why it is so important for us to have our hope grounded in something that is reliable. In life, we often envision that place as a person or group of people. Some people place their trust in family or friends. Some place their trust in their government, their job, or their bank account. As good as these options can be at times, they are subject to change and invariably fail at one time or another.

You may, however, find yourself without the support from your family or friends with what you are facing. You may not have an organization that you can place your trust in. Whether that is the case or not, it's important for you to have a personal answer to these questions: 1) Where does my hope reside? 2) Where can I find true hope?

Once you answer these questions, your hope will be firmly planted and will not be easily moved, no matter what side-effects or circumstances come your way.

DAVID AND HOPE

To see an example of how to do this, we're going to take another look at the life of David in the Bible. David faced many issues during his life. His family wasn't always reliable, and the king that he later served faithfully eventually gave way to paranoia and looked to have him killed. Regardless of what he faced, in his times of need David knew where his true hope came from and stated this in the book of Psalms:

> *I will lift up my eyes to the hills — From whence comes my help?*
> *My help comes from the Lord, Who made heaven and earth.*
> — Psalm 121:1-2

> *For You are my hope, O Lord God; You are my trust from my youth.*
> — Psalm 71:5

Since his youth, David had looked to God to be his hope. Being the youngest of Jesse's sons, David was sent to the fields to care for his family's sheep. He might have felt neglected at times, possibly unappreciated, and there probably would have been times of loneliness and times where fear tried to creep in. During these times, David placed his confidence in his Lord, trusting Him to be with him and care for him.

David's hope of defeating Goliath came from his trust in God. He believed that this result was possible because he had already seen the effect of God's presence in His life. As we read earlier in First Samuel chapter 17, David did indeed defeat Goliath and slay him. The event that he had hope for did come to pass, and the faith he had in God to be with him in the battle resulted in the victory he had hoped for. We even see this principle stated in Hebrews 11:1-2:

> *Now faith is the substance of things hoped for, the evidence of things not seen. For by it the men of old obtained a good report.*

BETWEEN HOPE AND A WISH

Understanding the difference between hope and a wish will change your life. It will help you to look at a given situation and better evaluate where you are truly at in it. Are you looking at the desired result you believe to be possible in your life? Then you are hoping. Make sure that your hope is based in God and His Word, and trust Him to bring that desired result to completion in your life.

Are you looking at the desired result as something that you see as not likely to happen or impossible? Then you are wishing. If you are wishing, your approach is lacking faith that what you desire will happen. You are in a place where your true expectations may be hindered by the need to protect yourself from disappointment.

If you find yourself in the land of wish, don't give up! You *can* move from wishing to hope. Remember, the difference between wish and hope is what your true expectation is and what it is founded on. This is where you can find true, biblical hope. I say "true, biblical hope" because the hope we find in the Bible is the only hope with a sure foundation. To get to the other side of whatever tunnel you are in, it will be *true, biblical hope* that will get you there, out into the open and the light that is found there. It is there that you will find God's results to the situation you are facing, and it is there that you will find your journey of faith through the hard times has made you stronger than ever. When God walks with your through a trial, He strengthens you and grows you with each successive step as you trust in Him.

WHAT IS BIBLICAL HOPE?

What is biblical hope? I say biblical hope, because how the Bible defines hope is different than many of the other definitions that you will find when consulting a dictionary. It's very important that you understand what the Bible has to say about hope, because the end of your tunnel is where hope is found. The ending that you desire is hope — your expected results — yet so often the relationship between hope and its related counterparts is either not fully explained or sadly, left out entirely. To have God's results, you have to understand how He works.

> **To have God's results, you have to understand how He works.**

As discussed earlier, hope — true biblical hope — is not wishing. It is not desiring something to take place; it is not being unsure or whimsical that it will take place. Biblical hope is based on something firm and can be obtained by keeping a grip on it until you see the results of what you have held on to hope for.

Biblical hope starts with a promise from God. You see, God knows you, and His desire for you is to excel in all He created you to be. He also knows that you will need help in this life, because your enemy — the devil — seeks to bring destruction in your life. His intent is to kill, steal, and destroy (*see* John 10:10). To combat this, God gives promises to you to keep your heart and mind for when the devil attempts to begin his cycle of destruction.

What is a promise? It is a statement of intent. When you make a promise, you are telling the other person what you intend to do in a situation. When a man and a woman make their marriage vows, they are making *promises* to each other. If you've ever been to a wedding, these promises may sound familiar:

"I will be faithful to you and you alone."

"I will stay with you in sickness and in health, for richer or for poorer, till death do we part."

These promises are made with the best of intentions, but people aren't always the best at keeping promises. You've probably experienced having a promise made to you that wasn't kept, or perhaps you have made promises you didn't keep. It's most often from these poor experiences that people base their distrust in promises and the hope that they should bring. Instead of trusting, they become jaded, hesitant, or resistant to putting their trust in the promises they hear.

Biblical hope is based in promises made by God. While other people may have fallen short in keeping their promises, you must remember that God isn't like them. In Numbers 23:19 (*NLT*) we are told:

> *God is not a man, so he does not lie. He is not human, so he does not change his mind. Has he ever spoken and failed to act? Has he ever promised and not carried it through?*

When God gives you a promise, He intends to carry it out. We see this in Jeremiah chapter 1, when God is reveals to Jeremiah His plans for him, and in verse 12, He reveals to Jeremiah this powerful truth:

> *Then the Lord said to me, "You have seen well, for I am [actively] watching over My word to fulfill it." (AMP)*

God watches over His word to fulfill it. When He speaks, His expectation is that what He has spoken will come to pass. He has invested Himself in His words. Why is this so important? Because God's words are a verbal expression of His character. God is not like you or me. He does not say something only to renege on it later. He does not make promises He cannot or will not keep. His character is expressed in those promises, and He watches over them because His character matters. It's in His character that we put our trust.

I have a beautiful wife who has promised to be faithful to me. I've rested in her promise for many years, because I've trusted in her character and her love for me. The promise is only as good as the person who made it. It is on them to keep it or break it. Our part is to trust.

All of God's promises are meant to deliver.

Which takes us back to biblical hope. Biblical hope is based on a promise. When you hear that promise, it brings with it the expectation of the promised result.

We see a precious example of this in Romans 10:9-10:

That if you confess with your mouth the Lord Jesus and believe in your heart that God has raised Him from the dead, you will be saved. For with the heart one believes unto righteousness, and with the mouth confession is made unto salvation.

The promise: If you confess with your mouth the Lord Jesus and believe in your heart that God has raised Him from the dead, you will be saved. The hope, or expected result, from this promise: Salvation. Righteousness in God's sight.

All of God's promises are meant to deliver. Some may take longer than others, but as we've seen earlier, God watches over His word to bring it to pass, to fulfill it. What we all wrestle with is what happens once we've heard God's promise in our situation and our expectation of seeing it come to pass.

To give you strength and understanding of how to see the promises of God come to pass in your life, we'll look at two people who were given promises that did not seem possible, but notice they didn't allow their circumstances to decide the final outcome — and you don't have to either.

WHEN GOD GIVES YOU A PROMISE THAT SEEMS LIKE ONLY A DREAM

In Genesis chapter 11, we are introduced to Abram, who was originally from the city of Ur in ancient Mesopotamia. He traveled with his father Terah, his wife Sarai, and his nephew Lot on a journey to the land of Canaan, but the family stopped along the way in Haran. While living in Haran, Abram's father Terah died. Living in a foreign land, his father now gone, Abram faced decisions that would shape the rest of his and his family's lives. It was against this backdrop that we read the words in Genesis 12:1-3:

> *Now the Lord had said to Abram:*
> *"Get out of your country,*
> *From your family*
> *And from your father's house,*
> *To a land that I will show you.*
> *I will make you a great nation;*
> *I will bless you*
> *And make your name great;*
> *And you shall be a blessing.*
> *I will bless those who bless you,*

And I will curse him who curses you;
And in you all the families of the earth shall be blessed."

This is the first recorded conversation that God had with Abram, and in it He made Abram, who was 75 at the time, the following promise: "I will make you a great nation."

In obedience, Abram took his family and his possessions and left Haran to travel to the land that God would show him. He journeyed to the land of the Canaanites, at which time God spoke to him again:

> *Abram passed through the land to the place of Shechem, as far as the terebinth tree of Moreh. And the Canaanites were then in the land. Then the Lord appeared to Abram and said, "To your descendants I will give this land."*
> — Genesis 12:6-7

God promised Abram that He would make him into a great nation and that He would give the land of the Canaanites to Abram's descendants. So Abram traveled and lived in the land, following wherever God led him, growing in wealth and influence due to God's blessing being on him. Later, God appeared to Abram again and spoke to him:

> *"...Do not be afraid, Abram. I am your shield, your exceedingly great reward."*
>
> *But Abram said, "Lord God, what will You give me, seeing I go childless, and the heir of my house is Eliezer of Damascus?" Then Abram said, "Look, You have given me no offspring; indeed one born in my house is my heir!"*
>
> *And behold, the word of the Lord came to him, saying, "This one shall not be your heir, but one who will come from your own body shall be your heir." Then He brought him outside*

and said, "Look now toward heaven, and count the stars if you are able to number them." And He said to him, "So shall your descendants be."

And he believed in the Lord, and He accounted it to him for righteousness.
— Genesis 15:1-5

It's against this backdrop that we find Abram — promised by God to be the father of a great nation and to have many descendants — still without a child of his own.

How can you have hope for an outcome that defies logic like Abram? From a natural perspective, based on what you are looking at, it may seem unreasonable to believe that you will have a favorable outcome. You might be thinking:

- *The tumor is too large and the cancer has spread.*
- *My debts seem insurmountable and there isn't a source of income to even make a dent.*
- *My marriage is crumbling and the lack of communication or care seem to be getting worse with each passing day.*
- *My child has gone their own way and rarely speaks to me.*
- *My life seems to be spiraling out of control, and I can't sleep, rest, or find peace.*
- *I feel so alone with no one to turn to and nowhere to go.*
- *I've longed for a child of my own, but now, in my later years, it is too late for my body to conceive.*

The circumstances say, even scream, that there is no hope for your situation. No hope. No light at the end of your tunnel — and there may not be, if you allow your circumstances and how they make you feel to dictate how you see your future. Yet biblical hope — the hope that is rooted in God faithfulness and His trustworthiness to do what He said He would do and be who He said He would be — can rise above and beyond what the natural world says is improbable or impossible. It was this hope that Abraham had, and you can have it as well.

In Genesis chapter 17, the Lord appeared to Abram to affirm His covenant with him to be a father of many nations. To signify this promise and serve as a reminder, the Lord changes Abram's name to Abraham, which means "father of multitudes." In Romans chapter 4, we read of this same Abraham, who had received a promise from God that he and his wife would have a child, even though they were old and she was barren. He had received the promise of descendants when he was 75, and now at 99 years of age, God has told Abraham that His blessing would be on the son that he and his 90-year-old wife bore. There was not a scenario in the world in which this was plausible. Yet Abraham had his eyes fixed beyond what the natural world could show him.

> *Therefore it is of faith that it might be according to grace, so that the promise might be sure to all the seed, not only to those who are of the law, but also to those who are of the faith of Abraham, who is the father of us all (as it is written, "I have made you a father of many nations") in the presence of Him whom he believed — God, who gives life to the dead and calls those things which do not exist as though they did; who, contrary to hope, in hope believed, so that he became the father of many nations, according to what was spoken, "So shall your descendants be." And not being weak in faith, he did not consider his own body, already dead (since he was about a hundred years old), and the deadness of Sarah's womb. He did not waver at the promise of God through unbelief, but was strengthened in faith, giving glory to God, and being fully convinced that*

what He had promised He was also able to perform. And therefore "it was accounted to him for righteousness."
— Romans 4:16-22

It is said of Abraham, "Who, contrary to hope, in hope believed, so that he became the father of many nations according to what was spoken, 'So shall your descendants be'" (v. 18).

Abraham hoped in God, contrary to the hope that was found in the natural world. The natural world said he and Sarah were far past the age of producing a child, but Abraham had God's promise that it would be so. Where the natural world said that a woman who was unable to conceive over many decades had a dead womb, God's promise said she would be the one who would not only conceive the child but carry the child and give birth to him.

You can have hope for God's results even when natural hope says it is impossible. You can have HOPE, against hope. What did Abraham do to have this type of biblical hope?

Verse 19 — He did not consider, or give final word to, his own body — even though he was almost 100 years old.

Verse 19 — He did not consider, or give the final word to, the deadness of Sarah's womb.

Instead, Abraham strengthened his faith:

And not being weak in faith, he did not consider his own body, already dead (since he was about a hundred years old), and the deadness of Sarah's womb. **He did not waver at the promise of God through unbelief, but was strengthened in faith, giving glory to God, and being fully convinced that what He had promised He was also able to perform.**
— Romans 4:19-21

As we've read, Abraham received a wonderful promise from God, and at the age of 99, he was visited by the Angel of the Lord who announced it was time for this promise to be fulfilled (*see* Genesis 18). By then Abraham was an old man, and his wife Sarah was an old woman, yet Abraham looked at the promise of God not only as *able* to happen, but as God's Word to him that it *would* happen — that God would be who He said He was to him and would do what He said He would do for him.

During one of my early consultations, my surgeon Dr. Johnson went over the initial scans of the tumor with me — its location, size, and possible methods of removal. He was kind during his presentation of the information but matter of fact about the complexity of the procedure that would be involved and the results that should be expected. As he explained the details of the proposed surgery, he spoke of the effects that the chemotherapy and radiation would have on my body, specifically in my crotch and posterior. These were not details I wanted to hear, as they did not hold hope for a normal life.

He explained that the tissue in the areas of treatment would be compromised from the chemo and further irradiation of the tissue. When the affected tissue would be removed, there would not be viable tissue left to reattach what was left of my rectum and my colon together. Medical experience had shown that reattachment of the compromised tissue led to complication, including rupture and possible death.

The situation I was facing called for a permanent colostomy, which would involve the sealing of my rectum and the installation of a permanent ostomy bag on my side that would be with me for the remainder of my life. Here was the question of my ongoing quality of life staring me straight in the face. I expected to live in the face of the aggressive cancer. Natural hope said that if I did survive cancer, I was looking at a permanent colostomy, yet I knew in my heart that God had a future for me that would involve me traveling the world speaking and ministering as well as writing books. I had His promise that He was my healer, and that where natural hope stopped, hope in the more than natural — the supernatural — was possible. I could *hope against hope*.

I listened to all Dr. Johnson had to say and then from a confidence that was grounded in my heart and not my head I told him that I would follow his advice but would trust God to provide healthy tissue where there needed to be. He smiled and told me he had never seen it happen before, but if it did, he would give God all the credit. I'm happy to say that God did indeed do the impossible in my situation and provided that healthy tissue where they expected none to be. The tumor was gone, and in the area where 28 radiation sessions had bombarded, no irradiated and compromised area of tissue was found. I was told it was "pristine"! Dr. Johnson was able to reattach my bowels and avoid the permanent colostomy. He gave God the credit for the miracle — with a smile on his face. God's goodness was displayed in the land of the living through what He had done in my body.

You can hear one of God's promises and allow it to roll around in your head as you analyze it and evaluate how plausible it is to actually come to pass. You can meditate on that promise and mentally go through the various scenarios that could play out and the results they would yield. That's how we are taught to process things, to be analytical and methodical in order to come to a plausible conclusion. Granted, we all know people who don't fit that mold, but in most places the teaching methods and curriculum point to this common reasoning and thinking.

The passage of time gives extended opportunities for looking at different facets of that promise, the promised results, and how it could **not** happen. Time has a way of chipping away at your confidence to receive what you can be waiting for, and as you've been reading in this book, you have hopefully learned that the enemy takes every opportunity to insert thoughts, people, and events into your path to shake you and draw you away from believing that God loves you and has a plan to see you through what you are facing. Not only does He have a plan to see you through, but He has a future for you to hope for, one that has purpose.

HOLDING ONTO GOD'S PROMISES BRINGS HIS RESULTS

Your hard times are not the end in God's eyes, and He doesn't want them to be the end in your eyes either. As we look again at Abraham's story, we see him in the place where you may find yourself. He had a promise from God — a promise so amazing and improbable in the eyes of others. Looking again at Genesis 15, we see the promise God made to Abraham:

> *And behold, the word of the Lord came to him, saying, "This one shall not be your heir, but one who will come from your own body shall be your heir." Then He brought him outside and said, "Look now toward heaven, and count the stars if you are able to number them." And He said to him, "So shall your descendants be." And he believed in the Lord, and He accounted it to him for righteousness.*
> — Genesis 15:4-6

God promised Abraham a son of his own blood and numerous descendants, and Abraham made the decision to trust God and take Him at His word. He trusted God to be who He said He would be to him and to do what He said He would do for him. Verse 6 even tells us that when God saw that Abraham looked upon Him as faithful and placed his trust in Him, He counted the position of Abraham's heart toward Him as righteous. This was based completely on Abraham looking to God and what He had to say as the truth in his situation, placing his trust in Him and his reliance on Him. That is what God is looking for in you and I as well — for us to place our trust in Him and our reliance on Him.

Notice again that Romans 4:20 says:

He did not waver at the promise of God through unbelief, but was strengthened in faith, giving glory to God, and being fully convinced that what He had promised He was also able to perform.

Abraham did not waver at the promise of God through unbelief. In layman's terms, Abraham did not go back and forth over whether God was able and willing to do what He had promised to do. Over time Abraham absolutely had opportunities for questioning thoughts to come to his mind about whether this promised child would ever come, but he didn't give in and kept his faith strong.

As we've discussed earlier in this book, opposing thoughts are going to come, but you have a choice in whether or not you will entertain them and come to believe them. They will come to take you off of your place of faith and bring into question what God has said about you and your situation. It's your choice to resist those thoughts or let them shape your thinking, causing you to doubt God's Word and His care for you. The same principles shared in this book follow after Abraham's pattern of not wavering.

Abraham was strengthened in his faith, and that kept him from wavering at what God had promised him. This strength kept him from falling into a place where he no longer believed that God would be who He said He would be to him and do what He said He would do for him. Abraham stayed fully convinced that God would fulfill what He had promised by "giving glory to God" (Romans 4:20).

I can remember going through treatment and the agony it was to use my bowels and eliminate through the treated areas. I'd have thoughts of how painful each trip to the bathroom would be and then I would dread having to go. It would have been easy to begin thinking of that colostomy bag and the relief it would provide me from the pain. It would have been acceptable to those around me to give in and change my expectations of what God was doing in my situation. However, I'm so thankful that in those early days, God reminded me of the call He had placed on my life and the dreams He had placed in my heart. He told me to: "Trust Him to be Who He said He would be to me and to do what He said He would do for me." During each trip to the bathroom, I would remind myself that this was not my destiny, but only a battle, a tunnel, that I was walking through to the other side. I would look in my Bible and see the things I had written over the years about what God had placed in my heart to do. They became the bright light of a lighthouse shining through the fog and darkness to my ship that was weathering a storm. I would thank God for His faithfulness and strengthen my faith.

When God first made His promise to Abraham, He took him outside under the night sky and had Abraham look into the heavens to see the innumerable stars and then spoke to him:

> *Then He brought him outside and said, "Look now toward heaven, and count the stars if you are able to number them." And He said to him, "So shall your descendants be."*
> — Genesis 15:5

"So shall your descendants be." Abraham understood that the child God promised him would be his first descendant, but as he looked at the countless stars in the sky, he saw that God's promise was of a greater magnitude than he could comprehend. God was seeing far into the future of the other side of Abraham's situation, showing him a representation of what He saw. Abraham saw the wonders of celestial creation before his eyes and understood that the same God who had placed those stars in the sky was the One who was making the promise to him. What God had promised Abraham was small in relation to all that God had done, yet He cared for Abraham so much that He was talking to him as a friend, giving him something tangible to refer back to when the trying times and thoughts of doubt came against him. Each gaze up into those stars would remind Abraham of God's promise to him and the hope he had in trusting God.

I've imagined Abraham having a difficult day, struggling with thoughts of doubt coming against him and then going out of his tent under the night sky to look at the stars. He would see those stars and be reminded of the majesty and greatness of his God and that nothing was too difficult for Him. Then as Abraham looked up into the night sky, he would think back to the goodness of God and all the times He had been with him to teach him, care for him, and lead him. I imagined him picking out a specific star that was always visible in the night sky and regarding it as his promised son. When he looked up in the night sky and saw all the stars, he would see hope — the settled expectation of God's words to him being fulfilled. He would look at his chosen star and say to himself and to God that he trusted in God's goodness and faithfulness to complete in his life what He had promised him. Abraham would thank God for all He had done in his life and what He was still doing on his behalf. As he glorified God, the thoughts of doubt would drift away and the temptation to waver would subside.

Even though Abraham didn't see from a practical point of view how God could take an old man and an old woman who had never been able to conceive a child and give them a child from their own bodies, he took God at His word. He placed his trust in God and saw his hope as having God's results, despite the fact that in the natural there was no reason for him to have hope he would see it happen.

In Romans 8:24-25, the apostle Paul explained:

For we were saved in this hope, but hope that is seen is not hope; for why does one still hope for what he sees? But if we hope for what we do not see, we eagerly wait for it with perseverance.

Abraham had true biblical hope, because even though he did not see the results of what God had promised him right away, he waited for God's promised results with perseverance. He stuck it out day after day trusting God's results to take place in his life. When thoughts of doubt circled in his mind, he persevered, expectantly waiting for his promised son with patience.

- He looked at his blessings around him and reminded himself of how good God had been to him, and he held onto his hope.
- He looked into the night sky and saw the stars that God had led him outside to see as he promised him descendants, and he held onto his hope.
- He spent time in prayer and fellowship with God, and he strengthened his hope.

Abraham saw with his own natural eyes that the son of promise was not in his tent, but that did not stop him from seeing in his heart the son God had promised him. He eagerly awaited the arrival of that son. It was not Abraham's thoughts that God had looked at and counted as righteousness. It was Abraham's heart toward Him, and from that same heart place Abraham believed in what God said, just as centuries later the father with the demonized boy believed Jesus when He told him with God all things were possible if he could believe they were. They both received God's results in their lives, just as you can when you place your trust in God's goodness and faithfulness.

> **There is no faith, no trusting in God, when you are waiting for a random, unspecified result.**

It is important to understand that faith, trusting in God, and hope go hand in hand. We read this in Hebrews 11:1-2:

> *Now faith is the substance of things hoped for, the evidence of things not seen. For by it the elders obtained a good testimony.*

What is "hoped for" is your desired result. You must have a desired result to have biblical hope, and biblical hope is specific. It is not a nebulous goal, and it is not a "throw it against the wall and see if it sticks" proposition. There is no faith, no trusting in God, when you are waiting for a random, unspecified result. Our goal should be to have God's results from His Word in our lives, and to receive those results, we must trust in God to deliver them and then wait with patience, expectantly awaiting their arrival.

In verse 1, we are told faith is a "substance," the realization or the confidence of things not seen. What has not been seen? The results of God's promise to you — that which you are "hoping for." It may not have arrived for you to see and experience yet, but you are counting on it as if it is on the way. You've made your request according to God's Word, your trust is in Him, and the resulting response has been dispatched and is on its way. You are not wondering if God heard you or whether He will decide to involve Himself in your situation; instead, you are certain He has heard you and has responded. You are simply waiting for His provision to arrive.

To put it personally: Faith, your trust in God to be who He said He would be to you and do what He said He would do for you, is all the evidence you need to be convinced that He will be personally involved in what you are hoping for.

Biblical hope, hope that trusts in God's goodness and faithfulness, will produce results. Whatever you are facing, it is not beyond God's desire or ability to step into and do amazing things. He is looking for the opportunity to respond to those who trust in Him. Now is your time to see Him as your answer and place your hope in Him.

CHAPTER 9
Remember You Are Walking in a Miracle

HAVE YOU BEEN through a time when the things you were facing seemed to be manageable, only to experience a sudden twist that throws you for a loop as everything around you seems to begin unraveling? Maybe you're in the middle of a fight and a move you make goes drastically different than what you had envisioned. When this happens, you're presented with the opportunity to be shaken and confused. You're faced with the question of whether to stay the course or alter your approach, and you may not have much time to make that determination.

When a crisis hits it does not care who you are, what you have going on, or whether you have the resources to deal with it. If you are going to overcome a crisis, you must decide not to fold at the first signs of resistance. It's like a running back in a football game who rushes to the line of scrimmage only to find there is no hole to run through — he must determine to make a *second effort* to push again and continue running the ball. He may change directions and look for another hole to run through, or he may redouble his efforts and plow through the blockers in front of him. In either case, he has a goal in mind, and he gives all he must to get closer to that goal. You could say the goal line and the end zone are the light at the end of his tunnel, and he presses on toward them to score.

That's the tenacity it will take for you to reach the other side of your tunnel. As you fight with the enemy that is bullying you, you can't fold when he lands a punch. Fighters are taught to counter punch, and a counter attack is required if you want to come out of your fight victorious. When you are hit, you must hit back, resisting the enemy's attempts to impose his will on you and take you out. Your tenacity and resilience are not what the enemy is expecting, and if you stand your ground, you will see the fight turn in your favor. Don't lose sight of the fact you are still standing, still fighting, and with God's help you *will be* victorious.

UNWANTED NEWS

A few weeks into my battle with cancer, I was scheduled for a PET scan to determine if the cancer had spread to other parts of my body. The type of cancer I was facing was known to spread aggressively, and the initial scans I had underwent showed the tumor went through the wall of my rectum and into the adjacent lymph nodes. I was trusting God to be healed of cancer, and I set myself to trust Him and to thank Him for healing me and the cancer being gone from my body. I wasn't flippantly throwing prayers to the wall hoping something would stick. I was convinced that God was healing me of cancer, and I was looking to the PET scan to show the cancer gone. I also had absolutely no desire to do chemotherapy or radiation treatments.

The day came for the PET scan, and I went in for the scanning process. I can honestly say I went in with an expectation that the scan would show the cancer was gone, and I was ready to give my testimony of God's healing power in my life. The technician laid me on a table that moved between two long tubes to perform the scan. The space was confined, but I was at peace. I don't particularly care for enclosed spaces, but I closed my eyes and mediated on God's faithfulness to me. He had already seen me through many tough spots in my life, and I expected nothing different in this latest ordeal. I actually nodded off a couple of times until the table would move and emit odd noises, jerking me awake. My plans for catching up on my sleep didn't come to fruition as I had hoped, but the process was bearable and over within an hour. I finished the scans and headed home, expectant of the good news I was going to receive at my next appointment with my oncologist.

My next oncology appointment came, and after I was weighed and had my vitals taken, my wife and I were led into an exam room to wait on the doctor. A few minutes later my oncologist walked into the room with a folder in her hand and a smile on her face. That moment I felt a bit of elation, and then she spoke these words:

"I have your scan results. They are good. We can work with this!"

My mind keyed in on the phrase: "We can work with this." I thought, *Work with what? I don't want to be working with any of this. The tumor was supposed to be gone!*

The doctor then proceeded to explain to my wife and me that the scan had come back reporting the only location in my body showing cancer to be was the tumor they had already discovered. There was no other cancer in my body even though this form was known to metastasize and spread aggressively, especially since it had been discovered encroaching on my lymph nodes. This was an unusual development on its own and encouraged the doctor that a possible treatment plan to attack the tumor could be devised and attempted.

I didn't share her excitement. My momentary elation disappeared, and in its place, I felt the onset of a wave of disappointment and dread. What I had been trusting for and expecting wasn't happening as I wanted. Looking back now from the other side of the tunnel, I did get what I was trusting for — it just didn't happen in the timing or manner I had been planning on. God was faithful to me, and He did heal me of cancer. The cancer that everyone anticipated would spread throughout my body was instead relegated to one location. Yet at that moment in the doctor's office, my tunnel seemed to get a lot longer and darker than it had seemed only minutes before.

You may relate to having some of these same feelings as you face your own trials. It is a natural response in this type of situation for disappointment to come and for dread, confusion, and anger to tag along for the ride. As I sat there in that room, my head begin to swirl with thoughts. The opportunity to be upset with God came, and as quickly as it came so did something I learned years before. It placed things in perspective for me and allowed me to be like that running back mentioned earlier and collect myself to make a second effort toward the healing I was trusting God to do in my body.

KEEPING SIGHT OF THE MIRACLE YOU ARE IN

Satan's tactic is to question what God has said and to use every means available in our lives to get us to question God as well. When my oncologist broke the news of the scan results to me, I had a choice to make. Would I let the news and its implications override what I knew about God and who He was to me? Would I trust in what Jesus had done for me on the Cross or allow my disappointment to be the perspective I moved forward with?

As these thoughts swarmed my mind, I was reminded of Peter and the night he walked on the water.

In Matthew 14:22-33 we read the account of Peter stepping out of a boat and walking on the surface of the water. Earlier in this passage, Jesus had fed a multitude of people and at the end of the day sent His disciples on to cross the Sea of Galilee while He dismissed the crowd and retired to the mountains to pray. Later that night, the weather over the Sea of Galilee changed, and Jesus walked across the water to rejoin His disciples.

> *Then Jesus commanded His disciples to get into the boat and go ahead of Him to the other side, while He sent the crowds away. When He sent the crowds away, He went up into a mountain by Himself to pray. And when evening came, He was there alone. But the boat was now in the middle of the sea, tossed by the waves, for the wind was turbulent.*
> — Matthew 14:22-24 (*MEV*)

One year I took my son and son-in-law on an open water fishing trip while our family was on vacation. The waters had been choppy because of a hurricane that was passing by, even though it was over 100 miles off the coast, but we were assured the night before by the boat captain that the weather would be fine for our trip. We got up early the next morning and headed to the marina where we boarded the boat and headed out. About an hour into the trip the winds picked up, and before we knew it, we were in waves that were over 5 feet high. That may not seem like a lot, but we were in a 28-foot boat! We had a powerful motor on that boat which enabled us to manage our way through the waves, and we wisely headed back to the marina. Turbulent winds stirred the water and had made the trip unsafe. This was the situation the disciples were facing as they watched the waves rise and fall across the Sea of Galilee.

The disciples had no motor to power their boat. They were relegated to men paddling with oars, straining with each stroke as they battled the waves that rocked their boat. Several of the men in that boat were experienced fishermen who understood sailing and seamanship. Doing everything they knew to do, they were still being overcome with the circumstances on the water they found themselves in.

You may be an experienced person, but it is possible to have life hit you with something that overwhelms you anyway. You might find yourself tossed around by waves and discover the rudder you are hanging onto as you try and steer your way through your mess isn't having much effect. Perhaps all you can do is row, and in your own strength you are straining to make progress. Jesus' disciples were facing the same type of situation, and the reality is, this can happen to anyone. Ultimately, it's how you respond to the situation that determines where you end up.

The account of this event in Mark 6 adds this important piece of information:

> *When evening came, the boat was in the midst of the sea. And He was alone on the land.* ***He saw them straining at rowing****, for the wind was against them.*
> — Mark 6:47-48

Even though Jesus had separated from them to go pray, He was still paying attention to His disciples. He may not have seemed near to them as they were fighting against the strong winds and the waves, but His disciples were still on His mind. He was aware of their plight and was still looking in their direction. When He saw they were facing trouble, He came to them. In the same way, He is watching over you, and although you will have moments where it may not seem like Jesus is there, you can rest assured He has not lost sight of you and who you are to Him.

After seeing His disciples struggle at sea, Jesus determined to help them, and He made the decision to move on their behalf. Notice He didn't go to the marina to get a boat and row to them. He didn't walk down to the shore and dive in, swimming to them. He took the most direct route available — even if that route meant that the normal, natural restrictions of gravity and physics would have to be set aside and overruled. What Jesus did was not natural, but He did not let natural law stop Him from coming to the aid of those He loved.

> **What Jesus did was not natural, but He did not let natural law stop Him from coming to the aid of those He loved.**

Jesus stepped out onto the stormy sea and made His way to the disciples. He walked on each ripple and wave that was in His path, sure-footed and determined to reach them. He was moving with purpose, just as He will in your life.

> *Now in the fourth watch of the night Jesus went to them, walking on the sea. And when the disciples saw Him walking on the sea, they were troubled, saying, "It is a ghost!" And they cried out for fear. But immediately Jesus spoke to them, saying, "Be of good cheer! It is I; do not be afraid."*
> — Matthew 14:25-27

When the disciples saw a figure walking through the waves toward them, they were awestruck. This was something unheard of, except possibly in old fishermen's tales. Just as in modern times we've had stories and legends about ghost sailors and ships, those type of tales may have existed among the people along the Sea of Galilee. The disciples became fearful and thought that it could be a spirit, and they cried out in fear.

As soon as Jesus heard their fear, He answered to calm it. He heard them over the noise of the wind and listened intently to hear them. He listens to hear you as well, and He will respond.

Jesus said, "Be of good cheer. It is I. Do not be afraid" (v. 27). It was as if He was saying: *"Guys! You can be happy and at rest. I am here now. There's no reason for you to be afraid!"*

Picture the disciples in a boat that is being tossed back and forth and taking on water as the waves splash against the sides of the boat. As they strain to keep their boat afloat and get it to safety, they see a figure coming across the water — on TOP of the water, waves and all. They are frightened and start to cry out in fear. We're not told what they were crying out, but it possibly included some form of:

"We're all gonna die!"

"Why me, God? Why me?"

"Bail Faster!!"

"Great, first a sinking boat, now a ghost is coming after us!"

What would you be crying out if you were seeing this?

Jesus called out to them to calm their fears, and there had to be a collective sigh of relief at His voice as well as consternation that Jesus was walking on the water toward them. They knew Him. He wasn't a ghost. Hours earlier He had been with them and miraculously fed a multitude, and now He was topping that miracle with walking on water. Just what matter of Man was He?

In the middle of the wind and the waves and the rowing and the stunning appearance of a figure walking across the water, Peter looked out at the figure and made a decision. He decided to respond. He called out to Jesus and said:

...Lord, if it is You, command me to come to You on the water.
— Matthew 14:28

Peter made the determination that he would rather be out on the water with Jesus than in the boat without Him. He was ready to go, but he wanted to know it was really Jesus. He also wasn't going to leave the boat and venture out onto the water unless He knew Jesus was in agreement with that action. He wanted Jesus to tell him what his next action should be and not assume ahead of Him.

It was when Jesus said *"Come"* that Peter left the boat and stepped out onto the water. The Bible has many examples in which God was consulted before an action or direction was taken. God's intentions for us are to grow us, heal us, and provide for us. This is revealed throughout the scriptures. He also has plans and purposes that are intertwined in His actions, and we are to seek Him so that we follow His plan and His timing in all we do.

Peter asked the question before he stepped out of the boat. He wanted to be where Jesus was, but he needed to know if he was going to step ONTO the water or sink INTO the water before he left the boat. Once he received Jesus' answer of confirmation, Peter made the decision to leave the boat and come to Him.

Can you visualize Peter lifting his leg up and over the side of the boat? Soon the rest of his body slides over the side to enter the water. The wet sensation that natural law said would accompany his action did not materialize. Instead of feeling the water rush over the tops of his feet, swirl around his ankles, and quickly rise up his legs and over his torso, Peter's feet rested ON TOP of the water. He wasn't hanging over the side of the boat. He was steadying himself with an arm as he stood next to it!

When he stepped out of that boat, he stood on top of the very same water that the disciples had feared would take their lives! As they made their way across the Sea of Galilee, they were very aware that if their boat were to capsize, the dark waters could very well be their end. Good swimmers they might have been, but the rolling waters could easily envelope them and they could drown. Now at Jesus' word, Peter was leaving the relative safety of their boat to go to the place where he had legitimate reason to be concerned for his life. We see in verse 29 that Peter left the boat and headed out onto the water to go to Jesus:

And when Peter got out of the boat, he walked on the water to go to Jesus.

Peter was taking one step at a time on top of the water toward Jesus. Then things began to change:

But when he saw that the wind was boisterous, he was afraid; and beginning to sink he cried out, saying, "Lord, save me!"
— Matthew 14:30

Verse 30 states: "When he saw that the wind was *boisterous*, he was afraid." As we saw in Chapter 4, Goliath was boisterous. Sennacherib was boisterous. Now Peter is facing his own boisterous situation. This is a tactic the enemy uses to take your focus away from what God has said and distract you from the victory that belong to you. This noise can be a bad report, aches and pains, an unexpected bill, or any other circumstance that comes against the Word of God being the standard in our lives. Any of these circumstances can come to you and do its best to shake your resolve, make you lose your focus, and attempt to usher in fear and doubt. This is what happened to Peter — and me and possibly you as well.

When Peter saw the wind was boisterous, noisy, and turbulent, he heard the noise it made, whistling and howling in his ears. He saw the effect it had on the water, causing waves to rise and fall and upsetting the surface of the sea making it uneasy, unstable. He felt the wind as it whipped around him, and at some point, he began to consider this wind and the effect it had on his surroundings to be a threat to his safety. Then verse 30 tells us *"...he was afraid."* Peter began to lose sight, his focus, on the fact that he was walking on the only things that could actually harm him. He began to reason in his mind about the wind's commotion and not the truth that he was already moving in a miracle, defying natural law — the same natural law that was allowing the wind to make noise, move water into waves, and change air pressure to cause the sensations he felt on his skin. Walking on top of the water, his position was *supernatural*, but he became distracted from that current reality and found himself drawn back to the natural condition of his surroundings.

As I sat in that exam room and heard the news that the tumor was still there, the doctor explained the proposed plan of chemo and radiation therapy, at least two surgeries, follow-up chemo, and ultimately no guarantee of the quality of life I might have afterwards. I was facing my own version of wind and waves just as the disciples faced and just like what you may be facing. I had several circumstances swirling around me telling me that my situation was grim and there wasn't much hope in what I was hearing. I was trusting God to heal me of this cancer, but the doctor was telling me that it was still there, and although they might be able to treat it and keep me alive, I would be wearing a colostomy bag the rest of my life in the best-case scenario. I felt my hope sinking.

Notice verse 30 says "beginning to sink." When circumstances come against us, we can be shaken, and we might even feel ourselves beginning to sink. I know because it has happened to me more times than I'd like to admit. Isn't it great to know that being shaken doesn't send us to the bottom *immediately*? Praise God, that didn't happen to Peter, and it doesn't have to happen to us. The scripture says that *he began* to sink. He didn't sink to the bottom like a rock. He *only began* to sink.

Peter was walking on top of the water when he began to see and hear the chaos around him, and he began to think about what it could do to him. At some point those thoughts began to take more of a place in his mind than his thoughts of walking on top of the water and reaching Jesus. The wind and waves roaring around him served as a constant reminder of all the times he had been out on the water or in the water as a fisherman. He knew that going under that water would rob him of the ability to breath, and if he remained under the waves too long the water would enter his lungs, and he would drown. He knew the heavy waves would drive him under the water over and over until he could no longer surface. A glance across the Sea of Galilee showed him wave after wave, and a glimpse of what was below him showed him the depth of the water he was crossing. We also must keep in mind that this was happening at night, in darkness except for the bit of moonlight or lightning that might have illuminated the scene from time to time. This was not a nice daylight stroll across the water — this was a stair-step walk over waves in the middle of the dark night. Think of your dark tunnel and understand that Peter's scene wasn't much better.

WHEN YOUR FAITH BEGINS TO WAVER AND HOW TO RESPOND

As Peter put one foot in front of the other his thoughts finally tipped from what he was miraculously doing to what might happen to him should he not continue on the top of the water. I picture this next part as a progression, as the scripture tells us he "[*began*] to sink" (v. 30).

Peter didn't quickly slip beneath the waves. Often it is the same situation when you begin to be overcome while walking through your tunnel — you don't lose heart overnight. The circumstances related to what you are going through weigh on your mind and slowly pull you down, further and further over time, until you are no longer seeing the hope that you are trusting God for.

As Peter walked on the water and began to give place in his thoughts to the wind and the waves around him, his confidence in his situation began to falter. The water that had been wet under his feet began to seep between his toes then cover his feet. Soon it was up to his ankles and then moved up to his calves. Peter realized that he was beginning to sink, and he knew from the sensations he was feeling that he was headed down below the waves where he would drown. It was at that moment that he called out to Jesus, "…Lord, save me!" (v. 30).

Notice Peter had enough presence of mind to cry out to the One who could save him. He didn't continue to sink and wallow in disappointment or self-pity. His walk on the water wasn't turning out the way he had envisioned, but he didn't cry out to Jesus, saying, *"This isn't fair! You're not being faithful!"* You would be surprised how often this is the first response people have when they find their situation is not going the way they want. They attribute their disappointment and trouble to God, when He is the author of neither. He is the solution to both. Peter knew Jesus

Peter did not let his situation override who he knew Jesus to be to him.

cared for him, and he called out from that place of trust. Peter did not let his situation override who he knew Jesus to be to him. When he cried out to Jesus, He was right there for him:

> *Immediately Jesus stretched out His hand and caught him, and said to him, "O you of little faith, why did you doubt?"*
> — Matthew 14:31

Immediately. We don't know how far away Peter was from Jesus when this happened, but we do know that *immediately* after Peter cried out, Jesus reached out His hand and caught him. Jesus was right there with Peter, and he's right there with you and me. What a beautiful picture it paints, as the Giver of the Word is also there to watch over His Word and preserve those who trust and act upon it. Jesus never leaves or forsakes us — *never*. He knows no other way to be than to be faithful.

I can think of many times over the course of my life where I've found myself faltering — beginning to sink — and I have cried out to Jesus. He was there immediately to catch me and strengthen me and to help me get to the end of that particular tunnel. He ushered me to the safe place He had for me, and Jesus is that present in your situation as well.

I have read the story of Peter walking on the water many times in my life, but it took me several years to see the practical wisdom in this story. For so long I had looked at this story as Peter's brave failure. He was brave enough to get out of the boat, but he had ultimately failed at walking on the water. It was only after I saw beyond the narrow view of Peter's apparent failure that I began to see how it mirrored my own struggles and how it provided a perspective that was applicable to approaching them and overcoming them.

It's a fact that Peter started out on his miraculous walk but along the way began to sink. Countless sermons have touched on this and on how Peter had taken his eyes off Jesus and caused himself to sink. Those are good and valid sermons, but they don't answer key questions I had as I read or heard the story.

- How did Peter take his eyes off Jesus?
- Since Peter apparently took his eyes off Jesus, was he required to physically be looking at Jesus to stay on top of the water?
- How far was Jesus from the boat when Peter started his walk?
- How did Peter get back to the boat?

Some of those answers are critical. Some had no bearing on his success, or yours. What I found was a direct path in the middle of Peter's stumble and encouragement on his walk back to the boat.

Whether Peter was physically looking at Jesus or not really has no bearing on whether he stayed walking on top of the water. What he was focused on had everything to do with it. You can't physically see Jesus today, but your focus can be on who He is to you and what He said He will do for you. In the midst of wave after wave of bad reports, pains, contentious thoughts and questions, your focus can stay on God's faithfulness. You can drown out the sound of the wind and the rolling waves with your attention to who God is to you and all that He has done and is doing in your life.

When Peter regarded the wind and the waves, he began thinking about all they could do to him. From his vast experience on the water as a fisherman, he knew how quickly the wind could stir up the waters and cause the waves to grow in size, frequency, and strength. As he watched the wind stirring up the strong, rolling waves that were buffeting their boat, he knew that going into that water would surely overwhelm him and he would drown. Walking on the water he was experiencing this in a way he never had before. He was in the middle of a situation that could easily take his life. Somewhere in this process he began to place more focus on what the waves and the water could do to him than what was actually happening — against all physical laws and experience, he was walking ON TOP of the thing that he was concerned would take him down. He was already walking in a miracle!

Sitting there in that exam room with my oncologist talking about the tumor and all the treatment plans she had in mind, I had my opportunity to regard my own version of "wind and waves." For a few moments her voice faded into a version of Charlie Brown's teacher, "Wa Waaa Wa Waaa Waaa," as I had a rush of emotion and thoughts hit me about what could be coming next. Then Peter's water walk came to my mind, and I remembered that even though the cancer was still there my hope was not gone. My hope was in God, and regardless of whether any cancer still showed up on the scans or was gone He was my Healer.

I reminded myself that I was already walking in a miracle. The doctors had expected the cancer to have spread throughout my body, but it was relegated to only the tumor they had previously found. The cancer wasn't spreading even though they had expected to find that it had. I chose to believe it was retreating and going away. Had it gone away as quickly as I wanted? Absolutely not! Yet I made the choice to focus on God being the answer to what I was dealing with. He was still the One who could see me through the sickness and heal my body. Symptoms and effects could hit my body, but it didn't change the fact that I was His child, He had a plan for my life, and that He was faithful. I reminded myself daily of what David said in Psalm 27:13:

I would have lost heart, unless I had believed that I would see the goodness of the Lord in the land of the living.

I believed that I would see the goodness of the Lord in the land of the living. Not when I was dead — I needed to see His goodness in my situation while I was *still alive*, here with all the other living people. As I reminded myself of these things, the oncologist's voice came back into focus. I was no longer overwhelmed with disappointment and dread. I was still disappointed and dreading the treatment she was proposing, but I was no longer overcome by it. I had an answer to this wind and wave, and I was determined to stay on top of what was trying to kill me.

I haven't always had that approach to trials. There was a time when I would stumble out on the water and sink down to my neck, crying and screaming for Jesus to grab me before I drowned or Jaws got me. He always reached out and grabbed me and pulled me up out of the water. I'd thank Him and go along my merry way, but I don't think I listened to what He had to say afterward many times and therein was my problem.

Notice in verse 31 Jesus reaches out and saves Peter and then asks him a pointed question:

Immediately Jesus stretched out His hand and caught him, **and said to him, "O you of little faith, why did you doubt?"**

For many years I had looked at this scripture as a mild chastisement from Jesus — "Awe, C'mon Peter! Why was your faith so weak that you allowed this to happen?" From the teachings I had grown up hearing and my own misperceptions of how Jesus looked at me, I had thought that Jesus was disappointed with Peter for not walking all the way on the water as He had. "Oh you of little faith" seemed to be attached to Peter's failure, but the phrase translated "little faith" is the Greek word *oligopistos* from the word *oligos* meaning *little* or *small* and *pistis*, which means *faith*. This means Peter had **little in quantity of faith**. His faith was there, but it wasn't abundant.

In the context of the story, Peter had exercised his faith and had walked on water. He had walked in a miracle by using his faith. He hadn't swum toward Jesus — he had walked on top of the water! He was operating on the word he had received from Jesus, but after he regarded the wind and waves as something that could overtake him, he became shaken and began to sink. We are the same way. If you aren't built up in the Word of God, remaining focused on the Word and what it truly means to you, you can be shaken.

When your faith is shaken, it can be like chips coming off a block of ice when it is struck. As the chips break off, the integrity of the block is compromised, and if it keeps happening, it will eventually fracture, fail, and shatter. Little faith, or faith that exists in a small quantity, cannot withstand the constant blows of fear unless it is strengthened. If you are not settled on God's Word and are not using it to evaluate all that is going on around you, your faith is being chipped away and reduced, and like Peter you will begin to slowly sink back under that which can really harm you. You might even continue to sink deeper and deeper under the power of the devil's lies until they engulf you, imprisoning you in an atmosphere that can eventually suffocate you.

Just like Peter, if you call out to Jesus, He will *immediately* reach out to catch you and strengthen you. Jesus took hold of His dear friend and then addressed him as "you of little faith" (v. 31). Understanding the meaning of this word "little" tells us Jesus was addressing Peter's need to grow his faith, not pointing out that it was *lacking quality*. For so long I had read this passage, heard it taught, and thought about it without ever seeing the truth in that small phrase. *Little* faith — not worthless, inconsequential, something to be ashamed of faith.

As stated earlier, the phrase "little faith" in this passage is the Greek word *oligopistos*, and in the four Gospels, it is used four other times as well. (*See* Matthew 6:25-34; Matthew 8:23-27; Matthew 16:5-12; and Luke 12:22-31.) In each of these passages, Jesus is teaching His disciples, and in the conversation He says to them, "O you of little faith." When He addresses His disciples in this manner, Jesus also asks them a question to help them each examine themselves and their perceptions. Jesus didn't use this phrase as a scathing indictment but as a way to accentuate His point to this group of twelve men that He was pouring His life into. He addressed them as a teacher would his pupils — those who still have much to learn.

An excellent example of this is found in Matthew 16:5-12.

The backdrop to this conversation is found in Matthew chapter 15, where Jesus ministered to great crowds of people and then performed a miracle of feeding 4,000 men (plus women and children) with seven loaves of bread and a few fish. He and His disciples had then taken a boat to the region of Magdala where they were met by Pharisees and Sadducees who challenged Jesus to prove Himself by performing a sign for them. After rebuffing the challenge, Jesus had counseled the disciples to beware of the motives of the Pharisees and Sadducees. This is where we find our example of those who still have much to learn:

> *Now when His disciples had come to the other side, they had forgotten to take bread. Then Jesus said to them, "Take heed and beware of the leaven of the Pharisees and the Sadducees."*
>
> *And they reasoned among themselves, saying, "It is because we have taken no bread."*
>
> *But Jesus, being aware of it, said to them,* ***"O you of little faith, why do you reason among yourselves*** *because you have brought no bread?* ***Do you not yet understand, or remember*** *the five loaves of the five thousand and how many baskets you took up? Nor the seven loaves of the four thousand and how many large baskets you took up?* ***How is it you do not understand that I did not speak to you concerning bread?*** *— but to beware of the leaven of the Pharisees and Sadducees."* ***Then they understood*** *that He did not tell them to beware of the leaven of bread, but of the doctrine of the Pharisees and Sadducees.*
>
> — Matthew 16:5-12

These men of "little faith" were constantly having their thinking and perspective challenged as Jesus taught them of the principles of the Kingdom of God. In the conversation above, Jesus was questioning their *understanding* of what He had been conveying to them. They were still thinking about a lack of bread even after Jesus had dealt with that lack in a miraculous fashion on multiple occasions! As well taught as they were, they still lacked understanding about much of what they had learned. This lack of understanding was the root of their "little faith," but it was not a disqualifying issue.

We must keep in mind the overall context of Jesus' ministry when we read these accounts, as there can be a tendency to attribute a gruffness to the specific interactions that weren't indicative of Jesus' regular manner. The gospels contain several pointed conversations between Jesus and the religious leaders of the day, and Jesus pulled no punches in being direct in His assessment of them or in the words He chose to say to them. Now think of the group of men that Jesus spent every day and night of three years with. He was loving, kind, and patient with them while also challenging them at times to help them see where they were in their understanding. There are instances in which He was very pointed with them as well, but the predominant way that Jesus dealt with them was through encouragement and love to see them grow into who He saw them capable of becoming.

Satan knows that faith, even small faith, has the potential to do amazing things...

This is important because the enemy will question the *quantity* and *quality* of your faith in order to chip away at it or get you to abandon it, but Jesus taught in Matthew chapter 17 that if you have faith the size of a mustard seed — which size-wise is very small — you can move mountains. Satan knows that faith, even small faith, has the potential to do amazing things, so when he sees that faith is present, he moves directly to negate that faith and to prevent it from growing. The faith that you have when you enter a trial may not seem like much, but your enemy understands it has the potential to carry you through to your victory.

It's because of this that negative thoughts often come to question your faith:

"You don't have enough faith to beat this. You've neglected things and it's too late."

"It's too late to build up your faith now. You'll just have to let things run their course."

"You may love God, but you've not been living in a way where you have any right to expect God to do anything for you."

"You've trusted God for small things, but this situation is far beyond where your faith is."

Do any of these statements sound familiar? They may all have a kernel of truth to them, but so do most lies the enemy uses to attack us. His tactic in these situations is to try and get us to focus on what we are going through and our own ability to influence or overcome it.

- Sitting in a doctor's office with a 5.5cm cancerous tumor growing in me — I was not equipped to overcome that tumor on my own.
- Left by your spouse to care for three children by yourself — your options appear very limited, and you don't know how you can pull it off.
- Looking at the pile of bills on your desk — you know you are in deep debt, and you don't see how you can dig your way out of the predicament you are in.

Satan fights dirty. It's who he is and how he goes about things. The only rules imposed on him are the ones that God has established, and that is why we must be strong in defending ourselves with God's Word. Those are the "rules of the ring" your enemy must follow — but he will do his best to convince you otherwise.

He says your faith is too small. It's stale. It's ineffective. If you don't answer — counterpunch — then he lands a blow that chips away at the faith that you have. Yet you do have an answer: "Even if my faith is the size of a mustard seed, I can move mountains!" An accusation has to be answered in order to nullify it. What you are trusting in isn't you — it's Jesus. Don't allow your enemy to draw you into where he prefers to fight, where you are the source of the answer. Keep your heart and mind fixed on who you are looking to for the answer — Jesus. Know how He feels about you, looks at you, and thinks about you. It will take away your enemy's ability to deceive you.

Now let's go back to Peter. He had been walking on the water when, after a time, his thoughts about the wind whipping around him and the waves rising and falling around and beneath him caused him to become concerned about what might happen to him. The enemy had used Peter's knowledge, his surroundings, and his imagination to chip away at Peter's faith until it began to fracture and no longer had the strength and singleness of thought that it once had. In relation to walking on the water, Peter had begun to become double-minded (*see* James 1).

Peter recognized that his solid position had begun to falter, and he cried out to Jesus to save him. He cried out to the Person who he knew cared for him and was able to take him to a place of safety, even if that place of safety was still out on the wind-driven waves of the Sea of Galilee. Jesus was there immediately to rescue him and then He asked him a question.

I have come to love the question that Jesus asked next, "… Why did you doubt?" (v. 31). Why do I love it? Because through studying this question I have come to realize the care and concern that Jesus had for Peter and, in turn, that He has for me as well. Jesus wasn't asking this question to show Peter how much he lacked. He asked Peter the question to help his faith get bigger and stronger. "Why did you doubt?" was a question that required Peter to have to look on the inside of himself to understand the core issues that caused him to regard the wind and the waves and begin to question the validity of the miracle he was walking in by the word of Jesus. He was walking on the water, wind whipping around him, but at some point, those circumstances began to assert themselves in his thinking, taking him into a place where he began to dread what they could do to him. He was no longer merely aware of their existence — he began to see them as the probable outcome of his steps of faith. Peter had walked to a place where he no longer was assured that his next step would be on top of the water because he had lost sight of the fact that he was already walking in a miracle. Jesus understood this and asked him that question to help open his eyes and heart to the answer. The man of "little faith" had walked on water, and Jesus wanted to strengthen his faith for the walk back.

We have no indication that Jesus carried Peter back to the boat. What we have is Peter and Jesus both walking on water and coming back to the boat and boarding it. Peter didn't sink. He didn't swim back. He wasn't carried back. He *walked* back.

Jesus' question, "Why did you doubt?" challenged Peter to look inside himself to see the root cause of his doubt so that it could be dealt with. Where did that conversation go after the question was asked? Scripture doesn't say, but by studying Jesus' interaction with people, we can see that He often asked questions to help locate where a person's thoughts were. I believe that the question He posed became a teachable moment that He took full advantage of to help Peter adjust his thinking.

I can see Jesus asking the question of wide-eyed Peter and Peter looking into the eyes of his master and seeing His stern yet loving look. His spirit was not beaten down; it was encouraged as Jesus looked to draw the answer out into the open so that it could be dealt with. I see Jesus putting His arm around Peter's shoulders as they turn toward the boat, maybe even giving a gentle squeeze of reassurance that all was well between them. On the walk back as Peter opened his heart to answer Jesus' question, Jesus listened thoughtfully and then answered Peter's thoughts in a manner that settled the matter for Peter, strengthening him and validating him.

Somewhere in that conversation Jesus would have reminded Peter that he had lost sight of *who* his trust was in. "Why did you doubt?" wasn't merely about Peter doubting that he was able to walk on the water any longer; it was about doubting that Jesus — who had called him out on the water — was able to ensure that he would make it to his destination on top of that same water. That's the component of taking your eyes off Jesus. It's not seeing Him physically; it's seeing Him in your heart as the focal point of how you evaluate your situation and His ability to see you through. Your faith in Him can be small, but if it is steadfast, it will not waver. Jesus' faith can carry you through, when your faith is fixed on Him. Hebrews 12:2 tells us that Jesus is the "author and finisher" of our faith. He looks on us with our "little faith," loves us, and teaches us so that He can grow our faith to new heights in Him.

As Peter and Jesus arrived at the boat and threw their legs over the side, they had both completed a journey — one with purpose. Peter had gone from feelings of being overwhelmed and failing to a sense of overcoming and purpose. The wet feet, wet legs, and soaked lower part of his cloak served as reminders of his moments of doubt, but they also served as reminders of how trust and focus could change his outcome. Like rings in a tree, Peter's wet limbs and cloak marked a place of growth in his life.

Sitting there listening to the doctor's report and proposed plan of action, I chose not to look at the waves of treatments, side-effects, and uncertainty that were all about me. They were waves rolling up and down, full of negative effects and possibly leading to a debilitating outcome. I was facing a tumor that was malignant and was drawing resources from the same body it was trying to destroy. I knew what could happen if I allowed cancer to take me under the surface and suffocate me with despair, fear, and no hope.

I also remembered that Jesus loved me and paid the price for my sin, taking a beating on His body so that I could have healing in my own. Where the doctors had expected to see metastasized cancer spread throughout my body, they only found one tumor. Jesus was (and is) my Healer, and instead of seeing that scanned image of the tumor and seeing cancer winning — I saw the healing grace of God already at work in my life. I was walking in a miracle, and just like Peter, I needed to keep reminding myself of that when the noise and waves were trying to get my attention and convince me that I was sinking. Cancer was receding, and if I kept my trust in who Jesus had said He would be to me and what He said He would do for me, I was going to make it to the other side and see His goodness manifest in my life — here in the land of the living. I sucked it up and walked out of that office determined to have God's results in my life. All things are possible to him who believes that they are in Jesus (*see* Mark 9:23).

This perspective set me free from the condemnation the enemy tried to bring to me when I would act on what the Word of God says in faith, only to see circumstance rear its ugly head and attempt to convince me that failure lay ahead. I faced many hard times, rough days, and screaming circumstances. Yet I knew that Jesus was watching me intently and was moving in a most supernatural way at my side, strengthening me as He took me to the other side. Wherever you are in your tunnel, Jesus can take your faith in Him and do miraculous things. Don't allow the enemy to tell you otherwise!

CHAPTER 10
The Key To Resisting the Devil

AS MENTIONED IN previous chapters, when you find yourself faced with a bully, you have the choice to run away or to stand and resist. In the case of the devil, he is not going to become tired of bullying you. Should you try and run away from him, he will pursue you. He is relentless. Once you enter a trying time, he will do all he can to continue to pile new thoughts and circumstances on you to completely dominate you. The devil isn't coming against you simply because it is his job. He's doing it because it gives him the utmost satisfaction.

To stop this cycle, you will have to stand your ground and resist the devil's advances against you. This may sound far away from where you are right now, but I can assure you that it is possible for you to not only stand your ground against the devil, but to also see him *run away from you*. The Bible is very clear about this in James 4:7, where we find a marvelous promise that also provides vital instruction:

> *Therefore submit yourselves to God. Resist the devil, and he will flee from you.*

James provided us with this hope: If we resist the devil, *he* will flee *from us*. There are opportunities each day for us to be tempted and influenced by the devil, and there are many people who succumb to this and feel like they have no hope. It seems like no matter how hard they try, they can't seem to shake the despair they feel. The bad habits they desire to end, the addictions that plague them, and the destructive behavior they can't escape all seem to have no resolution. Over many years in ministry, I've read or heard many heartbreaking stories from people who want to get out of the rut but can't seem to, and in almost every case, they are desperately looking for an answer. Centuries ago, James was talking to people who faced the same dilemma, and he tackled it head on by addressing their issues. James asked his readers where their issues were coming from and then provided answers that required them to do some self-evaluation. To understand how to walk in the victory James spoke of, we must first understand the obstacles in ourselves that must be overcome.

In James 4:1, James asked, "Where do wars and fights come from among you?" They come from the lusts that war in your body. That war going on inside you has two sides, and one appears to be winning. How do we know that? Because James went on to say:

You lust and do not have. You murder and covet and cannot obtain. You fight and war. Yet you do not have because you do not ask.

— James 4:2

Why were they fighting and warring? Because they desired to have something, yet they could not obtain it. Their response to not having what they wanted was to fight and to war until they finally got it. They were in a daily struggle trying to obtain what they wanted even to the point of hurting others and themselves. Does this sound familiar? I can look back at times in my life and honestly admit that I did the same thing. My thinking was off, and I did what I thought would help bring about what I was hoping for. In those times I made a mess, and in some cases, I even hurt others in the process.

TWO HINDRANCES TO ANSWERED PRAYERS

It's in the latter part of verse 2 that James points out the first of two keys we need to understand to effectively deal with our problems:

> *...Yet you don't have what you want because you don't ask God for it.*
>
> — James 4:2 (*NLT*)

I must admit this is one that I still struggle with at times. By nature, I am a planner, a protector, and a fixer. These are good traits to have when they are in balance, but if I don't pay attention, I find myself moving into one of those modes instead of pausing and asking God for guidance and help. Because of this I find myself not having what I need because I am not asking God for His help.

You may fall into this category as well. Some people don't ask God because they don't think He is listening. Others don't ask because they aren't sure that God cares. There are others who don't ask because they are too busy making their own plans. They'll go to God only if they run out of other options. Another issue could be that you don't want to bother God. I find myself in this place at times and have to be reminded that I am not bothering God — He is the one who instructed me to come to Him! James' audience included all of these types of people and many more. Ultimately, for them, you, and me, going without was due to not taking the time to ask God for His help.

Do you need His help today with what you are facing? That help you are asking for could be wisdom. It could be healing or finances. It could be for a relationship to be restored or for a job opportunity. His help could be any number of things, but if you never ask, you can't be upset when you don't get an answer or the result you wanted. God expects you to be an active participant in your life, and He openly encourages you to talk to Him.

The second scenario James covered hits home with all of us at one time or another:

> *And even when you ask, you don't get it because your motives are all wrong —you want only what will give you pleasure.*
> — James 4:3 (*NLT*)

James didn't pull any punches when he addressed this one. You can do your part in asking God for what you want but still not receive because your motives are wrong. In this case, your asking is focused only on what gives you pleasure.

> **God expects you to be an active participant in your life, and He openly encourages you to talk to Him.**

Let's put this in perspective. If *wrong asking* is based on asking with a motive that is self-serving and pleasing to you, then *right asking* must be based on a motive that is beyond yourself and what is pleasing to you. It has someone else in mind besides you.

When I was dealing with cancer, I had to watch myself as it was very easy to internalize what I was going through and make it all about me. I was miserable, tired, and in a great deal of pain. The longer I was on chemotherapy the foggier my mind was becoming. It would have been easy for me to expect everyone to cater to the sick fella and make allowances for my bad behavior. There were days when things were excruciating, and I was tempted to focus only on what I was going through and my feelings. I would purposefully remind myself of my wife, dutifully caring for me and our children while working to keep everything together. She had the tougher job because her future was much further up in the air than mine. I was expecting to live and not die. She was trusting God that I would live as well, but she was the one who had to live with the fallout of anything less than that outcome. Those thoughts have great weight, and it was a battle she fought bravely.

I could have let how my physical issues impacted me personally be the driving force behind my prayers. My actions would have been the barometer for where my prayers were. I would have been praying for relief, but I would not have focused on being like Jesus as I walked through the trial. You are not meant to be self-absorbed during hard times. That may be a bitter pill to swallow, but it is essential for you to realize that the devil would love for you to be self-centered and act as he would have you. Then you would not be in a place to be able to resist him and obtain God's results in your life.

Over my years of ministry, I've seen this countless times. People whose prayers are based on their emotional response to something they are facing tend to see themselves as victims, becoming self-centered and hurting others in the process. It is fine to have emotions and be engaged with them when you pray, but when they become the foundation of your requests instead of what God has said, *you are asking wrongly.*

We ask wrongly when we don't anchor our prayers in God's Words. Although, when we pray Scripture and ask according to His will, we know we are asking correctly. The apostle John addressed this in First John 5:14-15:

Now this is the confidence that we have in Him, that if we ask anything according to His will, He hears us. And if we know that He hears us, whatever we ask, we know that we have the petitions that we have asked of Him.

ASKING GOD FOR WISDOM WILL BRING REAL ANSWERS

God has a plan in every situation as well as a desired outcome, and when we get in line with His plan, we will see His results. We see examples of this throughout the Bible. As soon as God's people came in line with His plan, they began to see their purpose become clear and His results come to fruition in their lives.

In James 1:5, James also addressed what to do when you are unsure of what God's will is in your situation:

> *If any of you lacks wisdom, let him ask of God, who gives to all men liberally and without criticism, and it will be given to him.*

If you are unsure of what to ask for or how to ask according to God's will — ASK HIM! God isn't upset when you ask. He's delighted and will give you His answer to your need. He is for you!

Which takes us back to James' message. James had been instructing his readers, telling them that they weren't asking God for things correctly and that their motives were wrong. They caused harm to themselves and others because they were trying to get what they wanted by any means they could. It was at this point that James showed them how they veered off course:

> *You adulterers! Don't you realize that friendship with the world makes you an enemy of God? I say it again: If you want to be a friend of the world, you make yourself an enemy of God. Do you think the Scriptures have no meaning? They say that God is passionate that the spirit he has placed within us should be faithful to him.*
>
> — James 4:4-5 (*NLT*)

Somewhere along the way they had strayed from God's teachings and His ways of doing things and had begun operating and thinking like the world around them. They were no longer looking at their situations through God's eyes; they were evaluating it through the lens of how the world saw things and reacted. They were scraping and clawing toward their desires, doing all they could to make themselves happy even at the expense of others. When they had abandoned God's ways, their behavior was like a wife who no longer had affection for her husband and who he was, straying from him to find her satisfaction in another. They no longer knew how to pray correctly because they weren't praying with God's ways in mind. They didn't regard any plan or purpose He may have in their situations — their focus was all about themselves.

Have you been guilty of this approach? I'd say we all have at one time or another. Here's the beautiful thing: God knows you have and understands your weaknesses. He hasn't kicked you to the curb and looked for someone else to bless. He loves you and wants to restore you and His relationship with you. That's why James wrote in verse 6:

But He gives more grace. Therefore He says: "God resists the proud, but gives grace to the humble."

GOD GIVES GRACE

When you are ready to turn to God as your authority and compass, He will give you even more grace. Grace isn't some ethereal, nebulous thing. It is God's presence and power moving on your behalf.

For by grace you have been saved through faith, and this is not of yourselves. It is the gift of God, not of works, so that no one should boast.

— Ephesians 2:8-9

God stepped into a situation we couldn't resolve on our own. As these verses say, it was not of ourselves. Instead, it was a gift of God. By grace — in His presence and power — He intervened in your situation and made it possible for you to trust in Him to be who He said He would be and do what He said He would do so that you could be saved.

God gives grace — He steps into your situation to move in a way only He can, and He does it for your benefit.

On the other hand, God resists the proud. Those who choose to go their own way and act according to their own desires do so in pride. Pride says, "I don't want God," or, "I don't need God." Pride looks outside of God for answers and denies God's involvement by ignoring Him and His ways. When a decision is about you — your ability, your sufficiency, your wants — it is pride. God does not shower His blessings on the proud. Instead, He resists them because pride opposes Him. But those who humble themselves, who do not consider themselves to be the final authority on what is right and wrong and who recognize God and their need for Him, He gives grace to. That grace empowers them to live a life pleasing to God. It isn't easy, but His grace is there every step of the way to help.

SUBMITTING YOUR THOUGHTS AND ACTIONS TO GOD IS THE KEY

It is God's grace that empowers you to do what James says to do next, and in doing so, you will defeat the enemy when he assails your life.

> *Therefore submit yourselves to God. Resist the devil, and he will flee from you. Draw near to God, and He will draw near to you. Cleanse your hands, you sinners, and purify your hearts, you*

double-minded. Grieve and mourn and weep. Let your laughter be turned to mourning, and your joy to dejection. Humble yourselves in the sight of the Lord, and He will lift you up.
— James 4:7-10

When most people hear the word "submit," the first image that comes to mind is one of being dominated or lorded over by someone else. Sadly, in the church world the word "submit" has earned a bad reputation by some who have taught others to have loyalty and obedience toward them at any cost. In these environments, submission is often demanded and authority is never to be questioned. Because of this, the word "submit" is often treated as a four-letter word and has plugged many an ear as soon as it has been mentioned from the pulpit.

Here's the reality:

Submission is biblical. It has a blessing that is inherent in it. It is the key to defeating the enemy when he comes to assail you in life. You will not see the light at the end of the tunnel if you don't learn to submit to God. There's no way around it, but don't allow yourself to gloss over what we are about to discuss. It will not make you a slave. It will do the opposite — it will set you free!

Now that we've gotten that out of the way, let's dispel all the negative feelings you may have toward the word and look at it from the perspective of James chapter 4. It is your key to freedom, not a lock on a cage.

In James 4:7, we find a sequence of three things that occur. Let's think of them as a 1-2 combo followed by our enemy's reaction.

1) Submit to God.

I had heard people teach on submitting to God for most of my life, and I was very aware that I needed to be doing it. I knew that there were blessings that flowed from it and that it was pleasing to God. I had even been taught that living a life that pleases God is to live a life submitted to Him, but I had never really heard what that looked like in practical terms.

It was only after I began to learn more about dealing with fear and thoughts that this passage in James took on a whole new dimension for me and provided the practical approach that I had been searching for.

James chapter 4 is about how we think and how we correspondingly act. Right thinking leads to right acting. It is a theme throughout the book of James. With that in mind, let's take a deeper look into what submitting to God on a daily basis actually looks like.

We saw that the people James was referencing had gotten to a place where they thought and acted like everyone else in the world around them. Because of this, they were allowing ungodly thoughts to reside in their minds until they became their new way of thinking. Their thoughts were no longer centered on what God had to say or what His ways were. Instead, they acted in accordance with a worldly mindset, and a myriad of problems ensued. There was no resistance to the inroads the devil had made in their thinking, and he in turn stayed involved, wreaking havoc in and through them.

To submit to God, you need to change your way of thinking. Paul wrote about how to do this in Romans 12:2 (*MEV*):

> *Do not be conformed to this world, but be transformed by the renewing of your mind, that you may prove what is the good and acceptable. Don't copy the behavior and customs of this world, but let God transform you into a new person by changing*

the way you think. Then you will learn to know God's will for you, which is good and pleasing and perfect.

If you are to be able to truly submit to God, then you need to renew or change your mind from one way of thinking to another. You have to gain a different *perspective* in order to see things as God sees them. In Romans 12:1 Paul pleads with his readers to present themselves as a "living sacrifice" to God. A living sacrifice doesn't *die* on the altar, but it does *live* out its life with the commitment that dying on the altar would take. Each day is approached with a dedication to pleasing the one that the sacrifice is being made to. In the life of a believer, the tables have been turned upside down from old sacrificial practices, as God Himself made the sacrifice of Jesus to pay your price. Now He does not require you die for Him, but instead, He requires you to *live* for Him. Living for Him will require you to see things as He does and act as He would have you act.

Paul, like James, explained that you must change your way of thinking from that of how the world around you thinks to the way that God thinks — to His Word and His Ways. You need to know how God would have you think and act and then live according to it. Paul encouraged that as you do so, you will learn how to find and know God's will for your life. While his wording is somewhat different than that of James, the message is still the same. When you learn God's ways and live according to them, you position yourself to know and live in God's will. Part of God's will for your life is to not live in fear and

A living sacrifice doesn't *die* on the altar, but it does *live* out its life with the commitment that dying on the altar would take.

defeat. He wants you to live a life of strength and purpose — one that confronts the enemy and drives him out. You are to not only recognize the devil's attempts to influence your life, you are to resist them steadfastly until he is the one who folds, gives in and runs away.

WHAT SUBMITTING TO GOD DAILY LOOKS LIKE

As I stated earlier, I knew about submitting to God and was quite willing to do it, but I wasn't sure how to approach it on a daily basis. How was I able to know that I was "submitting" to God while I was going through my day. It seemed to me like most of my evaluations of how I was doing were after the fact. I could look back over my day and see where I had done OK and where I knew I had missed it. Then one day I had submission explained to me in a whole new way, and it revolutionized the way I looked at it.

Previously I had looked at submission as bowing to another's power or authority, and there is a concrete truth in that definition. Yet that definition didn't address how I did it from hour to hour, day to day, month to month. As I learned to look at submission not as just an act, but also a process, things became clear.

When you went to school there were homework assignments and tests involved. You would do your best to give the answers that you believed were correct, and then you would hand in, or *submit*, your work for review by the teacher. The teacher knew the correct answers and had been working to teach you what they were, why they were correct, and how to understand them. The teacher's goal was to solidify that working knowledge in you for success in your life.

Once your papers were in the teacher's possession, he or she would review your answers against the "key" of correct answers

The Key To Resisting the Devil

and then grade the work, pointing out the wrong answers that needed correction. The goal was that you would know all the right answers or grow into knowing them as mistakes were pointed out, explained, and corrected.

In the same way, you can *submit* to God minute by minute, hour by hour, day by day, by taking what you think about a situation and bringing it to Him for review. What He says about the issue should be the final authority on what you think and do. To make your life easier, He has even provided you the "key" for the tests up front, giving you His Word, the Bible, as your guide. You honestly are being given an open book test!

When you are in a situation where you are tempted to lie to further your interests, you can submit that response and check it against what the Bible says to know whether that action is acceptable in God's eyes (*see* 2 Timothy 2:15; 3:16-17). When you weigh your response with what God has said and choose to act in accordance with it, that is submitting to God. You do it thought by thought, act by act, and as you continue this submission process, you are also actively renewing your mind to the things of God. Over time your continued submission of your thoughts and actions to the ways of God build a mindset that no longer easily considers every thought that comes your way. Many thoughts will be shot down before they have a chance to even land. Amazingly, as you are deliberately place your focus on God and His way of thinking and doing things, you will find you are already in the next phase of what James wrote in James 4:7.

2) Resist the devil.

In a practical sense, resisting the devil is exactly what it sounds like, but it occurs on a mental and spiritual level. The devil isn't physically grabbing you and manhandling you like a wrestler from the WWE — he is insidiously working behind the scenes to influence you through thoughts, people, and situations to turn you from the things of God and to convince you to follow after your own desires. It is what he has done from the beginning, and what he has enticed countless others to do. If he can find a place to insert himself and hold on, he will do all he can to attack your body, your mind, and all that you are. As it states in John 10:10, he comes to kill, steal, and destroy. He has nothing good in mind for you.

Each time a thought comes that doesn't line up with God's ways and you swat it away, you are actively resisting **the devil**.

- When you are walking on the beach and you choose not to look at all the women in skimpy bikinis — you are resisting the devil.
- When your coworker comes up to you to share the latest gossip and you excuse yourself from conversation — you are resisting the devil.
- When you hold your tongue instead of speaking harshly — you are resisting the devil.
- When you are feeling low and sad and you choose to leave the alcohol alone — you are resisting the devil.

There are a myriad of real-world scenarios you can come up with, and in each of these cases, there is a response that puts God's ways first. This is the basis for resisting the devil.

When you habitually place what God says and thinks as the foremost "key" to evaluate your decisions by, you make it harder and harder for the devil to have his way with you. Eventually, there will come a point when he will make the choice to leave you alone. This is the result of habitually submitting to God and resisting the devil.

3) He (the devil) will flee from you.

Your steadfast resistance to the devil's assaults on your life not only waste his time and thwart his plans — **it does so much more**. When you are living a life submitted to God, you are walking closely with Him. In fact, in verse 8, James describes this relationship and the fruit that comes from it:

> *Draw near to God, and He will draw near to you....*

The devil flees not only because you resist Him, but because of *where* you are and *who* is with you. When you submit to God, you draw near to Him, and when you draw near to Him, you partake of His goodness and His protection. A wonderful picture of this is given to us in Psalm 91 (*NLT*):

> *Those who live in the shelter of the Most High*
> *will find rest in the shadow of the Almighty.*
> *This I declare about the Lord:*
> *He alone is my refuge, my place of safety;*
> *He is my God, and I trust Him.*
> *For He will rescue you from every trap*
> *and protect you from deadly disease.*
> *He will cover you with His feathers.*
> *He will shelter you with His wings.*
> *His faithful promises are your armor and protection.*
> *Do not be afraid of the terrors of the night,*
> *nor the arrow that flies in the day.*
> *Do not dread the disease that stalks in darkness,*
> *nor the disaster that strikes at midday.*
> *Though a thousand fall at your side,*

> **When you are living a life submitted to God, you are walking closely with Him.**

> *though ten thousand are dying around you,*
> *these evils will not touch you.*
> *Just open your eyes,*
> *and see how the wicked are punished.*
> *If you make the Lord your refuge,*
> *if you make the Most High your shelter,*
> *no evil will conquer you;*
> *no plague will come near your home.*
> *For He will order His angels*
> *to protect you wherever you go.*
> *They will hold you up with their hands*
> *so you won't even hurt your foot on a stone.*
> *You will trample upon lions and cobras;*
> *you will crush fierce lions and serpents under your feet!*
> *The Lord says, "I will rescue those who love Me.*
> *I will protect those who trust in My name.*
> *When they call on Me, I will answer;*
> *I will be with them in trouble.*
> *I will rescue and honor them.*
> *I will reward them with a long life*
> *and give them my salvation."*

All of this is a result of a person choosing to live in "the shelter of the Most High" (v. 1). When you align yourself with God, submitting to His ways in what you say and do, you are not the person the devil wants anything to do with. You can rest in God's shadow as He is your "place of safety" (v. 2), and as verse 4 says, "…He will shelter you with His wings. His faithful promises are your armor and protection." God is right next to you, so close He can cover you with His wings. Picture that for a moment, how close a baby bird is to its mother to be able to be covered by her wings. That is how near God draws near to you when you draw near to Him.

In Jesus' encounter with the devil in the wilderness, He proved His submission to God, and after refusing to give Satan any place, we read in Luke 4:13 (*NLT*):

> *Now when the devil had finished tempting Jesus, he left him until the next opportunity came.*

The devil will flee the scene and wait to see if another prime opportunity arises to test your level of submission to God, but you are the deciding factor in whether he will be successful.

HUMILITY TOWARD GOD BRINGS HIS GRACE

James concludes his teaching on this subject with a wonderful promise for the person who humbles themselves before God and submits to Him:

> *Humble yourselves in the sight of the Lord, and He will lift you up.*
> — James 4:10

When you humble yourself before God, He gives you grace. We now see that His grace does something specific — it lifts you up. Even when things look bleak and it seems you are only going lower and lower, you have a promise that you will be lifted up if you humble yourself before God. Each blow the enemy lands against you may stun you. It may stagger you. Yet you don't have to end up lying on the ground, because God Himself will lift you up. No matter how rough things look or hard they seem, God is for you!

The apostle Peter wrote of this as well in First Peter 5:6-7 (*NLT*):

> *So humble yourselves under the mighty power of God, and at the right time He will lift you up in honor. Give all your worries and cares to God, for He cares about you.*

Notice that Peter says, "…And at the right time He will lift you up in honor." When you are going through hard times, each passing second seems like it should be "the right time." I know for myself that I faced many times when I thought it was the "right time" for my cancer tunnel to be over, but I had to discipline myself not to get caught up when things were not going as I wanted. I had to focus on the last part of verse 7 — "…for He cares for you." I rested in the reality that God cares for me more than even I care for myself. His sense of timing is perfect, and if you allow Him to direct your path throughout your situation your "right time" will come, and you will see His results in your life as He lifts you up.

Another way to understand this is to think of an orchestra. Imagine yourself sitting in your prime seat, waiting quietly for the performance to start. You hear the different musicians warming up and practicing softly. Then the conductor walks across the stage to the podium. With a few taps to the podium with his baton, he gains the musicians' attention. He then swings his baton in motion to *set the timing of the piece*, and the music begins. As long as the musicians stay in the timing that the conductor has set, the music sounds beautiful. The conductor's timing is essential for the piece to sound as it should.

Just as important, that timing is essential for each of the different instruments to come in and play their parts at their assigned time in the song. Those musicians play their part "at the right time" (v. 6). The Bible also speaks of "appointed times" and "right times" in the plan of God (*see* Genesis 18:14; Psalm 75:2; Habakkuk 2:3; Galatians 4:4-5). When you are going through your tunnel, the symphony of Heaven is playing, and if you trust in God and humbly wait for His timing, you will play your part right on time, and He will lift you up as you do.

God cares for you and yearns for you to come alongside Him to learn from Him. He isn't looking for mindless automatons to follow His bidding. God doesn't want minions — He longs for you to be in a deep, personal relationship with Him just as He first instituted in the Garden of Eden with Adam and Eve. He knows that as you walk closely with Him and follow His ways, you are safest from the evil designs that the devil has for your life. Submitting to God isn't servitude; it is a self-defense regimen. Think of it as spiritual karate to defeat your enemy. When you practice the art of holding up your thoughts to God's Word and ways and then acting accordingly, you are putting yourself in a position for peace, protection, and success. There is no exploitation. Instead, there is an impartation of God's character into your life that produces blessing.

CHAPTER 11
Seagulls and Bad Thoughts

SEVERAL YEARS AGO, my wife and I went away for a few days at the beach. There's something about the sounds of the surf rolling into the shore that is relaxing, and we both enjoy taking it in and unwinding. One afternoon we were out on the beach, and we noticed the group of ladies next to us had ordered sandwiches and fries for lunch. As they dove into their meals, we became aware that we weren't the only ones that had noticed the meals. The seagulls had noticed as well.

We watched as the gulls slowly floated by, their eyes intent on the ladies' hands moving to and fro with French fries dangling from their fingertips. The ladies were oblivious to what the gulls had in mind. My wife and I looked at each other and thought, "Surely not?" and then one brave gull swooped in on the ladies. He deftly snatched a French fry from one of their waving hands and quickly flew away with his prize, leaving us astonished and the lady who had the fry pilfered from her shocked.

Emboldened by their friend's success, several gulls followed, swooping in and trying to grab fries from the ladies' hands while other gulls gathered at their feet. We watched the frenzy ensue, culminating when a gull landed on one of the ladies' plates! It was like the scene from a Hitchcock movie as the gulls swooped in over and over, stealing fries, bread, and any bit of composure that the ladies had possessed. The ladies were screaming, running in circles, and throwing their food away from them in hopes that the birds would leave them. As food began to litter the sand around their palapa, even more birds showed up. It was as if they had opened a sidewalk café for all the birds flying by.

By now there was quite a commotion going on. Women were screaming, birds were squawking, and sand was flying — and mothers were grabbing their children and fleeing the scene. My wife and I looked at each other trying to decide the best course of action, then we grabbed our towels and ran at the birds, waving the towels up and down to chase the birds away. The birds were reluctant to leave at first, but after a couple of passes they relented and flew away.

The remaining scene was quite a spectacle. We had a group of wide-eyed ladies — hair disheveled, mascara running — who were visibly shaken. Their plates and the remnants of their meals littered the sand. Beach chairs and loungers were flung about the area, leaving everything in their place in total disarray. We watched as the ladies nervously gather up their items and quickly left the area, calling it a day. What had started out for them as a nice day at the beach had turned into a nightmare that left them shaken, disheveled, and still hungry. It was in many ways a microcosm of how life can turn upside down on you at a moment's notice.

My wife and I moved away to a quieter area and sat in disbelief of what we had just witnessed. It had been crazy. Those gulls had swooped in with no fear. Even the screams of the ladies had done little to faze them as they took the food out of their hands and off their plates. Since the screams and flailing hadn't been directed at them, the gulls had disregarded it and went about their heist.

When those gulls were swooping in, stealing food and terrorizing those ladies, all of the noise and movement that the ladies were generating wasn't directed *at* the birds. We recognized that since it wasn't directed **at** the birds, the birds disregarded it and went about their mayhem. Yet when my wife and I went toward those same birds, making noise and waving our towels *at* them, they relented and left. It left an impression on me that moving and making noise without a plan or intention could do little more than expend energy without achieving any desired result. Does this sound familiar?

Sometime later I remembered that afternoon on the beach and realized how well it illustrated what happens to us in life. We start out with a direction or idea in mind, only to have events and circumstances drastically change what we thought we were going to experience. Along with that, those birds reminded me of a key principle that helped me in dealing with and overcoming thoughts that had bullied me over the years.

DEALING WITH MY OWN FEAR

I lost my mother in a car wreck when I was 12. I had gone to school that day knowing that I would be getting my report card, and I was excited about showing it to her later in the evening. It was a day in late January, cold with some snow and ice in the forecast. As the day wound to a close, I boarded my bus for the ride home with my report card with straight A's in hand. Just as I was beginning to find a seat, one of my teachers climbed onboard and called for me to come with them. I obediently got off the bus and followed the teacher back inside the school and down the long hall to the principal's office.

I had no idea why I was being called to the principal's office, but my school experience told me it wasn't good. As the door opened, I saw the principal standing in the room, along with my sister-in-law. They had me sit down and then as gently as possible broke the news to me that my mother had been killed earlier in the afternoon in a car accident. Her car had left the icy roadway on her way to work and ended her life.

I am the youngest of five children, and I was very close to my mother. In the span of a few seconds, she had been removed from my life. I was a 12-year-old kid who would be going through the rest of life without his biggest advocate. She had always encouraged me to think big, and to never let others make me feel that I was less. I can remember her looking in my eyes and telling me that I had it in me to be special. I was a scrawny, small, red-headed kid, but she made me feel like I wasn't defined by my looks. She reminded me that who I was on the inside was most important, and she encouraged me to look to God to find my true worth. With this news I would never look her in the eyes again or hear her voice. I was devastated.

Her voice. I had missed the school bus that morning and my brother-in-law had to take me to school. Mom had been upset with me and expressed her displeasure to me for missing the bus. Those were the last words I heard from her voice. I am so thankful that I remembered all the other things she had said, but for years it hurt to know that her last words to me were disappointment in me. From this I made a commitment to tell my loved ones often what they meant to me. I wanted to ensure they always have those words to hold onto, just as I had. Those words were a lifeline to me in hard times.

After the meeting in the principal's office, I was taken to meet the rest of my family at the local funeral home. I was placed on a pew in the empty viewing room while the rest of my family met with the funeral director and mortician to make arrangements. I sat there on that old pew, in shock and lightly sobbing. I felt lost. I already missed my mom. I felt so alone. Raising my head, I saw an old velvet picture of Jesus kneeling in prayer in the Garden of Gethsemane hanging on the wall in front of me. It was one of those old pictures with a backlight included to imitate a halo over His head. As I sat there staring at the picture, I wondered aloud at what I would do now and whether or not she had suffered. At that moment I felt a peace come over me that washed away my despair, and I heard this echo inside me:

"She is with me now. Everything will be OK."

It was the first time I had ever had God speak to me, and I recognized the peace those words brought to me. Over the following days when the despair and depression of grieving would begin to overwhelm me, I would remember that voice and those words:

"She is with me now. Everything will be OK."

Everything was going to be OK.

During the subsequent funeral visitation, I stood in the receiving line with my family. I was next to my brother who had taken me into the backyard those years earlier to teach me to defend myself. Near the end of the evening, he leaned over to me and remarked at how proud he was of me, that I was standing there so strong and composed. That meant a lot to me, and when I was much older, I realized that I had been able to stand there that evening like that because I had held onto what I had been told:

"She is with me now. Everything will be OK."

I didn't see it then for what it was, but in hanging on to what God had said I was using a prime tactic in my battle with the enemy. It was years later that I came to understand the importance of keeping what God says as the standard by which my thoughts are measured and judged.

MY BREAKTHROUGH DEALING WITH FEAR

For several years after losing my mom, I dealt with fear of losing those close to me. During those years I didn't understand what was transpiring or the source of my apprehension until one day when I heard a siren in the distance, and I realized the first thought that came to me was wondering if my wife had been in a wreck. It was at that moment that things became clear, as if a curtain had been pulled back, and I suddenly understood that fear was dominating my thoughts and taking me to a place in my mind where the outcome was negative and oppressing. My first thoughts were of harm, despair, and tragedy almost every time I heard a siren, saw smoke in the distance, etc. I understood that losing my mom those years ago was the root of my fear, and I needed to learn how to combat that fear. I found the foundation of my answer in Second Corinthians 10:4-5 (*MEV*):

> *The weapons we fight with are not the weapons of the world. On the contrary, they have divine power to demolish strongholds. We demolish arguments and every pretension that sets itself up against the knowledge of God, and we take captive every thought to make it obedient to Christ.*

I realized I had a fear problem when it came to losing a loved one. That fear was constantly bullying me, taking my peace from me like it was my lunch money, and I was an easy score. It was so developed and entrenched that it could indeed be described as a "stronghold." I understood that like any other castle or fortified tower, it was constructed of building blocks, and from Scripture, I knew those blocks could be identified as *thoughts*. Those thoughts connected together to form a cohesive train of thought that built on itself and built on itself until it finally became a stronghold — a fixed way of thinking in my mind.

Armed with this understanding, I thought back to those ladies on the beach — they were carefree and ready for an afternoon of relaxation. Then the first gull swooped in to upset and rob from them, and once it had its desired effect, others joined in the mayhem. Now replace those gulls with thoughts. A thought presents itself, and if it is left unchecked, it can upset and rob you. Once it has had its way, other thoughts related to it swoop in to do the same and soon you are overwhelmed. Your mind and emotions become just as those ladies, shaken and disheveled, making you want to pack it in and leave defeated.

Friend, you don't have to pack it in and leave! You can stand your ground and win, but it will take work and tenacity. God has reserved your place on the beach for you, but it is up to you to defend it and thrive.

Once I recognized that I was dealing with a fear problem, I set out to seek God on how to combat that fear and overcome it. Those are key steps in the journey of freedom from what assails you: to recognize the issue, learn to combat it, and in combating it, overcome it.

To combat fear or anything else that assails you, you must learn this key and make it part of your life:

You must answer a thought with what God says.

Those thoughts that come to your mind to torment and bring fear are in effect the "arguments" or "imaginations" that Paul spoke about in Second Corinthians 10:4-5. When they come to you, they "exalt themselves" against the knowledge of God, but what does that really mean? The thought effectively presents itself as the predominant truth in your mind, even lifting itself above what God has to say. It presents itself in a personal way — intent on challenging you to the core. If you are sick, you might encounter a thought that something evil is going to come and take your health, saying:

> "Well, things don't look good for you. You can't be looking to God to protect you or your health. You are at my mercy, and you're too far gone to be hoping for a change. You can try and pray, but don't expect something wonderful to happen. Besides, you mess your prayers up, and by the time you are done, your words fall to the ground, lifeless. God may love you, but don't get your hopes up. It will all be over eventually."

You must realize that those words are either true or they are a lie, and Scripture tells us that when thoughts are "exalting" themselves or giving themselves the highest place in your mind, even over the knowledge of God, they are a lie. That thought is portraying an outcome of hopelessness to you. It is attempting to settle into your mind so that it can form a foundation for other similar thoughts to come and build a structure of thinking that eventually becomes a stronghold. It effectively becomes just what it is called — a *strong hold* on your way of thinking that you are unable to break free from in your own strength.

> **Each time you answer a thought and cast it down, it is no longer available for the next lying thought to build upon.**

What is this knowledge of God these arguments are saying they are higher than? The knowledge of God is the He is who He says He is and He will do what He says He will do. It is *His Word*. When those arguments are held up against God's Word, they are exposed as what they are — **A LIE**. Don't believe the lies. Instead, use God's Word to expose them and refute them, rendering *them* the lifeless words that have fallen to the ground.

Remember, a stronghold is built one stone at a time, and a thought can be related as equivalent to one of those stones. Each time you answer a thought and cast it down, it is no longer available for the next lying thought to build upon. They fall to the ground like rubble, and if you do not pick them back up, they will remain there, easily avoided and passed over.

ANSWERING BULLYING THOUGHTS

Those arguments that say, "What you are facing is more powerful than God's ability to move in your life," will hang in the air and attack you like those birds did those ladies that day on the beach. They will continue to circle and swoop, only leaving you when you make the decision to stand up to them. Think of each thought as a bully who will continue to harass you until you stand up to it. You must make the decision to answer its accusation with determination.

Take that bullying thought and its statement and hold it up for comparison to what God has said. Evaluate the statement and judge it's validity by God's Word. When you take hold of that thought and evaluate it, you are taking it captive and making it subject to "the obedience of Christ" (2 Corinthians 10:5). This is your first step in preventing a stronghold from being built in your mind or in tearing down a stronghold that already exists.

Our earlier discussion on submitting to God is foundational in how we take captive every thought to make it obedient to Christ and learn to put this into practice in our daily lives. Each thought that comes to us we are to hold up to be evaluated against our knowledge of God and His Word. It is that standard we need to use to filter out thoughts, ideas, and arguments that are contrary to what God has said. Understanding this, you can see why Satan works so diligently to keep people from knowing what God has said and adhering to it. He knows that a mind submitted to God is one that will see through the propositions and lies that he brings — and if he can't fool you, he will be forced to flee.

Your mind is the most prized territory in your life to occupy in your battle. Your enemy knows this and uses a wide array of attacks to gain this high ground and its strategic importance. He understands that if he can keep this place of influence, he can dictate what happens on the battlefield below.

> **Your mind is the most prized territory in your life to occupy in your battle.**

As with any battle, there are strategic moves that are made to take advantage of the circumstances at hand. It is important that the defending army is well prepared and equipped for any action it may find itself in. Most importantly, it must engage the enemy in order to hold its ground and maintain control of its territory. In the same way, your fight will require you to put up a defense or you will lose the ground that belongs to you. Your enemy comes to kill, steal, and destroy, and just as he wasn't satisfied with merely observing Job's life, he isn't interested in a sight-seeing tour of yours. His intentions are the same — to wreak havoc and do all he can to turn you against God while destroying your life.

Like those birds on the beach that day, the attack often begins with a single, probing thought. As the first gull swooped in to grab a French fry, he wasn't confronted in a forceful manner, and he regarded the lack of a response as the opportunity to come in and impose his will. He wanted to take what those ladies had. After his initial success, he saw their lack of response as an invitation to come in for more and brought other gulls along to take as much as they could.

It would have been so much easier to shoo that first gull away. He would have been persistent for a while, but had the ladies waved their towels at him, he would have left — he would have *fled* from the situation if he wasn't having his way in it. It is the same with our thoughts. You can have thoughts and situations that occur in life that can get you worked up, but at some point, you have to compose yourself and focus your energy on what is upsetting you. You must confront that which disturbs you if you want to overcome it. When the enemy inserts himself into your thought life, you must act decisively.

When the thought comes, recognize it for what it is and *take action*. Submit your mind and that thought to God. Then rule on how that thought stands up to what God has said in His Word. Here is an example so you can see this in action:

The thought says: "What you are facing is more powerful than God is in your life."

You can respond: "What I'm facing isn't the most powerful factor in my life. God's Word tells me, *'You are of God, little children, and have overcome them, because* **He** *who* **is** *in you* **is greater** *than* **he** *who* **is** *in the world'* (1 John 4:4). In fact, I'm also told that nothing is impossible when God is involved — *'With man this is impossible, but not with God; all things are possible with God'* (Mark 10:27)."

The thought says: "You are all alone."

You can respond: "I'm not all alone. Jesus said, *'I will never leave you nor forsake you'* (Hebrews 13:5)."

The thought says: "God won't help you or your health. You are at the mercy of this situation, and you can't defend yourself against what is coming. Face it, you're helpless."

You can respond: "The Bible tells me that Jesus has already done something about my health — *'Who Himself bore our sins in His own body on the tree, that we, having died to sins, might live for righteousness—by whose stripes you were healed'* (1 Peter 2:24). I know that I am not defenseless, because God's Word tells me that He is with me and watching over me —

'Because you have made the Lord, who is my refuge, even the Most High, your dwelling place, no evil shall befall you, nor shall any plague come near your dwelling; for He shall give His angels charge over you, to keep you in all your ways' (Psalm 91:9-11)."

The thought says: "God isn't able or willing to help you. You're too far gone to be looking to God for help."

You can respond: "Colossians 1:13-14 says, *'He has delivered me from the power of darkness and conveyed me into the kingdom of the Son of His love, in whom I have redemption through His blood, the forgiveness of sins.'* I am no longer subject to the kingdom of darkness or under its control. In fact, Colossians 2:15 says, *'Having disarmed principalities and powers, Jesus made a public spectacle of them, triumphing over them in it.'* Jesus has disarmed you and made it a public showing that you no longer have that power over me.

"Romans 8:37-39 tells me that *'Yet in all these things we are more than conquerors through Him who loved us. For I am persuaded that neither death nor life, nor angels nor principalities nor powers, nor things present nor things to come, nor height nor depth, nor any other created thing, shall be able to separate us from the love of God which is in Christ Jesus our Lord.'* I am not under your control. I am not a *victim*. I am a *victor* through Jesus and what He has done for me. I resist your attack, and I refuse your lies. Nothing can separate me from God's love for me, not lying thoughts, imperfect wording in my prayers — nothing!"

This is what it looks like to defend yourself and assert your place from God's Word. It's a war waged in your mind and in the spirit, and you have it in you to beat the fears that assail you. Fill yourself with the scriptural responses to the thoughts that you are wrestling with and then use those scriptures to lay hold of and throw down those thoughts when they come to rob you of your peace. It's in this way that you can answer those thoughts and take them "captive" or restrict them so that they no longer run rampant in your mind, stealing your peace and your sleep — just like those gulls stole those ladies' fries. Take your knowledge of God and run at those troubling thoughts just like my wife and I did that day with our towels. Wave your promises at them and stay at it until they relent and go away. As you grow in this, you will learn to chase away those thoughts before they cause mayhem in your life.

In Luke chapter 4 we see this on display, as Jesus deals with Satan's arguments by casting them down with what God's Word had to say on the matter. In the next chapter, we'll peel back yet another layer of this teaching, but as of now, I've given you the basics to help you begin to fight back. God is faithful — He's faithful to me, and He's faithful to you.

CHAPTER 12
Jesus' Pattern for Resisting the Devil

THERE IS NO better example of resisting the devil than the one Jesus gave us in Luke chapter 4. It is important to remember that Jesus was living in this world as a human being, and as such He was facing trials and temptations just like you and I do. This is explained in Hebrews 2:17-18 (*NLT*):

> *Therefore, it was necessary for him to be made in every respect like us, his brothers and sisters, so that he could be our merciful and faithful High Priest before God. Then he could offer a sacrifice that would take away the sins of the people. Since he himself has gone through suffering and testing, he is able to help us when we are being tested.*

Jesus dealt with the same emotions you do. He dealt with the same physical conditions — dirt, heat, cold, hunger, thirst — and life gave Him a steady stream of opportunities to be disappointed, to be prideful, and to be spiteful. He chose to pass on those opportunities because He was totally submitted to God and His ways.

In this chapter, we'll explore the events surrounding Jesus' temptation in the wilderness in Luke 4 and the keys to how He resisted Satan's advances and saw him leave defeated. While the wilderness that Jesus walked through was, in fact, an actual wilderness, it is also symbolic of the hard times we face in life — the *tunnels* each of us face. Just as a physical wilderness has a beginning and an end, so does the tunnel you are facing, and each requires steady movement on your part to reach the other side.

There are three main points to understand in the pattern Jesus followed for resisting and defeating the enemy. To consistently resist the devil, you will need to understand them and put them into practice. They will require you to grow in God, and that growth will make you more stable, strong, and resilient. Those points are:

1) Jesus knew who He was to God.

2) He knew what God's Word said about Him.

3) He knew how God's Word applied to Him.

Point number one may sound simple, but it is the foundation to your ability to walk in the things of God. I know I am Michael, son of Emory and Norma, and grandson of Frank (on both sides), and you have a mother and father and a grandfather as well. I'm a minister who has worked as a project manager, IT manager, and retail store manager. You probably have a job, an education, and a resume of some fashion as well. Those details are important, but they don't move the needle when it comes to dealing with the devil when he inserts himself into your life. You have to know who you are to God.

Jesus was the son of Joseph and Mary and the grandson of Heli. His father was a craftsman, and he had trained as a craftsman as well. None of those things impressed Satan, but Jesus understood His deeper identity that did.

Jesus understood He was special in God's eyes, and that He was in fact God's Son. He was in a relationship with God on a familial level; He wasn't just an acquaintance. Jesus understood that in this familial relationship, God's protection and provision belonged to Him, and He was not subject to Satan's whims. His *position* was that of a Son, and all the benefits that came with it were His. What He was convinced of would be what He would eventually act on, and the same is true for you and me.

In Luke 3:21-22, we find that Jesus had come to the Jordan River where John the Baptist was baptizing people after they repented for their sins and asked God to forgive them. Jesus came to John and asked to be baptized, and afterward John took Jesus into the water and baptized Him.

> *One day when the crowds were being baptized, Jesus himself was baptized. As he was praying, the heavens opened, and the Holy Spirit, in bodily form, descended on him like a dove. And a voice from heaven said, "You are my dearly loved Son, and you bring me great joy."*
>
> — Luke 3:21-22

Jesus was baptized and then the Holy Spirit descended on Him just as a voice from Heaven said, *"You are My dearly loved Son."* After the completion of His baptism, Jesus felt compelled by the Holy Spirit to go out in the wilderness for an intense time of solitude and fasting (*see* Luke 4:1).

The landscape of Judea and its surrounding regions are not what the average camper thinks of when imagining a "wilderness." There were no grand forests and streams. This was a hot, arid place where vegetation could be scarce. It was hot in the daytime and could become very cold at night. Moreover, this wilderness was known for its wild beasts, which included vipers, jackals, scorpions, hyenas, bears, wolves, leopards, and on rarer occasions, even lions. This was not a scenic trip where Jesus was going to become one with nature. There were no sweat lodges for Him to retreat to or to seek a spiritual experience in. He was heading to a lonely, dangerous place. This is where Jesus went after the Holy Spirit descended on Him and a voice from Heaven verified His Sonship.

We read the following in Luke 4:1-2:

Then Jesus, being filled with the Holy Spirit, returned from the Jordan and was led by the Spirit into the wilderness, being tempted for forty days by the devil. And in those days He ate nothing, and afterward, when they had ended, He was hungry.

Jesus went into the wilderness and was tempted by the devil for 40 days. This wasn't a 40-day fast that ended and then Satan appeared to pop three quick questions — this was 40 days of heat, hunger, thirst, and the prospect of being attacked by wild animals. It was a relentless experience.

The tunnel you are in can be relentless. The pressure never seems to let up, as something potentially harmful may seem to be around every turn. It will try your resolve and seek to deprive you of your strength and peace.

Dealing with cancer was a relentless experience. I was fatigued by the tumor and sickened by the treatment the doctors were giving me. Radiation burns caused using the bathroom to feel like I was passing lava and broken glass. At one point it became so bad that after each trip to the toilet I would have to sit in a bathtub of lukewarm water in order to get the irritation to stop. I had sores in my mouth, and the skin on my palms and the bottoms of my feet was peeling off — the side effects, pain, and exhaustion never took a moment off. It was grueling at every level.

What you are going through may seem relentless as well. It probably feels as if there is no break to the cascade of events that fall upon you and try to drag you down. There are many others who have experienced their own version of what you are feeling, but most importantly, Jesus has experienced what you are feeling, and He understands what it is like to be tried physically, emotionally, and spiritually.

Each day Jesus was in the wilderness He was faced with hunger and thirst and various thoughts about what He should do about it surely came to His mind. He was faced with fear and had to decide whether He would give in or refuse to allow it a place in His thoughts. He probably was faced with thoughts of packing it in and heading back to civilization before He had accomplished what He had gone into the wilderness to do. Each day He was bombarded with thoughts on these subjects and many others. This kind of relentless assault on His mind and body was meant to wear Him down, and it is a tactic the enemy uses to weaken you at every level in an attempt to sap your resolve and get you to loosen your grip on hope. The devil knows that if he can get you to lose sight of your hope — your light at the end of the tunnel — he can close in and steal from you the goodness God has in store for you. Satan used the same approach with Jesus when he tempted Him in the Judean wilderness.

At the end of the 40 days in the wilderness, Satan visited Jesus and made three separate attempts to convince Jesus to alter His thinking and His course. He moved in at when he perceived Jesus would be the weakest, most vulnerable, and more easily persuaded.

Satan's first attempt was disguised as temptation to deal with Jesus's hunger —— but it was about much more. We read about it in Luke 4:3:

> *The devil said to Him, "If You are the Son of God, command this stone to become bread."*

Notice Satan poses a question, *"If You are the Son of God"*, and then adds a qualifying action to it. This is often a tactic he uses to draw you into a performance-based reality that questions your status in the eyes of God. If you aren't settled in who you are in God's eyes, Satan will offer up a test with the hope of watching you fail. He will then take that failure and use it to bombard you with feelings of doubt, unworthiness, and hopelessness. He is all about creating *opportunities* for himself to take advantage of and try to deceive you and convince you of anything that is contrary to God's Word.

When Satan made his proposal to Jesus to prove Himself, it didn't work because Jesus hadn't forgotten who He was in God's eyes. He hadn't forgotten the day at His baptism in the Jordan River when the Holy Spirit descended on Him and a voice from Heaven said He was God's "dearly loved Son." Jesus saw through the devil's question and answered in the most fitting way — with more of what God had said:

> *But Jesus answered him, saying, "It is written, 'Man shall not live by bread alone, but by every word of God.'"*
> — Luke 4:4

That verse is such a wonderful answer. Jesus didn't need to prove Himself to anyone, especially not to Satan. The enemy was using the situation to directly challenge Jesus' *identity* in God's eyes. He was looking for the opportunity to cause Jesus to divert from what God had said about Him and to insert a replacement thought. Since God had already testified Jesus' Sonship, Jesus held firm to what God had said about Him and then there was no further need to address it. When Jesus answered, He was essentially saying to Satan:

"I'm sustained not merely by food, but by every word that God says about Me. I know that He has declared to Me that I am His dearly loved Son, and those words are what testify of who I am. My life is found in His words, and I have no need to do anything else to prove to you what I already know to be true."

You don't have to get dragged into proving who you are to God either. When you accept Jesus as your Lord and Savior, you became a child of God. From that moment on, God looks at you as His own, and He is your Father. Make a decision to learn who you are in Christ and know it as truth. You have an *identity* in God that is based on what *He says about you*.

> **You have an *identity* in God that is based on what *He says about you*.**

It is important to take the time to unpack the rest of Jesus' answer, as it illustrates the other two points of Jesus' approach.

1. Jesus knew Scripture and quoted it.

2. Jesus knew specifically what the background of that particular scripture was and how it applied to Him — and Satan.

The scripture Jesus used is from Deuteronomy 8:1-5, and in context it reads:

> *Every commandment which I command you today you must be careful to observe, that you may live and multiply, and go in and possess the land of which the Lord swore to your fathers. And you shall remember that the Lord your God led you all the way these forty years in the wilderness, to humble you and test you, to know what was in your heart, whether you would keep*

His commandments or not. So He humbled you, allowed you to hunger, and fed you with manna which you did not know nor did your fathers know, that He might make you know that man shall not live by bread alone; but man lives by every word that proceeds from the mouth of the Lord. Your garments did not wear out on you, nor did your foot swell these forty years. You should know in your heart that as a man chastens his son, so the Lord your God chastens you.

Let's dissect this passage to bring out some key elements that answer why Jesus was in the wilderness, what God did for Him while He was there, and what symbolic test Jesus passed when He didn't change the stones to bread as Satan requested.

First, why was Jesus in the wilderness? According to verse 2 of this passage, the children of Israel had been led in the desert for a purpose:

And you shall remember that the Lord your God led you all the way these forty years in the wilderness, to humble you and test you, to know what was in your heart, whether you would keep His commandments or not.

The Children of Israel had been a group of complainers since God had delivered them from Egypt. Their trek in the wilderness took much longer than normal because they had refused to enter the land God wanted to give them. When some who had spied out the promised land, most of them reported it would be hard to take. They did not place their trust in God, and instead of stepping into His promise, they shrank from it (*see* Numbers 14). Because of their lack of trust in God to do what He had promised, God sent the children of Israel into the wilderness to weed out the generation of those who would not trust Him and follow His commandments.

Verses 3-5 go on to tell us:

So He humbled you, allowed you to hunger, and fed you with manna which you did not know nor did your fathers know, that He might make you know that man shall not live by bread alone; but man lives by every word that proceeds from the mouth of the Lord. Your garments did not wear out on you, nor did your foot swell these forty years. You should know in your heart that as a man chastens his son, so the Lord your God chastens you.

In Exodus chapter 17, we see another example of the attitude of the people as they traveled. Their reliance on God was for preservation in the moment and was not grounded in trusting Him to care for them when circumstances were trying:

Then all the congregation of the children of Israel set out on their journey from the Wilderness of Sin, according to the commandment of the Lord, and camped in Rephidim; but there was no water for the people to drink. Therefore the people contended with Moses, and said, "Give us water, that we may drink."

So Moses said to them, "Why do you contend with me? Why do you tempt the Lord?"

And the people thirsted there for water, and the people complained against Moses, and said, "Why is it you have brought us up out of Egypt, to kill us and our children and our livestock with thirst?"

— Exodus 17:1-3

The children of Israel were in an arid area with no visible source of water to meet their needs. In verse 2, we are told that they "contended" with Moses. This word can also be translated as "chided" and carries the meaning of being *argumentative*. The

Israelites found themselves in dire circumstances, and they confronted Moses about their unhappiness with the situation. They so quickly forgot the many times God had been faithful in the past and focused only on their current plight.

When things get tough and you don't see a readily available solution, you can lose perspective. This can cause you to become disrespectful, frustrated, and argumentative. If these behaviors are left unchecked, they can become an attitude that flows through all you think and do. This was the current of emotions that was flowing through the children of Israel. They were in great need of water, yet instead of looking to God to meet that need, they allowed their frustration to turn into a disrespectful attitude that shaped their thoughts, words, and actions.

> *So Moses cried out to the Lord, saying, "What shall I do to this people? They are almost ready to stone me."*
> — Exodus 17:4

The people's attitude had taken them to the point of being angry at God and Moses, His representative, and they were ready to kill Moses. To them, the blame had to be laid at someone's feet, and since Moses was tangible and present, they looked at him as the object on which they could to take their frustrations out.

When you are going through a hard time, frustration can cause you to lash out at those around you. These people may be other victims of what you are going through, or they may simply be there to help — and unfortunately close enough to become an unwitting target. It's important that you realize this and not cause harm to others in an attempt to find some form of satisfaction or momentary relief. The old adage "hurting people, hurt people" is true. Don't allow yourself to go down that path.

The children of Israel had come to this place, and Moses was entreating God for an answer. Notice his request was for an answer regarding the people, not just the issue of water. Moses understood

> **They had a *reliance on God*, but not a *relationship* with God.**

that the plight they were in had overcome the Israelites and was shaping their response. He understood they were looking at their situation and allowing it to influence them. They had no reliance on God as someone they could trust even though He had proven Himself over and over. He was someone who had provided for them, but when that provision wasn't obvious anymore, they were consumed with fear. They had a *reliance on God*, but not a *relationship with God*.

> And the Lord said to Moses, "Go on before the people, and take with you some of the elders of Israel. Also take in your hand your rod with which you struck the river, and go. Behold, I will stand before you there on the rock in Horeb; and you shall strike the rock, and water will come out of it, that the people may drink."
>
> And Moses did so in the sight of the elders of Israel. So he called the name of the place Massah and Meribah, because of the contention of the children of Israel, and because they tempted the Lord, saying, "Is the Lord among us or not?"
> — Exodus 17:5-7

Notice in verse 7 the children of Israel had tested the Lord with their complaints about a lack of water because of their attitude, saying, "Is the Lord among us or not?" They were still stuck in a place of requiring God to show His faithfulness to them at every turn in order for them to believe He was with them. To them, their identity was shaped by the next day's provision, not by what God had said about them. He often called them His Chosen People and spoke of how He would go before them, protect them, and provide for them. Yet they did not see their value in being "His Chosen People," an identity that no other people on the face of the earth could claim. They were judging His presence and intentions in their lives by their next drink, meal, or battle won, and because their identity was not based in His words to them, they were easily dissuaded from the provision He had promised them when it did not appear at the first sign of need.

Jesus, however, did not fall into this trap in the wilderness. He knew that bread alone wasn't going to sustain Him for that day, let alone the rest of His life. He knew His position of strength was to hold fast to His identity as God's Son because in that identity, He had a relationship with the One who could meet His every need.

If you have accepted Jesus as God's Son and your Savior, then you are a child of God. That is your identity in God's eyes. You may be reading this while you are sick, poor, broken, or in the midst of some other trial, and the enemy is likely trying to convince you to look at your situation and evaluate who God is to you by how things look and feel. But remember, Jesus was hungry and weak when He was asked to turn stones into bread. You can be like Him and look beyond how you feel at this moment and, instead, recognize that God said you belong to Him. You are His child. You don't have to jump through some hoop the devil has set up to prove that. Your proof is in what God has said about you. You answer the devil's questions and accusations by trusting Him in the middle of what you are going through, not by blaming Him for it. He is the answer to what you are going through; He is not the cause of it.

When you approach your trials in this way, you are:

1) Standing firm in your knowledge of who you are in God's eyes, just as Jesus did.

2) Affirming God's Word, what He has said about you, in your life.

3) Acting upon that Word and applying it to your situation and your life.

You are following Jesus' pattern for resisting the devil, and as you stand firm in your resistance, you will find that the devil will leave you, just as he did in the wilderness with Jesus. Remember, even Jesus was tempted by Satan in three different ways. Don't be surprised when your enemy is persistent. Meet his persistence with a settled heart and a resolute attitude. Remind yourself of who you are to God and how God loves you — and remind your enemy of this as well. Resist the devil, and he will flee.

CHAPTER 13

Trusting God When Things Aren't Going as You Had Expected

HAVE YOU EVER been through a trial in which you have done everything you know to do, yet nothing seems to have changed, or perhaps the situation even took a turn for the worse? This can cause you to begin to question your approach. You might begin to look for the step you may have missed or the missing piece of the equation that will produce the results you desire to see.

In ministry I often see people shaken to the core by what appears to be the lack of results in their life as they make their way through the tunnel they are in. Most of the time, they are completely sincere in their love for God, and they are doing what they know to do to see His results in their situation. Those are some of the hardest questions to respond to because even after one 10- or 20-minute conversation, you don't know the details and nuances involved in their particular situation well enough to answer their questions. What you do know is that God is faithful and His Word is true. This is your plumb line, and everything must be measured against it.

Trusting God is not a formula. There are principles that apply to trusting God and seeing His results in your life, but there is no special recipe to put together in your faith kitchen to get your miracle after 45 minutes in the oven at 375 degrees. Remember, trust in God is based in your relationship with Him. We know that Jesus is the same yesterday, today, and forever (*see* Hebrews 13:8), He does not change (Malachi 3:6), and He does not lie (Numbers 23:19). That is our baseline and the foundation of our trust in Him. We can then use our knowledge of who He is and our trust in Him as the standard that we compare things to and build our lives upon.

Trusting God is not a formula.

In those times when you are searching for what your next step should be or where you might have missed it, remember that you are one half of this relationship. Jesus is on the other side, and His desire is for you to be in harmony with Him so that you can receive all that He paid for on the Cross. He is not stingy with His love and provision. He is looking for those who see Him for Who He is, those who will trust Him to be who He said He would be to them and to do what He said He would do for them, so He can pour out His love and goodness on them. It's not about qualifying somehow or jumping through hoops — it is about coming to a place of trusting God to be good because His Word says so.

Many years ago, when my oldest daughter was 17 months old, she contracted a dangerous staph infection. We had been diligent to follow the doctor's instructions, but the infection continued to progress. We prayed over her and did all that we knew to do, but her condition only worsened. In a matter of days, she was at a place where she had to be admitted to the hospital for further treatment. The area on her neck where the staph infection was presenting had grown large and needed to be treated with IV antibiotics and other medicines.

That same morning my wife went into labor with our second daughter. I found myself admitting my oldest daughter to the hospital for treatment for the staph infection and admitting my wife to the Labor and Delivery ward for the impending birth of our baby girl. Our families lived two states away, so help was limited. Our niece and a neighbor helped care for our son while we dealt with the circus of events that was unfolding.

It was a busy afternoon riding elevators up and down between the two hospital departments. On one floor the doctors and nurses were working to install a stent into my daughter's neck to drain the staph infection. On another floor they were prepping my wife to give birth. I stayed with my oldest daughter until the nurses from the Labor and Delivery ward called and asked for me to come up and check in. Then, late in the afternoon the call came for me to hurry and be with my wife for the birth of our little girl, and I did make it in time to be with my wife as our newest baby girl came into the world. After spending precious time with them, I headed back to the children's ward to be with my oldest daughter.

To make matters even more interesting, the children's ward was under construction, and the only room they had to put us in was a make-shift arrangement made up of a children's bed with chrome rails, a television, and two basic plastic and metal chairs. No other adult-sized furniture was available. I sat in those plastic and metal chairs for the next 3 days. Each night I pushed them together and slept in them as much as I was able to, as they had a tendency to slowly slide apart and, after a couple of hours, dump me on the floor. I would groggily push them back together and try to go back to sleep. Needless to say, I did not get much sleep those nights in the hospital.

The TV in the room made the waiting a bit more bearable. I had it and the occasional trip to see my wife and new baby girl to take my mind off my little girl in that chrome-railed bed, hooked to IV antibiotics while a stent drained nasty yellow-green fluid from her neck. It was agonizing to see her suffering. I would comfort her as I could, but at 17 months old, she could only understand a certain amount of what I was saying. I did my best to make her sterile, scary surroundings a bit less frightening by holding her little hand, stroking her head, and letting her know that Daddy loved her very much.

After the second day in the hospital, I was beginning to have several questions as to why things were the way they were and why I hadn't seen a change. In that make-shift room, I had time to sit and do some soul searching. I was in ministerial school at the time, and in my mind, things were supposed to be working differently than what I was seeing and experiencing. I was doing everything I knew to do, everything I had been taught to do, but I wasn't seeing any results.

As I sat there in my less than comfortable chair watching TV, I began asking myself and then God why things weren't working. Sitting there staring at the TV, I heard God speak to my heart. He reminded me that I had to be honest with myself and then He could be honest with me. When you are not being honest with yourself, you can't truly receive what He has to tell you and instruct you in. He wants to show you where you are in order to instruct you and take you to a higher place in Him. This is what we see in Matthew chapter 14 when Jesus talked to Peter after walking on the water, and there are other examples in Scripture as well.

I had been sitting there for days, admittedly shaken, wondering why my little girl wasn't getting better. I was praying for her healing. I was speaking God's Word over her, and I had laid hands on her in Jesus' Name. I was tithing. I had been reading my Bible. I was doing all the things I knew to do, but I was not seeing any results.

Sitting in that little room, I made the choice to be honest with myself and honest with God. It's important to realize you aren't going to fool God. He isn't deceived by your Oscar-worthy acting performance looking like you have things all together. The Bible tells us that He knows the hearts of men (Acts 1:24), and it is only in that place of honesty that God can shine light onto the areas of your thoughts and actions so that you can make corrections and align yourself with His purposes and His ways. That is where His blessings are found. I found my way to that place of honesty there in that hospital room.

Sitting in that uncomfortable chair, I had to admit that I had learned many things about walking in faith. I had learned about God's will to heal and praying His Word in my situation. I had understood the importance of giving to God from what He had given me. I had applied myself to many things, but I was still striving to see them work together and bring steady results in my life. I had learned a lot *about* faith, but my situation was requiring me to not only know about it, but to actually have it.

It was then that I realized I had been learning the components of faith — all of which are very scriptural and valid — but in learning those components, I had lost sight of the simplicity and importance of having a relationship with God.

> *He has shown you, O man, what is good; And what does the Lord require of you but to do justly, to love mercy, and to walk humbly with your God?*
>
> *— Micah 6:8*

While I was trying to do many things right, I had lost sight of the Person I was in relationship with. This can happen with your family, your friends, or your spouse as well as in your relationship with God. Somewhere along the way I had put more focus on doing what I thought God required of me than on who I was to Him and who He was to me. My trust in Him was beginning to be predicated on my obedience to Him. I had allowed my thinking to get backwards.

Your obedience to Him should be a result of your trust in Him.

As I realized my error, I asked for His forgiveness and for Him to show me where I was in my situation with my little girl and how to resolve it. I can still hear those words spoken to my heart as if it were today:

"What can you say right now over this situation and expect it to happen?"

Several things came to mind. There was a part of me that thought to say something that sounded full of faith. Maybe if I showed I was expecting big results, God would be pleased and make them happen. But I knew that I had to be honest with myself because God already knew my heart. As I took an inner inventory of where I was at with things, I located what I could honestly say I believed and could expect to see come to pass.

I must admit it did not come out sounding as a strong as I thought a man of faith should sound. Where I was at wasn't even that my daughter would be healed and leave the hospital that day. If I had been required to state this in front of a group of classmates, I might have been embarrassed. In all honesty, it would have been embarrassing to admit it to even a group of family or friends. Here I was alone with God, whom I most wanted to impress and please, and this is what I was honestly able to say:

"That she would be fine, we would be out of the hospital in four days, and that the scar on her neck would not be able to be seen."

That was all I had. It wasn't much of a faith statement, but I was being honest. And oh, how God loves honesty and integrity. They are a part of His character.

On the inside, in my spirit, I heard Him reply:

"And that is what you shall have. Your faith works where your heart is settled."

This brought to mind Mark 11:22-24:

So Jesus answered and said to them, "Have faith in God. For assuredly, I say to you, whoever says to this mountain, 'Be removed and be cast into the sea,' and does not doubt in his heart, but believes that those things he says will be done, he will have whatever he says. Therefore I say to you, whatever things you ask when you pray, believe that you receive them, and you will have them.

It all made sense to me then.

- *Whoever says...and does not doubt in his heart, but believes those things he says will be done, he will have whatever he says.*
- *Whatever things you ask when you pray, believe that you receive them, and you will have them.*
- *Your faith works where your heart is settled.*

It was then that I fully realized I had been doing all the right things waiting for my desired result to happen, but I honestly hadn't been settled in the fact that they **would** happen. I was stuck in believing they **should** happen. There is a difference in those two places, and only by studying God's Word and spending time with Him can you bridge the gap between the two.

THERE'S A LIGHT AT THE END OF YOUR TUNNEL

CAUGHT IN NO MAN'S LAND

When you are going through a tunnel situation, the enemy seeks to catch you in the land of "It *should* happen." His age-old tactic is to get a person to question what God has said and to manipulate them once God's Word is questioned. This is the "No Man's Land" in the walk of faith. A working definition of this area would be: *No man's land is land that is unoccupied or is under dispute between parties who find it unoccupied out of fear, uncertainty, or lack of controlling authority.*[7]

No man's land is an area where fear and uncertainty keep you from laying claim to and occupying the ground you are standing on. The enemy knows he has no rightful claim to it, but as long as he can keep you from understanding and asserting your rights, and although he has no controlling authority, he continues to operate as he wills in that territory.

> **Yet you must understand you haven't failed your test until you have given in or given up.**

The uncertainty of knowing and trusting in Who you belong to and what His promises to you are leaves you questioning the current results instead of expecting God's results in your situation.

This is a common response.

That is why the enemy continually attacks in this way — because he knows it works in many cases. He will bully you into not standing for your rights and, instead, impose his will as he is able. Yet you must understand you haven't failed your test until you have given in or given up.

I was in no man's land sitting in that rickety chair in the little hospital room. I had been focusing on what *should* happen instead of settling in my heart what *would* happen. In my time with The Lord, I was honest about my uncertainty, and He helped me clear it up. With the response I gave Him, I wasn't going to make it to the church platform the next Sunday to give my testimony, but it was an honest response.

And I received what I was settled on.

My little girl and I left the hospital after 4 days. She no longer had the staph infection, and that scar from the stent is so unnoticeable that even today as a grown woman she has trouble finding it. God met me where I was and took me to a higher place in my walk with Him. I didn't have it all figured out in my head, but He moved on the trust He found in my heart. In doing so He laid a foundation in my life that has seen me through many trials. What I learned directly impacted how I walked through my battle with cancer, and I came out the other side healed and cancer free.

When people ask why they haven't seen the results they are looking for it is so hard to respond in a way that I feel really gives them the answer they are seeking. The situation they are going through has its own nuances that only God knows, and without sitting and talking with those involved, there is no way to really know where they are at with what they are facing and how they truly see God in the midst of it. That is why it is important that you understand the principles shared in the pages of this book. Each of us has our own set of strengths and weaknesses. We each carry unique experiences that shape how we see and hear things. It is that uniqueness that makes you so special and qualifies you to represent the hope found in Jesus to a world that is crying out for help. It is that uniqueness that the enemy will seek to exploit and destroy because he knows the potential you carry to impact the world for God's glory, but you can send him on the run by recognizing who you are and building on the level of trust that is in your heart.

The enemy will stir thoughts and events in your life to keep you unsettled in your mind and in your heart, trying to get you to ask:

What more can I do?

Should I have done something different?

Have I missed something?

Is it too late for me?

Does God really care about me?

Remember, the enemy's aim is to do as he has done to Eve, Job, and countless others throughout history — to manipulate your circumstances and cause you to question God's goodness, His faithfulness, and His love for you. He knows if he can get you to question these things long enough, you may cast away or abandon your trust in God.

In the early years of the Church, Paul wrote to his readers about the need to hold onto what they had believed regarding Jesus. Pressure was coming for them to change their beliefs and renounce their faith in Jesus as the Messiah, the Son of God. In Hebrews 10, believers were given these words of encouragement to hold on to and stay their course:

> *Let us firmly hold the profession of our faith without wavering, for He who promised is faithful. And let us consider how to spur one another to love and to good works. Let us not forsake the assembling of ourselves together, as is the manner of some, but let us exhort one another, especially as you see the Day approaching.*
>
> — Hebrews 10:23-25

The author of Hebrews was telling these early believers when times are tough and things aren't going well they can make the choice to hold on tightly to the hope — the results — that they had been speaking and trusting God for. There was no need for them to waver in that trust because He (God) who made the promise to them is faithful to keep His promises.

The writer also encouraged these believers to think of how to encourage one another in their lives to love and do good. They were not to withdraw from each other but maintained fellowship to encourage each other and pray for one another. This also indicates there were some who withdrew or forsook other believers as trials came.

We are the Body of Christ, and we can't forsake the importance of gathering with one another. We are meant to be connected. It is understandable for you to withdraw if your condition is such that you are unable to attend church or meet with other believers, but it is quite another situation when you withdraw in general from being with and talking to other believers. We are to be a source of encouragement to each other, and when you withdraw, you lose that critical link and become isolated. When you become isolated, you are effectively wearing a large sign around your neck that says "PREY" and the enemy will gleefully come in for the kill.

Isolating yourself is a critical mistake. I can't stress enough how detrimental this is. Do not allow it.

When I was battling cancer, I was blessed with a good church that we attended each Sunday until I was no longer able to make the trip. Each week we would come and those who knew us would check to see how I was doing. There were those in the church that were regularly praying for me and my family.

I also was blessed to work in a ministry that was a second family to us. They prayed for us, took care of us, and encouraged us as we walked through the dark tunnel of cancer. We were not alone because we chose to allow others to join us in our fight. When days were tough, they were encouraging us to hold fast to our trust in God to heal my body and meet our needs. It came in the form of a call, a text, an email, or someone stopping by our house — we were strengthened by those who rallied around us in faith during that trying time.

I found that as I placed my trust in God and looked to Him to be the solution to my problem, things began to get easier to deal with. I was physically a wreck with radiation burns causing bathroom visits to be excruciatingly painful along with the shingles in my mouth and throat — and with the exception of keeping my hair, I was literally experiencing every side effect listed on the chemotherapy chart for the compound I was given. I even had a few side effects that both the oncologist and the nuclear medicine doctors said they had not seen. Yet even while I was going through those painful times, as I grew in trusting God, I found that things became simpler. I was no longer trying to check off every item I could think of — the rounds of chemo had made it harder for me to concentrate to even do that. Instead, I focused on knowing God was who He said He would be to me and would do what He said He would do for me. My reliance was on who He was to me and who I was to Him.

I woke up each morning and thanked God for another day and His faithfulness to me. I thanked Him that I was going to see His goodness in my body and that the cancer was not staying in my body. I thanked Him for His love, His grace, and His mercy and stated that He was not the cause of my problem — He was my solution. In Him was My hope.

I understood that true hope is found in God and so is true rest — even in the middle of hard times.

TRUSTING GOD IS RESTFUL

When you are going through one of life's tunnels, peace and rest don't seem like they are available to you, but they are.

You may be wondering how in the middle of battling cancer you can have peace. Peace is born of trust. When you are trusting God, taking Him at His Word that He loves you and cares about you, you can...*rest*.

In John chapter 14, Jesus talked to His disciples about His departure from them and the coming of the Holy Spirit, who would be to them exactly whom Jesus had been when He walked among them. Having Jesus near had been a wonderful experience for the disciples, as they knew He loved them and took care of them. Jesus had proven that during His time with them. They had faced deadly storms and even demonic forces, but Jesus had been there to preserve them and bring peace to their lives. They could lay down their heads at night and rest peacefully because they knew He was with them, and in verses 25-27, Jesus addressed their concern of what the coming days would be like for them without Him:

> *These things I have spoken to you while being present with you. But the Helper, the Holy Spirit, whom the Father will send in My name, He will teach you all things, and bring to your remembrance all things that I said to you. Peace I leave with you, My peace I give to you; not as the world gives do I give to you. Let not your heart be troubled, neither let it be afraid.*
> — John 14:25-27

Jesus made a point to tell them that He gave *His peace* to them. His peace is inseparable from His presence. He is the Prince of Peace (*see* Isaiah 9:6), and His peace is established as who He is and all He stands for. Jesus assured them He was not giving His peace as the world does — a possible reference to the common use of the greeting "peace be with you." What He was giving them was not a mere cordial statement, it was representative of *who He was* to them.

> **His peace is inseparable from His presence.**

Understanding this, we can begin to understand why Jesus told the disciples not to let their hearts be troubled or afraid. He gave His peace to them to counter any troubling thoughts that might have led them to fear. He was careful to tell them "let not." Jesus drew attention to the fact that they would have situations arise that would put them in a place where their hearts could become troubled and afraid. By telling them "let not," He was reminding them to fight off the thoughts that would bring an unsettled heart and fear. They each had a choice in how they could respond to the trials ahead of them, and Jesus was telling them, the remedy for their situation was His peace and all that it stood for.

In Paul's letter to the church in Philippi, he explained to his readers a practical approach to receiving the peace of God in their lives:

> *Be anxious for nothing, but in everything by prayer and supplication, with thanksgiving, let your requests be made known to God; and the peace of God, which surpasses all understanding, will guard your hearts and minds through Christ Jesus.*
> — Philippians 4:6-7

When Paul wrote, "Be anxious for nothing…let your requests be made known to God," he was speaking about a relationship of trust in which the person asking could be at peace because he trusted who he was making the request of. That *peace of God* would guard his heart and mind through Christ Jesus. Through Jesus we as believers are righteous in God's eyes. We are no longer enemies of God but are sons and daughters. We are at peace with God, and His peace is with us, guarding our hearts and minds.

It guards our hearts and minds by answering the questions the enemy brings. You might be wondering, *How does it pass all understanding?* Because even in the middle of your trial when nothing seems to be working, you can look to God and know He loves you and is moving in your situation. To the outside world, it can look bleak, like you have no reason to hope, but your trust in God and the peace that comes with it passes, or goes beyond, the understanding the world has when they look at your situation. Your calmness in the middle of your tunnel makes no sense to others, but it is grounded in the trust you have in God to be who He said He would be to you and do what He said He would do for you. It's that trust that brings you to a place of rest.

The essence of resting in God has been stated throughout this book: You can rest by trusting God to be who He said He would be and do what He said He would do.

It was during my battle with cancer that I came to understand resting in God was not some complex spiritual exercise. It was really about finding my way back to looking at God as someone who was more invested in my future than even I was. He expects us to follow after Him and His ways, growing each day to be more like Jesus. We are even encouraged in Scripture to become mature in the faith. God isn't sitting on His throne withholding His blessing from you until you check all the boxes on His miracle eligibility requirements list. What God is looking for is a person who will take Him at His word and expect His integrity to always come through.

When you come to the place where you trust God and take Him at His word, you enter a place where that trust covers the questions that nag you and the thoughts that seek to torment you. You might be aware of your surroundings and your circumstances, but you aren't consumed by them. Instead, you have a confidence in God that gives you strength and peace. Your energy isn't taken up by worry and supposition. You are settled in your heart — you are at a place of *rest*.

CHAPTER 14
Strengthening Your Faith To Receive God's Results

AS WE'VE DISCUSSED throughout this book, God desires to walk through your situation with you and see you to the other side to His results. We've also discussed that your enemy, the devil, will try an array of tactics to steal your hope and attempt to get you to settle for less than what God has for you, to the point of, as John 10:10 tells us, to steal, kill, or destroy.

We've looked at how the devil is persistent in his attacks — merciless and determined to have his way if you let him. We've also looked at practical approaches to resisting him and his attacks — ones that you can take to yourself and put into practice on a daily basis. You have the ability to resist him, and in resisting him, God will give you the grace to carry you through whatever you are facing.

Adding to the lessons you've been taught over the previous pages of this book is an important factor in sustaining your endurance and patience until you see the results of your trusting God to be who He said He would be and do what He said he would do. We read about it in the story of Abraham in Romans 4:20-21:

> *He did not waver at the promise of God through unbelief, but was strengthened in faith, giving glory to God, and being fully convinced that what He had promised He was also able to perform.*

Abraham *strengthened* his faith.

Strengthening your faith as you walk through the tunnel of your situation is vital to you getting to the other side and walking in the light of what God has for you. The circumstances, thoughts, and voices that harass you as you walk through things have to be answered. Not answering them allows them to grow louder, stronger, and more suffocating. Oh, but answering them with faith in God's Word — what He has said — will bring you strength, peace, determination, and even joy in the midst of what you are going through.

When I would hear teaching about strengthening your faith, I came to understand the principle of it but struggled to find a clear definition of what that looked like for me to put it into practice. How could I quantify it in a way that would make sense to me but also to others? I found the basis of my answer in Romans 10:17: *"So then faith comes by hearing, and hearing by the word of God."*

Faith comes by hearing, and hearing by the word of God. **Faith *comes*.** Faith doesn't mysteriously appear. It's not a wispy vapor. It comes on purposefully once we hear and hear the Word of God.

I was reminded of growing up as a kid in a rural area and how on summer nights we would go out into the yards and the fields in our neighborhood and catch lightning bugs. To you they might be called fireflies. We would take a glass mason jar with a lid and poke small holes in the lid to allow air to flow but not large enough to let the lightning bugs escape. We would watch the area intently for the quick twinkle of light against the dark backdrop of the surroundings or sky and then run to the location to try and snatch the lightning bug up when it twinkled again.

It made for an evening of fun as we ran from place to place trying to anticipate where the lightning bug would light up next, hoping to grab it and place it into the glass jar where it would continue to twinkle off and on for our enjoyment. Even to this day I enjoy going out with my grandchildren to catch an occasional lightning bug. My grandkids are amazed by the bugs and how they light up, and my kids are still impressed that other than being slower, I still have the bug-catching skills they benefited from when they were young.

Receiving, building, and strengthening your faith isn't like running from place to place hoping for faith to show itself long enough for you to snatch it into your hand. Too often people take that approach and go from church to church, meeting to meeting, seeking God to show up and do something for them. God certainly moves every day in the lives of people who attend services and meetings, but if you want to develop your own faith, you will have to do the **hearing** for yourself. Faith comes by *hearing*, and that will be your own personal hearing.

The word used for "hearing" in Romans 10:17 carries the connotation of more than the mere sense or act of hearing audibly. It relates to a deeper understanding of what is being heard and acting upon it. In Matthew 13:13 and 16, Jesus spoke of this distinction:

> *Therefore I speak to them in parables, because seeing they do not see, and hearing they do not hear, nor do they understand.... But blessed are your eyes for they see, and your ears for they hear.*

The Hebrew word *shama* is translated as "hear" in our English Bible translations, but it carries a greater meaning than simply hearing audibly. In the Hebrew language, there are far fewer words than in our English language, thus a word carries a deeper, wider meaning. In Hebrew it was understood that to "hear" one heard audibly, comprehended what was heard, embraced it, and then acted in obedience to it. This is the picture of what Jesus was referring to when He spoke of **hearing.** In the verses above, there were people who heard Jesus teach, yet did not **hear** and truly comprehend what He said. This could be true because even though they heard the words that were spoken, they did not take the message to heart or act upon it. They merely processed it audibly and mentally and moved on.

Most parents can relate to this. As they can tell their child to clean their room or do the dishes, the child acknowledges that they heard the request, but with a quick check later, the parents find that the room is still messy or the dishes are still dirty. It could be said that the child was hearing but did not hear. There was no embracing of what was heard, no action, and no obedience. We can speak God's Word and have those sounds register in our ears and our mind, recognizing the words, but until we meditate on those words and have them come alive to us, they are really only sounds and words.

I can think of the many times that God's Word has become alive to me at a deep level, moments in which I had a strong conviction and became settled that it was the truth in my situation. From that place the words I spoke were not only what I would like to see happen, they were what I was expecting to see happen. I wasn't speaking things to convince myself. I was convinced and was consequently speaking what I expected to see happen in my life. Those words became part of my thinking, and I acted upon them.

Understanding this, we can look back at Romans 10:17 and see that faith comes by hearing — hearing audibly, comprehending what was heard, embracing it, and then acting in obedience to it. So if faith comes by hearing, what is it that you are hearing will produce faith in your life? Let's look at the *New Living Translation* of the verse: *"So faith comes from hearing, that is, hearing the Good News about Christ."*

Faith comes from hearing the good news about Jesus. That good news is the Word of God. Faith comes when you hear the good news from God's Word, comprehend it, embrace it, and act in obedience according to it.

- You receive faith to be saved when you hear the good news of God's love for you and believe that Jesus paid the price for your sin to bring you into fellowship with God.

- You build and strengthen your faith as you hear more of God's Word regarding His love for you, of His character, and His ways and act on them.

Understanding that this is so much more than a physical, auditory exercise but instead one that involves your spirit, let's look at four ways you can "hear" so that you can build and strengthen your faith.

READ YOUR BIBLE

God gave his Word for our benefit, and in Psalm 19:7-9 (*NLT*), David spoke of the perfection and benefits of God's Word:

The instructions of the Lord are perfect, reviving the soul.
The decrees of the Lord are trustworthy, making wise the simple.

The commandments of the Lord are right, bringing joy to the heart.
The commands of the Lord are clear, giving insight for living.
Reverence for the Lord is pure, lasting forever.
The laws of the Lord are true; each one is fair.

The apostle Paul also wrote to Timothy and explained this further in Second Timothy 3:16-17 (*NLT*):

All Scripture is inspired by God and is useful to teach us what is true and to make us realize what is wrong in our lives. It corrects us when we are wrong and teaches us to do what is right. God uses it to prepare and equip his people to do every good work.

As you read God's Word you will learn about His character and His Ways. All scripture has importance, and as your read your Bible, you can expect God to speak to you from its pages and reveal Himself to you. The Bible is more than words on a page, it is a Holy Spirit-inspired representation of God, full of wisdom and life, given to us out of an indescribable love by God to benefit us. Read His Word to *hear*, and you will see your life change.

SPEAK GOD'S WORD

We have already seen that faith comes by hearing. That hearing is to take place deep down in your spirit, taking root in you and growing. To build and strengthen your faith, don't only read and listen to God's Word, but personally SPEAK His Word as well. The Bible places an emphasis on saying, as we can see in Romans 10:9-10:

That if you confess with your mouth the Lord Jesus and believe in your heart that God has raised Him from the dead, you will be saved. For with the heart one believes unto righteousness, and with the mouth confession is made unto salvation.

We also find Jesus giving instruction to speak in Mark 11:22-24 as well:

*So Jesus answered and said to them, "Have faith in God. For assuredly, I say to you, **whoever says** to this mountain, 'Be removed and be cast into the sea,' and does not doubt in his heart, but believes that those things **he says** will be done, he will have whatever he says. Therefore I say to you, whatever things you ask when you pray, believe that you receive them, and you will have them."*

Speaking and saying is important because it takes a thought and puts breath into it. You can have many thoughts going through your head, but what you speak takes on a new dimension. Speaking God's Word brings it to a greater place of focus in your life. Many people read out loud to comprehend better. Most people say what they are memorizing over and over to commit it to memory. Along with reading your Bible and meditating on it to gain understanding, speaking those same words out loud can release your faith to see them come to pass. When you speak God's Word, your heart is strengthened, peace comes to your mind, the devil trembles, and angels take notice and move according to His spoken word (*see* Psalm 103:20).

PRAY

Depending on your upbringing and experiences, your idea of what prayer is can land in several different areas. Let's simplify it — not to diminish its importance, but to put it into a true biblical context.

Prayer is communicating with God. It is meant to be a conversation, with each side speaking and listening. Conversation builds relationship, and prayer is a vital part of building your relationship with God. It doesn't have to be flowery or deeply intellectual. It's key ingredient is to be humble and heartfelt, open and honest, as you talk with God. Remember that God so loved you that He gave a part of Himself in Jesus to pay the price for your sin and bring you back into fellowship with God (*see* John 3:16). From this great act of love, it is easy to see that God is extremely invested in having a relationship with you, so don't let the devil try to convince you otherwise.

You can have dedicated times of prayer, and you can have spontaneous times of prayer. The main thing is that you have an active, running dialogue with God about what you are facing, what He has to say about it, and how you can walk with Him to the other side. It is not odd or creepy to talk to your friend or loved one throughout the day, so don't allow yourself to be deceived into thinking that you can't spend time talking to God in the same way. As you walk through trials, you can lean on Him in the moment and in dedicated times as well. A read through the gospels will show Jesus as an in-the-moment Savior to many who talked freely with those who followed him. If you have accepted Him as your Lord and Savior, the Holy Spirit lives inside you to lead you, teach you, and empower you to live the life that God has ordained for you (*see* John 14:15-18,25-26; 16:7,12-14).

Conversation builds relationship, and prayer is a vital part of building your relationship with God.

(If you have not accepted Jesus as your Lord and Savior but would like to, a prayer of salvation can be found in the back of this book.)

The baptism in the Holy Spirit also brings a new dimension to prayer. Praying in the spirit (also referred to as praying in tongues or praying in your prayer language), provides several benefits to your prayer life, as it allows you to pray according to God's will (*see* Romans 8:26-27), it edifies your spirit (1 Corinthians 14:4; Jude 1:20-21), and it prays out unknown things that have to do with your future (1 Corinthians 14:2).

(A more detailed explanation of the baptism in the Holy Spirit and how to receive it can be found in the back of this book.)

As you go through your trial, it is without question a time in which the devil will be talking to you through your thoughts, your circumstances, and through other people. Spending time in prayer puts you in a place of talking to God, hearing from Him, and receiving strength and grace to be patient and make it to the other side of your tunnel where the light shines bright. Make prayer a part of your life and choose God's narrative to be the one that you walk through hard times by.

PRAISE AND WORSHIP

Offering up praise and worship to God is an important part of strengthening your faith, as it magnifies the One who has the answer to what you are going through and reduces your view of the size of your situation in relation to Him. David provides an example of this in Psalm 27:6:

And now my head shall be lifted up above my enemies all around me;
Therefore I will offer sacrifices of joy in His tabernacle;
I will sing, yes, I will sing praises to the Lord.

David looked at his plight of being surrounded by enemies that were intent in doing him harm and turned his focus to God.

Worship Him because He is worthy of it.

Even if things aren't looking great, you should be focused on your hope — the light at the end of your tunnel — and seeing God's results. You thank God for His faithfulness and His goodness, giving Him praise for all He has done and is doing. Praise Him for His love for you and His hand on your life. Thank Him that He will be who He said He would be to you and do what He said He would do for you.

It is also important that you worship God because of who He is, not only because of what He has done for you or is doing for you. Give thanks to Him for His faithfulness and goodness in all He has done for you. Worship Him because He is worthy of it.

We worship God in deep admiration and awe of His righteousness, holiness, and power. David spoke of this in Psalm 29:1-2 (*NLT*):

> *Honor the Lord, you heavenly beings; honor the Lord for His glory and strength.*
> *Honor the Lord for the glory of His name. Worship the Lord in the splendor of His holiness.*

When you do this, you are magnifying Him over your situation and circumstances. Your perspective of what is possible changes. Hope rises in your heart as you see God's greatness in relation to what you are facing, and your problems seem smaller and smaller in comparison to Who He is. Jesus, the One who fed multitudes with a few loaves and fish, the One who healed the sick, cast out evil spirits, and even raised the dead — He is well able to do the miraculous in your life as well. As you glorify Him and His name, fear retreats, hope rises, and your faith is energized.

LEARNING FROM DAVID ABOUT STRENGTHENING YOUR FAITH

The book of Psalms is full of David's thoughts while he was going through many trials and hardships on his journey from being a shepherd boy in the hills near Bethlehem to reigning as king of the nation of Israel. He faced betrayal, hunger, fear, depression, and the many other emotions that come with them. As you read through these Psalms, you will see a pattern that he follows and learn how to take this same approach to strengthen your own faith.

How did David strengthen his faith? He reminded himself constantly of who God was to Him and who he was to God. He reminded himself of God's majesty, His faithfulness, and His goodness — and he spoke of those things with an understanding of how they applied to him. David saw God's character in how God interacted with him. They were not only virtues that David recognized from a distance — they were his experience in his relationship with God as he worshipped Him and trusted in Him.

When you read Scripture and find it is talking about who you are in Jesus and what you have in Him, read it and insert "I" or your name as you do. This is the perspective David wrote the bulk of his Psalms from. They were about him and to him, and once they were written down, he shared them with others. They were David's personal reflections on who God was, what he was going through, and what God had done in His life. Strengthening your faith involves doing the same. As your enemy seeks to drain your faith, wearing it down with each new circumstance, report, or unhelpful thought, you can choose to see God in each of those areas and remind yourself of who He is. As we've discussed earlier, the devil will resist your stand of faith to get you to move away from it. When you strengthen your faith, you are pushing back, and in doing so, you will be the one left standing strong.

When you are walking through a situation that is taking time to resolve, your enemy will make the most of every moment to try and move you off your place of faith. As we discussed, he will do all he can to chip away at your faith, and if you leave him unchallenged, you will find yourself wavering. Your faith might begin to weaken — and that is why you must strengthen it. Often as I've talked with people who at one point started out strong in trusting in God and hoping for a wonderful outcome to their situation, I have heard many times that the constant pressure of what they were facing began to make them weary and Satan swooped in like a seagull to take God's blessing from their hand.

In most of cases, the weariness is allowed to settle in because people neglect to strengthen themselves in God. They neglect reading God's Word and reminding themselves of who He is. They neglect reminding themselves of what Jesus has done for them and who they are in Him. Just as we saw in Peter's example, they lose sight of the hope they were trusting in Jesus for and allow the circumstances around them to begin to convince them of the outcome they will receive.

We might all find ourselves there at one time or another — but you don't have to stay there. Whether you are strong in your faith and apply yourself to stay strong or waver in your faith from the constant barrage of what you are facing, the principles for strengthening your faith work the same. The wonderful news is that Jesus is not standing to the side watching you as a passive observer, grading you on your approach and whether or not you can stick your landing. In the same way He treated Peter in the Sea of Galilee, He is right there next to you to take your hand and bring you back up on top of the water — and then to strengthen you so that you can walk on top of that water back to the boat.

Let's look again at Psalm 27, which is an excellent example of David strengthening his faith and talking to himself as he did. Take special notice of some of the points he makes as he reminds himself of God's goodness, his responsibility to walk according to God's ways, and the blessings that come from obedience in his relationship with God.

> *The LORD IS MY LIGHT AND MY SALVATION;*
> *Whom shall I fear?*
> *The LORD IS THE STRENGTH OF MY LIFE;*
> *Of whom shall I be afraid?*
> *When the wicked came against me*
> *To eat up my flesh,*
> *My enemies and foes,*
> *They stumbled and fell.*
> *Though an army may encamp against me,*
> *My heart shall not fear;*
> *Though war may rise against me,*
> *In this I will be confident.*
>
> — Psalm 27:1-3

We read in First and Second Samuel about several situations David faced. It is believed that David wrote this Psalm concerning the persecution he suffered from King Saul or in response to the betrayal of his son Absalom who rebelled and tried to take David's kingdom. David spoke of the wicked people coming against him and that an army encamped against him. Does this sound like what you've been facing? Are you confronted by constant opposition from others?

In the midst of such trying times, David said, "My heart shall not fear." He was experiencing peace that surpasses understanding — peace in the middle of circumstances that should have caused him fear and worry. Yet he said his heart would not fear because "in **this** I will be confident". What was he confident in? "The Lord is my light and salvation" (v. 1).

David was talking to himself when he said, "Whom shall I fear?" He was speaking words to himself that put his situation into perspective in relation to who God was. You can look at these verses and see that perspective:

> *When the wicked came against me*
> *to eat up my flesh,*
> *Though an army may encamp against me,*
> *Though war may rise against me,*
> *My heart shall not fear;*
> *In this I will be confident.*
> *The Lord is my light and my salvation;*
> *The Lord is the strength of my life;*
> *Whom shall I fear?*
> *Of whom shall I be afraid?*
> *My enemies and foes,*
> *they stumbled and fell.*
>
> — Psalm 27

David was confident. He trusted in the Lord to be the strength of his life. He knew God would be His strength and protect his life. He was the light in the middle of the darkness David was facing, and God will be the same for you in your own situation.

David went on to speak of what was most precious to his heart, and it wasn't receiving relief from his trials. It was his relationship with the One who was the strength of his life.

*One thing I have desired of the LORD,
That will I seek:
That I may dwell in the house of the LORD
All the days of my life,
To behold the beauty of the LORD,
And to inquire in His temple.
For in the time of trouble
He shall hide me in His pavilion;
In the secret place of His tabernacle
He shall hide me;
He shall set me high upon a rock.*

— Psalm 27:4-5

David's desire was to know God, to remain in His presence, to behold His majesty, and to learn from Him. David knew that his relationship with God was the most important thing, as it was the "one thing I have desired of the Lord, that I will seek."

When you make your relationship with God your focus in life, everything else of importance in life will be found there. Jesus shared this wisdom with His disciples when He told them this in Matthew 6:31-34:

Therefore do not worry, saying, 'What shall we eat?' or 'What shall we drink?' or 'What shall we wear?' For after all these things the Gentiles seek. For your heavenly Father knows that you need all these things. **But seek first the kingdom of God and His righteousness, and all these things shall be added to you.** *Therefore do not worry about tomorrow, for tomorrow will worry about its own things. Sufficient for the day is its own trouble.*

Remember what we read in Romans 4:20 about Abraham? It says:

He did not waver at the promise of God through unbelief, **but was strengthened in faith, giving glory to God,** *and being fully convinced that what He had promised He was also able to perform.*

Abraham followed the principle we are talking about as he gave glory to God, praising Him and worshiping Him, and he was strengthened in his faith. He was strengthened to the point that he became fully convinced God was able to perform that which He had promised him.

When looking at Abraham, David, Peter, or other heroes of faith in the Bible, we can see they all struggled with situations that were beyond their own means to overcome, but they placed their trust in God and saw Him meet them where they were to take them to the place of faith He had for them. They didn't start out as faith giants, and you won't either — but they spent time growing in a relationship with God, and over time they benefited from the same principles that have been laid out in this book. For each man, it can be said:

- He came to understand the devil's tactics and how the enemy would attempt to convince him that God was not able to deliver what He had promised.
- He came to understand that God was willing and able to move in his situation and that He would do as He had promised.
- He came to understand what true hope in God was, and he placed his full trust in God.
- He remembered that he was walking in the miraculous each day with God, and while his situation and circumstances did not change, he kept his focus on God's faithfulness.

- He learned to combat the many thoughts that came to his mind to try and convince him that what God had promised to him would not actually happen.

- He kept his heart humble before God and submitted his thoughts and actions to God's words and God's ways. In doing so he resisted the devil's repeated attempts to draw him into sin and unbelief.

- When things did not go as he expected, he did not blame God or turn away from Him. Instead, he continued to worship God and give Him the glory and the honor He deserved. This kept his faith from wavering, and he did, indeed, see God's promise to him fulfilled.

You can come to that same place as well and see God be who He said He would be to you and do what He said He would do for you.

THE SENTRY IN THE SKY

Remember the story in Chapter 9 about the seagulls swooping in on that group of ladies and the chaos and mayhem the gulls caused? A few years after that unforgettable day, my wife and I were at the same beach, and as I sat there admiring the rolling waves and beautiful sky, I eventually noticed something had changed. We had been to this place many times, but something was different this time. As I tried to put my finger on the difference, my wife pointed out that all the seagulls that had normally floated around the beach looking for their chance to swoop in were curiously absent. I spent the better part of the afternoon wondering why they were gone and then the answer appeared — quite literally. I heard a slight swoosh to my left, and when I looked up, I saw a hawk perched on the top of the palapa next to us. He stood on the post, majestic in his watchful pose.

As I looked at the hawk, I knew I had the answer as to where the seagulls had gone. With this hawk in the area, the seagulls had moved on to another place where they felt less threatened. The hawk was a bird of prey and a natural enemy to the sea gulls, and the gulls wanted nothing to do with it. The hawk was now the master of the skies over our beach, the sentry standing watch and chasing the seagulls away from the area. Any bird that came nearby would have to contend with the hawk, and it would be the hawk's decision whether it stayed or not. It was if that hawk had become a gatekeeper to the area over our heads.

I learned from the hawk's trainer that the owners of the resort had contracted with him to have the hawk patrol the skies over the resort's stretch of beach. This wasn't some random hawk that had found a stretch of beachfront property to frequent. This was a deliberate arrangement made to control the nuisances that had been at work for many years.

Thinking back to the gulls that had swarmed those ladies that day and the mayhem that ensued, it was easy to see the contrasting situations, and how they apply to our own thought lives. When we have nothing in place to guard our minds and our thoughts, we can be bombarded by one thought after another. Yet these thoughts don't remain random. Like thoughts attract other like thoughts, and soon they form ideas — just like those seagulls came together, or flocked, and then terrorized those ladies. One gull grabbed a fry, and as soon as the others saw its success, the rest descended to join the action.

As we saw in Chapter 9, all the screaming and crying of the ladies didn't have any effect on the birds. Instead of chasing them away, the chaos fed into their attack, as the hysteria only made the women more disorganized and unable to put up any real defense. That is what happens to you and me when we live oblivious to the fact that we have a real enemy who wants our fries, our plate, our peace, and anything else he can take. If we make no preparations or plan of defense for confronting fear and worry, then we often face a surprise attack and end up screaming and crying in our own right. Hysteria comes in different forms — it can be frantic or it can leave a person frozen, unable to move or make a decision.

The owner of the resort understood where the source of his problem was originating from and made the decision to invest in a solution to bring peace of mind for himself and those he was entertaining. He looked outside of himself for a resource that could help and introduced the hawk to patrol the skies over the beach.

Think of the beach as your mind, and the skies above as the area where thoughts present themselves. When the skies are unpatrolled, thoughts can fly in undeterred, and as soon as a situation presents itself, a thought will swoop in and wreak havoc, presenting itself for consideration. If that thought isn't shooed away, it settles in and makes itself at home. Soon other thoughts of the same nature are attracted to land as well. As they group together, they form a cohesive idea that becomes much more difficult to dislodge.

Enter the hawk. He has been brought in for the purpose of patrolling the skies above the beach. In the case of your thought life, the hawk is the Word of God. As you engage it and allow it to patrol your thought life, it protects your mind and fends off thoughts that are contrary to it.

THERE'S A LIGHT AT THE END OF YOUR TUNNEL

It is so important that you understand that the hawk doesn't appear out of the blue and faithfully patrol on its own. There is time invested by its handler into bonding and training with it. In the same way, attending church and listening to teaching or music on their own will not place that watcher in the skies of your mind to help keep you at peace. You have to spend time studying God's Word and listening to what He has to say so you can bond with it and let it train you how to think. Then you must apply God's Word and ways to your life in order for them to take their place in confronting thoughts that are contrary to them and chasing those thoughts away.

As the prophet Isaiah instructed in Isaiah 26:3:

You will keep him in perfect peace, Whose mind is stayed on You, Because he trusts in You.

This is how it is rendered in the *New Living Translation*:

You will keep in perfect peace all who trust in You, all whose thoughts are fixed on You!

You must take deliberate steps to have this protection, but oh, what a precious thing it is to have in your life! To keep your mind "stayed" on God, to have your thoughts fixed on God, you will have to strengthen your faith — and by keeping your thoughts on Him and His ways, you in turn will be strengthened. This isn't an either/or situation. God designed it as a reciprocal dynamic, where the energy and focus you put on reminding yourself who God is and who you are to Him is in turn built up by you receiving an increasing awareness of who He is and who you are to Him. Abraham strengthened his faith and gave glory to God. The more he looked at God and glorified who He was, the stronger Abraham became convinced that God could and would do what He had promised to him — regardless of how things looked in the natural.

It's my great desire that you can take what you have learned in the pages of this book and make them part of who you are and how you go about life. I know as I've learned them in my own life, they have been instrumental in me making it to the other side of many a tunnel situation, some longer and darker than others. The light at the end of your tunnel is assured when your trust is placed in Jesus. He will meet you where you are to take you to what He has for you, and you will see His salvation.

If you can learn to trust God and take Him at His word, the possibilities for your life are big and bright, as the apostle Paul wrote in First Corinthians 2:9 —

Eye has not seen, nor ear heard,
Nor have entered into the heart of man
The things which God has prepared for those who love Him.

RESOURCES
Take a Trip Down to the Brook

AS WE READ back in Chapter 4, on his way to facing Goliath, David stopped at a brook and selected five smooth stones to take into battle with him. There was practical significance of choosing smooth stones, as he needed smooth projectiles for the most aerodynamic and accurate missiles to fire against his enemy. Rough stones with edges would not exit the sling in a reliable manner and wouldn't be predictable in their flight toward a target. Stones taken from a brook would be well worn by the passing water, making them ideal for this job.

David gathered those stones into a pouch and kept them with him until the time that they were needed. He didn't merely grab the first five stones he found. He took time to study the stones he would be using to ensure that that he had held them, tested them with his fingers, and became acquainted with their feel. In a sense, he came to know those stones.

Stones taken from a brook would be well worn by the passing water, making them ideal for this situation, but why did he need five of them? I could understand having a backup or two in case of a miss – but five?

As I read through First and Second Samuel, I came across information that put everything in perspective. When David went out to meet Goliath, there were actually four other giants in Philistia who were fighting the Israelites during the time of Saul and David. In reading the passage below keep in mind that a Gittite was a person from the Philistine city of Gath:

> *When the Philistines were at war again with Israel, David and his servants with him went down and fought against the Philistines; and David grew faint. Then* **Ishbi-Benob, who was one of the sons of the giant**, *the weight of whose bronze spear was three hundred shekels, who was bearing a new sword, thought he could kill David. But Abishai the son of Zeruiah came to his aid, and struck the Philistine and killed him. Then the men of David swore to him, saying, "You shall go out no more with us to battle, lest you quench the lamp of Israel."*
>
> *Now it happened afterward that there was again a battle with the Philistines at Gob. Then Sibbechai the Hushathite killed* **Saph, who was one of the sons of the giant**. *Again there was war at Gob with the Philistines, where Elhanan the son of Jaare-Oregim the Bethlehemite killed* **the brother of Goliath the Gittite**, *the shaft of whose spear was like a weaver's beam.*
>
> *Yet again there was war at Gath, where there was a man of great stature, who had six fingers on each hand and six toes on each foot, twenty-four in number;* **and he also was born to the giant**. *So when he defied Israel, Jonathan the son of Shimea, David's brother, killed him.*
>
> **These four were born to the giant in Gath, and fell by the hand of David and by the hand of his servants.**
> — 2 Samuel 21:15-22

Five stones for five giants. Whether David was aware of the other giants or simply picked up the five stones without knowing about them, it is an encouraging part of the story that carries practical application for us today. When we face situations that seem daunting or ones that taunt us and attempt to convince us that there is no hope, we can be just like David and trust God to not only deliver us from the threat but to deliver the threat into our hands. We are not only meant to escape, but to be victorious.

When David faced Goliath, God had prepared him well for what laid ahead of him. David gathered those stones into a pouch and kept them with him until they were needed. He didn't merely grab the first five stones he found. He took time to study the stones he would be using to ensure that he had held them, tested them with his fingers, and became acquainted with their feel. In a sense he came to *know* those stones.

We can do the same with God's Word — taking His promises and placing them in our hearts and minds. It's only when they have been taken into our hands, handled, and examined that we gain familiarity with them that will allow us to use them properly. We are then prepared to draw them out as needed and use them effectively.

In the following pages you will find a topical list of scriptures — a brook, if you will — that you can reach into to find and pull out the stones (scriptures) you need to combat any assault on your mind you might face due to the circumstance and situations that attempt to oppress you.

Just as David did, take these stones and become acquainted with them, understanding how they fit in your hand and how to use them to stand against the enemy, and obtain the victory that God has for you.

SMOOTH STONES

Addiction / Freedom:
John 8:31-32
Then Jesus said to those Jews who believed Him, "If you abide in

My word, you are My disciples indeed. And you shall know the truth, and the truth shall make you free."

John 8:36
Therefore if the Son makes you free, you shall be free indeed.

Romans 6:14
For sin shall not have dominion over you, for you are not under law but under grace.

Romans 8:2
For the law of the Spirit of life in Christ Jesus has made me free from the law of sin and death.

Galatians 5:1
Stand fast therefore in the liberty by which Christ has made us free, and do not be entangled again with a yoke of bondage.

Adversity:
Psalm 16:8
I have set the Lord always before me; Because *He is* at my right hand I shall not be moved.

Psalm 34:4
I sought the Lord, and He heard me, and delivered me from all my fears.

Psalm 46:1
God *is* our refuge and strength, a very present help in trouble.

Psalm 107:19-20
Then they cried out to the Lord in their trouble, a*nd* He saved them out of their distresses.
He sent His word and healed them, and delivered *them* from their destructions.

Psalm 145:18-19
The Lord *is* near to all who call upon Him, to all who call upon Him in truth.
He will fulfill the desire of those who fear Him; He also will hear their cry and save them.

Isaiah 40:31
But those who wait on the Lord shall renew *their* strength;
They shall mount up with wings like eagles,
They shall run and not be weary,
They shall walk and not faint.

John 16:33
These things I have spoken to you, that in Me you may have peace. In the world you will have tribulation; but be of good cheer, I have overcome the world.

Romans 8:37
Yet in all these things we are more than conquerors through Him who loved us.

Anxiety / Worry / Stress:
Psalm 29:11
The Lord will give strength to His people; the Lord will bless His people with peace.

Psalm 37:7
Rest in the Lord, and wait patiently for Him; do not fret because of him who prospers in his way, because of the man who brings wicked schemes to pass.

Isaiah 26:3
You will keep *him* in perfect peace, *whose* mind *is* stayed *on You*, because he trusts in You.

THERE'S A LIGHT AT THE END OF YOUR TUNNEL

Matthew 11:28-30
Come to Me, all *you* who labor and are heavy laden, and I will give you rest. Take My yoke upon you and learn from Me, for I am gentle and lowly in heart, and you will find rest for your souls. For My yoke *is* easy and My burden is light.

John 14:27
Peace I leave with you, My peace I give to you; not as the world gives do I give to you. Let not your heart be troubled, neither let it be afraid.

Romans 15:13
Now may the God of hope fill you with all joy and peace in believing, that you may abound in hope by the power of the Holy Spirit.

Philippians 4:6-7
Be anxious for nothing, but in everything by prayer and supplication, with thanksgiving, let your requests be made known to God; and the peace of God, which surpasses all understanding, will guard your hearts and minds through Christ Jesus.

1 Peter 5:6-7
Therefore humble yourselves under the mighty hand of God, that He may exalt you in due time, casting all your care upon Him, for He cares for you.

Authority / Resisting and Overcoming the Devil:
Ephesians 1:19-23
And what is the exceeding greatness of His power toward us who believe, according to the working of His mighty power which He worked in Christ when He raised Him from the dead and seated Him at His right hand in the heavenly places, far above all principality and power and might and dominion, and every name that is named, not only in this age but also in that

which is to come. And He put all things under His feet, and gave Him to be head over all things to the church, which is His body, the fullness of Him who fills all in all.

Ephesians 6:16
Above all, taking the shield of faith with which you will be able to quench all the fiery darts of the wicked one.

Colossians 1:13
He has delivered us from the power of darkness and conveyed us into the kingdom of the Son of His love.

Colossians 2:10
And you are complete in Him, who is the head of all principality and power.

James 4:7
Therefore submit to God. Resist the devil and he will flee from you.

1 John 4:4
You are of God, little children, and have overcome them, because He who is in you is greater than he who is in the world.

Boldness:
Psalm 27:14
Wait on the Lord; be of good courage, and He shall strengthen your heart; wait, I say, on the Lord!

Acts 4:29-31
Now, Lord, look on their threats, and grant to Your servants that with all boldness they may speak Your word, by stretching out Your hand to heal, and that signs and wonders may be done through the name of Your holy Servant Jesus. And when they had prayed, the place where they were assembled together was

shaken; and they were all filled with the Holy Spirit, and they spoke the word of God with boldness.

Romans 8:31
What then shall we say to these things? If God *is* for us, who *can be* against us?

Ephesians 3:11-12
According to the eternal purpose which He accomplished in Christ Jesus our Lord, in whom we have boldness and access with confidence through faith in Him.

Philippians 4:13
I can do all things through Christ who strengthens me.

2 Timothy 1:7
For God has not given us a spirit of fear, but of power and of love and of a sound mind.

Hebrews 4:16
Let us therefore come boldly to the throne of grace, that we may obtain mercy and find grace to help in time of need.

Hebrews 13:5-6
Let your conduct *be* without covetousness; *be* content with such things as you have. For He Himself has said, "I will never leave you nor forsake you." So we may boldly say: "The Lord *is* my helper; I will not fear. What can man do to me?"

Character and Integrity:
Psalm 25:21
Let integrity and uprightness preserve me, For I wait for You.

Psalm 41:12
As for me, You uphold me in my integrity, and set me before Your face forever.

Proverbs 22:1
A *good* name is to be chosen rather than great riches, loving favor rather than silver and gold.

Acts 24:16
This *being* so, I myself always strive to have a conscience without offense toward God and men.

Children and Parenting:
Genesis 18:19
For I have known him, in order that he may command his children and his household after him, that they keep the way of the Lord, to do righteousness and justice, that the Lord may bring to Abraham what He has spoken to him.

Exodus 20:12
Honor your father and your mother, that your days may be long upon the land which the Lord your God is giving you.

Deuteronomy 6:7
You shall teach them diligently to your children, and shall talk of them when you sit in your house, when you walk by the way, when you lie down, and when you rise up.

Psalm 127:3-5
Behold, children *are* a heritage from the Lord, the fruit of the womb *is* a reward. Like arrows in the hand of a warrior, so *are* the children of one's youth. Happy *is* the man who has his quiver full of them; they shall not be ashamed, but shall speak with their enemies in the gate.

Proverbs 22:6
Train up a child in the way he should go, and when he is old he will not depart from it.

Isaiah 54:13
All your children *shall be* taught by the Lord, and great *shall be* the peace of your children.

Ephesians 6:1-4
Children, obey your parents in the Lord, for this is right. "Honor your father and mother," which is the first commandment with promise: "that it may be well with you and you may live long on the earth." And you, fathers, do not provoke your children to wrath, but bring them up in the training and admonition of the Lord.

Colossians 3:20
Children, obey your parents in all things, for this is well pleasing to the Lord.

Confidence:
Psalm 20:7
Some *trust* in chariots, and some in horses; but we will remember the name of the Lord our God.

Proverbs 3:26
For the Lord will be your confidence, and will keep your foot from being caught.

Jeremiah 17:7
Blessed *is* the man who trusts in the Lord, and whose hope is the Lord.

1 Corinthians 15:58
Therefore, my beloved brethren, be steadfast, immovable, always abounding in the work of the Lord, knowing that your labor is not in vain in the Lord.

Philippians 1:6
Being confident of this very thing, that He who has begun a good work in you will complete *it* until the day of Jesus Christ.

Philippians 4:13
I can do all things through Christ who strengthens me.

Hebrews 10:35
Therefore do not cast away your confidence, which has great reward.

1 John 4:17
Love has been perfected among us in this: that we may have boldness in the day of judgment; because as He is, so are we in this world.

1 John 5:14-15
Now this is the confidence that we have in Him, that if we ask anything according to His will, He hears us. And if we know that He hears us, whatever we ask, we know that we have the petitions that we have asked of Him.

Contentment and Satisfaction:
Psalm 37:3
Trust in the Lord, and do good; dwell in the land, and feed on His faithfulness.

Philippians 4:1
Therefore, my beloved and longed-for brethren, my joy and crown, so stand fast in the Lord, beloved.

1 Timothy 6:6
Now godliness with contentment is great gain.

Hebrews 13:5-6
Let your conduct *be* without covetousness; *be* content with such things as you have. For He Himself has said, "I will never leave you nor forsake you." So we may boldly say: "The Lord *is* my helper; I will not fear. What can man do to me?"

Destiny and Purpose:
2 Chronicles 16:9
For the eyes of the Lord run to and fro throughout the whole earth, to show Himself strong on behalf of *those* whose heart *is* loyal to Him.

Psalm 138:8
The Lord will perfect *that which* concerns me; Your mercy, O Lord, *endures* forever;
Do not forsake the works of Your hands.

Proverbs 16:3
Commit your works to the Lord, and your thoughts will be established.

Jeremiah 29:11
For I know the thoughts that I think toward you, says the Lord, thoughts of peace and not of evil, to give you a future and a hope.

Jeremiah 33:3
Call to Me, and I will answer you, and show you great and mighty things, which you do not know.

Habakkuk 2:2-3
Then the Lord answered me and said:
"Write the vision and make *it* plain on tablets,
That he may run who reads it.
For the vision *is* yet for an appointed time;

But at the end it will speak, and it will not lie.
Though it tarries, wait for it; because it will surely come, it will not tarry."

1 Corinthians 2:9-10
But as it is written:
"Eye has not seen, nor ear heard, nor have entered into the heart of man
The things which God has prepared for those who love Him."
But God has revealed *them* to us through His Spirit. For the Spirit searches all things, yes, the deep things of God.

Ephesians 2:10
For we are His workmanship, created in Christ Jesus for good works, which God prepared beforehand that we should walk in them.

Direction:
Psalm 25:4-5
Show me Your ways, O Lord; teach me Your paths. Lead me in Your truth and teach me, for You *are* the God of my salvation; on You I wait all the day.

Psalm 31:3
For You *are* my rock and my fortress; therefore, for Your name's sake, lead me and guide me.

Psalm 32:8-9
I will instruct you and teach you in the way you should go; I will guide you with My eye.
Do not be like the horse *or* like the mule, w*hich* have no understanding,
Which must be harnessed with bit and bridle, else they will not come near you.

THERE'S A LIGHT AT THE END OF YOUR TUNNEL

Psalm 37:5
Commit your way to the Lord, trust also in Him, and He shall bring *it* to pass.

Psalm 37:23
The steps of a *good* man are ordered by the Lord, and He delights in his way.

Psalm 61:1-2
Hear my cry, O God; attend to my prayer.
From the end of the earth I will cry to You, when my heart is overwhelmed;
Lead me to the rock that is higher than I.

Psalm 73:23-24
Nevertheless I *am* continually with You; You hold *me* by my right hand.
You will guide me with Your counsel, and afterward receive me *to* glory.

Proverbs 3:5-6
Trust in the Lord with all your heart, and lean not on your own understanding;
In all your ways acknowledge Him, and He shall direct your paths.

Proverbs 16:3
Commit your works to the Lord, and your thoughts will be established.

John 16:13-15
However, when He, the Spirit of truth, has come, He will guide you into all truth; for He will not speak on His own *authority*, but whatever He hears He will speak; and He will tell you things to come. He will glorify Me, for He will take of what is Mine

and declare *it* to you. All things that the Father has are Mine. Therefore I said that He will take of Mine and declare *it* to you.

Romans 8:14
For as many as are led by the Spirit of God, these are sons of God.

Romans 12:1-2
I beseech you therefore, brethren, by the mercies of God, that you present your bodies a living sacrifice, holy, acceptable to God, *which is* your reasonable service. And do not be conformed to this world, but be transformed by the renewing of your mind, that you may prove what *is* that good and acceptable and perfect will of God.

Colossians 1:9-10
For this reason we also, since the day we heard it, do not cease to pray for you, and to ask that you may be filled with the knowledge of His will in all wisdom and spiritual understanding; that you may walk worthy of the Lord, fully pleasing *Him*, being fruitful in every good work and increasing in the knowledge of God.

James 1:5
If any of you lacks wisdom, let him ask of God, who gives to all liberally and without reproach, and it will be given to him.

Diligence:
Proverbs 10:4
He who has a slack hand becomes poor, but the hand of the diligent makes rich.

Proverbs 21:5
The plans of the diligent *lead* surely to plenty, but *those of* everyone *who is* hasty, surely to poverty.

THERE'S A LIGHT AT THE END OF YOUR TUNNEL

John 8:31-32
Then Jesus said to those Jews who believed Him, "If you abide in My word, you are My disciples indeed. And you shall know the truth, and the truth shall make you free."

1 Corinthians 9:24-27
Do you not know that those who run in a race all run, but one receives the prize? Run in such a way that you may obtain *it*. And everyone who competes *for the prize* is temperate in all things. Now they *do it* to obtain a perishable crown, but we *for* an imperishable *crown.* Therefore I run thus: not with uncertainty. Thus I fight: not as *one who* beats the air. But I discipline my body and bring *it* into subjection, lest, when I have preached to others, I myself should become disqualified.

1 Timothy 4:8
For bodily exercise profits a little, but godliness is profitable for all things, having promise of the life that now is and of that which is to come.

Hebrews 12:1
Therefore we also, since we are surrounded by so great a cloud of witnesses, let us lay aside every weight, and the sin which so easily ensnares *us,* and let us run with endurance the race that is set before us.

Faith and Trusting God:
Matthew 17:20
So Jesus said to them, "Because of your unbelief; for assuredly, I say to you, if you have faith as a mustard seed, you will say to this mountain, 'Move from here to there,' and it will move; and nothing will be impossible for you.

Mark 10:52
Then Jesus said to him, "Go your way; your faith has made you well." And immediately he received his sight and followed Jesus on the road.

Mark 11:23-24
For assuredly, I say to you, whoever says to this mountain, "Be removed and be cast into the sea," and does not doubt in his heart, but believes that those things he says will be done, he will have whatever he says. Therefore I say to you, whatever things you ask when you pray, believe that you receive *them*, and you will have *them*.

John 11:40
Jesus said to her, "Did I not say to you that if you would believe you would see the glory of God?"

Romans 4:19-21
And not being weak in faith, he did not consider his own body, already dead (since he was about a hundred years old), and the deadness of Sarah's womb. He did not waver at the promise of God through unbelief, but was strengthened in faith, giving glory to God, and being fully convinced that what He had promised He was also able to perform.

Romans 10:17
So then faith *comes* by hearing, and hearing by the word of God.

2 Corinthians 5:7
For we walk by faith, not by sight.

Galatians 2:20
I have been crucified with Christ; it is no longer I who live, but Christ lives in me; and the *life* which I now live in the flesh I live by faith in the Son of God, who loved me and gave Himself for me.

Hebrews 11:1
Now faith is the substance of things hoped for, the evidence of things not seen.

Hebrews 11:6
But without faith *it is* impossible to please *Him,* for he who comes to God must believe that He is, and *that* He is a rewarder of those who diligently seek Him.

Hebrews 11:11
By faith Sarah herself also received strength to conceive seed, and she bore a child when she was past the age, because she judged Him faithful who had promised.

James 1:5-6
If any of you lacks wisdom, let him ask of God, who gives to all liberally and without reproach, and it will be given to him. But let him ask in faith, with no doubting, for he who doubts is like a wave of the sea driven and tossed by the wind.

1 Peter 5:8-9
Be sober, be vigilant; because your adversary the devil walks about like a roaring lion, seeking whom he may devour. Resist him, steadfast in the faith, knowing that the same sufferings are experienced by your brotherhood in the world.

1 John 5:4
For whatever is born of God overcomes the world. And this is the victory that has overcome the world — our faith.

Faithfulness:
Proverbs 28:20
A faithful man will abound with blessings, but he who hastens to be rich will not go unpunished.

Matthew 25:21
His lord said to him, "Well *done*, good and faithful servant; you were faithful over a few things, I will make you ruler over many things. Enter into the joy of your lord."

Luke 12:42-44
And the Lord said, "Who then is that faithful and wise steward, whom *his* master will make ruler over his household, to give *them their* portion of food in due season? Blessed *is* that servant whom his master will find so doing when he comes. Truly, I say to you that he will make him ruler over all that he has.

Luke 16:10-12
He who *is* faithful in *what is* least is faithful also in much; and he who is unjust in *what is* least is unjust also in much. Therefore if you have not been faithful in the unrighteous mammon, who will commit to your trust the true *riches?* And if you have not been faithful in what is another man's, who will give you what is your own?

1 Corinthians 4:2
Moreover it is required in stewards that one be found faithful.

1 Corinthians 15:58
Therefore, my beloved brethren, be steadfast, immovable, always abounding in the work of the Lord, knowing that your labor is not in vain in the Lord.

1 Corinthians 16:13
Watch, stand fast in the faith, be brave, be strong.

2 Timothy 1:12
For this reason I also suffer these things; nevertheless I am not ashamed, for I know whom I have believed and am persuaded that He is able to keep what I have committed to Him until that Day.

2 Timothy 4:7
I have fought the good fight, I have finished the race, I have kept the faith.

Favor:
Psalm 5:12
For You, O Lord, will bless the righteous; with favor You will surround him as *with* a shield.

Psalm 89:17
For You *are* the glory of their strength, and in Your favor our horn is exalted.

Proverbs 3:3-4
Let not mercy and truth forsake you; bind them around your neck,
Write them on the tablet of your heart, *and* so find favor and high esteem
In the sight of God and man.

Proverbs 12:2
A good *man* obtains favor from the Lord, but a man of wicked intentions He will condemn.

Dealing With Fear:
Psalm 23:4
Yea, though I walk through the valley of the shadow of death, I will fear no evil;
for You *are* with me; Your rod and Your staff, they comfort me.

Psalm 27:14
Wait on the Lord; be of good courage, and He shall strengthen your heart;
Wait, I say, on the Lord!

Psalm 112:7-8
He will not be afraid of evil tidings; his heart is steadfast, trusting in the Lord.
His heart *is* established; he will not be afraid, until he sees *his desire* upon his enemies.

Proverbs 1:33
But whoever listens to me will dwell safely, and will be secure, without fear of evil.

Isaiah 41:10
Fear not, for I *am* with you; be not dismayed, for I *am* your God. I will strengthen you, yes, I will help you,
I will uphold you with My righteous right hand.'

Isaiah 43:1-2
But now, thus says the Lord, who created you, O Jacob, and He who formed you, O Israel:
"Fear not, for I have redeemed you; I have called *you* by your name; you *are* Mine.
When you pass through the waters, I *will be* with you; and through the rivers, they shall not overflow you. When you walk through the fire, you shall not be burned, nor shall the flame scorch you."

John 14:27
Peace I leave with you, My peace I give to you; not as the world gives do I give to you. Let not your heart be troubled, neither let it be afraid.

Romans 8:15
For you did not receive the spirit of bondage again to fear, but you received the Spirit of adoption by whom we cry out, "Abba, Father."

2 Timothy 1:7
For God has not given us a spirit of fear, but of power and of love and of a sound mind.

Hebrews 2:14-15
Inasmuch then as the children have partaken of flesh and blood, He Himself likewise shared in the same, that through death He might destroy him who had the power of death, that is, the devil, and release those who through fear of death were all their lifetime subject to bondage.

Hebrews 13:5-6
Let your conduct *be* without covetousness; *be* content with such things as you have. For He Himself has said, "I will never leave you nor forsake you." So we may boldly say:

"The Lord *is* my helper;
I will not fear.
What can man do to me?"

1 John 4:18
There is no fear in love; but perfect love casts out fear, because fear involves torment. But he who fears has not been made perfect in love.

Forgiveness:
Isaiah 1:18
"Come now, and let us reason together," says the Lord,
"Though your sins are like scarlet, they shall be as white as snow;
Though they are red like crimson, they shall be as wool."

Matthew 5:44
But I say to you, love your enemies, bless those who curse you, do good to those who hate you, and pray for those who spitefully use you and persecute you.

Matthew 6:14-15
For if you forgive men their trespasses, your heavenly Father will also forgive you. But if you do not forgive men their trespasses, neither will your Father forgive your trespasses.

Mark 11:25
And whenever you stand praying, if you have anything against anyone, forgive him, that your Father in heaven may also forgive you your trespasses.

John 3:16-17
For God so loved the world that He gave His only begotten Son, that whoever believes in Him should not perish but have everlasting life. For God did not send His Son into the world to condemn the world, but that the world through Him might be saved.

Romans 12:18
If it is possible, as much as depends on you, live peaceably with all men.

Ephesians 1:7
In Him we have redemption through His blood, the forgiveness of sins, according to the riches of His grace.

Colossians 1:13-14
He has delivered us from the power of darkness and conveyed *us* into the kingdom of the Son of His love, in whom we have redemption through His blood, the forgiveness of sins.

Colossians 3:13
Bearing with one another, and forgiving one another, if anyone has a complaint against another; even as Christ forgave you, so you also *must do*.

1 John 1:9
If we confess our sins, He is faithful and just to forgive us *our* sins and to cleanse us from all unrighteousness.

God's Love:
Psalm 86:15
But You, O Lord, *are* a God full of compassion, and gracious, longsuffering and abundant in mercy and truth.

John 3:16
For God so loved the world that He gave His only begotten Son, that whoever believes in Him should not perish but have everlasting life.

Romans 5:5
Now hope does not disappoint, because the love of God has been poured out in our hearts by the Holy Spirit who was given to us.

Romans 5:8
But God demonstrates His own love toward us, in that while we were still sinners, Christ died for us.

Ephesians 2:4-5
But God, who is rich in mercy, because of His great love with which He loved us, even when we were dead in trespasses, made us alive together with Christ (by grace you have been saved).

Ephesians 3:14-19
For this reason I bow my knees to the Father of our Lord Jesus Christ, from whom the whole family in heaven and earth is named, that He would grant you, according to the riches of His glory, to be strengthened with might through His Spirit in the inner man, that Christ may dwell in your hearts through faith; that you, being rooted and grounded in love, may be able to comprehend with all the saints what *is* the width and length and

depth and height — to know the love of Christ which passes knowledge; that you may be filled with all the fullness of God.

1 John 4:8-10
He who does not love does not know God, for God is love. In this the love of God was manifested toward us, that God has sent His only begotten Son into the world, that we might live through Him. In this is love, not that we loved God, but that He loved us and sent His Son *to be* the propitiation for our sins.

1 John 4:16-19
And we have known and believed the love that God has for us. God is love, and he who abides in love abides in God, and God in him.

Grace:
Romans 3:24
Being justified freely by His grace through the redemption that is in Christ Jesus.

Romans 4:16
Therefore *it is* of faith that *it might be* according to grace, so that the promise might be sure to all the seed, not only to those who are of the law, but also to those who are of the faith of Abraham, who is the father of us all.

Hebrews 4:16
Let us therefore come boldly to the throne of grace, that we may obtain mercy and find grace to help in time of need.

James 4:6
But He gives more grace. Therefore He says: "God resists the proud, but gives grace to the humble."

THERE'S A LIGHT AT THE END OF YOUR TUNNEL

Grief:

Psalm 34:18
The Lord *is* near to those who have a broken heart, and saves such as have a contrite spirit.

Psalm 147:3
He heals the brokenhearted and binds up their wounds.

Matthew 5:4
Blessed *are* those who mourn, for they shall be comforted.

John 14:1
Let not your heart be troubled; you believe in God, believe also in Me.

2 Corinthians 1:3-4
Blessed *be* the God and Father of our Lord Jesus Christ, the Father of mercies and God of all comfort, who comforts us in all our tribulation, that we may be able to comfort those who are in any trouble, with the comfort with which we ourselves are comforted by God.

2 Corinthians 5:8
We are confident, yes, well pleased rather to be absent from the body and to be present with the Lord.

1 Thessalonians 4:14-18
For if we believe that Jesus died and rose again, even so God will bring with Him those who sleep in Jesus.

For this we say to you by the word of the Lord, that we who are alive *and* remain until the coming of the Lord will by no means precede those who are asleep. For the Lord Himself will descend from heaven with a shout, with the voice of an archangel, and with the trumpet of God. And the dead in Christ will rise first. Then we who are alive *and* remain shall be caught up together with them in the clouds to meet the Lord in the air. And thus we shall always be with the Lord. Therefore comfort one another with these words.

Revelation 21:4
And God will wipe away every tear from their eyes; there shall be no more death, nor sorrow, nor crying. There shall be no more pain, for the former things have passed away.

Guilt:
Psalm 103:12
The Lord *is* near to those who have a broken heart, and saves such as have a contrite spirit.

Isaiah 43:25
I, *even* I, *am* He who blots out your transgressions for My own sake; and I will not remember your sins.

Romans 5:1
Therefore, having been justified by faith, we have peace with God through our Lord Jesus Christ.

Romans 8:1
There is therefore now no condemnation to those who are in Christ Jesus, who do not walk according to the flesh, but according to the Spirit.

2 Corinthians 5:17
Therefore, if anyone *is* in Christ, *he is* a new creation; old things have passed away; behold, all things have become new.

Hebrews 8:12
For I will be merciful to their unrighteousness, and their sins and their lawless deeds I will remember no more.

1 John 1:9
If we confess our sins, He is faithful and just to forgive us *our* sins and to cleanse us from all unrighteousness.

Healing:
Psalm 30:2
O Lord my God, I cried out to You, and You healed me.

Psalm 103:1-5
Bless the Lord, O my soul; and all that is within me, *bless* His holy name!
Bless the Lord, O my soul, and forget not all His benefits:
Who forgives all your iniquities, Who heals all your diseases,
Who redeems your life from destruction, Who crowns you with lovingkindness and tender mercies,
Who satisfies your mouth with good *things, so that* your youth is renewed like the eagle's.

Psalm 107:20
He sent His word and healed them, and delivered *them* from their destructions.

Proverbs 3:7-8
Do not be wise in your own eyes; fear the Lord and depart from evil.
It will be health to your flesh, and strength to your bones.

Proverbs 4:20-23
My son, give attention to my words; incline your ear to my sayings.
Do not let them depart from your eyes; keep them in the midst of your heart;
For they *are* life to those who find them, and health to all their flesh.

Keep your heart with all diligence, for out of it *spring* the issues of life.

Isaiah 53:4-5
Surely He has borne our grief and carried our sorrows;
Yet we esteemed Him stricken, smitten by God, and afflicted.
But He *was* wounded for our transgressions, *He was* bruised for our iniquities;
The chastisement for our peace *was* upon Him, and by His stripes we are healed.

Romans 8:11
But if the Spirit of Him who raised Jesus from the dead dwells in you, He who raised Christ from the dead will also give life to your mortal bodies through His Spirit who dwells in you.

Galatians 3:13
Christ has redeemed us from the curse of the law, having become a curse for us (for it is written, "Cursed *is* everyone who hangs on a tree").

1 Peter 2:24
Who Himself bore our sins in His own body on the tree, that we, having died to sins, might live for righteousness — by whose stripes you were healed.

3 John 2
Beloved, I pray that you may prosper in all things and be in health, just as your soul prospers.

Hope:
Psalm 3:3
But You, O Lord, *are* a shield for me, my glory and the One who lifts up my head.

THERE'S A LIGHT AT THE END OF YOUR TUNNEL

Jeremiah 29:11
For I know the thoughts that I think toward you, says the Lord, thoughts of peace and not of evil, to give you a future and a hope.

Romans 5:5
Now hope does not disappoint, because the love of God has been poured out in our hearts by the Holy Spirit who was given to us.

1 Corinthians 15:56-58
The sting of death *is* sin, and the strength of sin *is* the law. But thanks *be* to God, who gives us the victory through our Lord Jesus Christ. Therefore, my beloved brethren, be steadfast, immovable, always abounding in the work of the Lord, knowing that your labor is not in vain in the Lord.

Hebrews 6:19
This *hope* we have as an anchor of the soul, both sure and steadfast, and which enters the *Presence* behind the veil.

Long Life:
Exodus 20:12
Honor your father and your mother, that your days may be long upon the land which the Lord your God is giving you.

Psalm 91:15-16
He shall call upon Me, and I will answer him; I *will be* with him in trouble;
I will deliver him and honor him. With long life I will satisfy him, and show him My salvation.

Psalm 118:17
I shall not die, but live, and declare the works of the Lord.

Proverbs 3:1-2
My son, do not forget my law, but let your heart keep my commands;
For length of days and long life and peace they will add to you.

Proverbs 10:27
The fear of the Lord prolongs days, but the years of the wicked will be shortened.

Ephesians 6:2-3
"Honor your father and mother," which is the first commandment with promise: "that it may be well with you and you may live long on the earth."

1 Peter 3:10
He who would love life and see good days, let him refrain his tongue from evil,
and his lips from speaking deceit.

Overcoming Depression:
Psalm 16:11
You will show me the path of life; in Your presence *is* fullness of joy;
At Your right hand *are* pleasures forevermore.

Psalm 103:1-5
Bless the Lord, O my soul;
And all that is within me, *bless* His holy name!
Bless the Lord, O my soul,
And forget not all His benefits:
Who forgives all your iniquities,
Who heals all your diseases,
Who redeems your life from destruction,
Who crowns you with lovingkindness and tender mercies,
Who satisfies your mouth with good *things*,
So that your youth is renewed like the eagle's.

John 15:11
"These things I have spoken to you, that My joy may remain in you, and *that* your joy may be full."

THERE'S A LIGHT AT THE END OF YOUR TUNNEL

John 16:22-24
Therefore you now have sorrow; but I will see you again and your heart will rejoice, and your joy no one will take from you. And in that day you will ask Me nothing. Most assuredly, I say to you, whatever you ask the Father in My name He will give you. Until now you have asked nothing in My name. Ask, and you will receive, that your joy may be full.

Romans 15:13
Now may the God of hope fill you with all joy and peace in believing, that you may abound in hope by the power of the Holy Spirit.

Philippians 4:4
Rejoice in the Lord always. Again I will say, rejoice!

James 1:2-4
My brethren, count it all joy when you fall into various trials, knowing that the testing of your faith produces patience. But let patience have *its* perfect work, that you may be perfect and complete, lacking nothing.

1 Peter 1:8-9
Whom having not seen you love. Though now you do not see *Him*, yet believing, you rejoice with joy inexpressible and full of glory, receiving the end of your faith — the salvation of *your* souls.

1 John 1:4
And these things we write to you that your joy may be full.

Prayers Heard:
2 Chronicles 7:14
If My people who are called by My name will humble themselves, and pray and seek My face, and turn from their wicked

ways, then I will hear from heaven, and will forgive their sin and heal their land.

Psalm 145:18
The Lord *is* near to all who call upon Him, to all who call upon Him in truth.

Mark 11:24
Therefore I say to you, whatever things you ask when you pray, believe that you receive *them,* and you will have *them.*

John 16:23-24
And in that day you will ask Me nothing. Most assuredly, I say to you, whatever you ask the Father in My name He will give you. Until now you have asked nothing in My name. Ask, and you will receive, that your joy may be full.

Romans 8:26-27
Likewise the Spirit also helps in our weaknesses. For we do not know what we should pray for as we ought, but the Spirit Himself makes intercession for us with groanings which cannot be uttered. Now He who searches the hearts knows what the mind of the Spirit *is,* because He makes intercession for the saints according to *the will of* God.

Ephesians 3:14-20
For this reason I bow my knees to the Father of our Lord Jesus Christ, from whom the whole family in heaven and earth is named, that He would grant you, according to the riches of His glory, to be strengthened with might through His Spirit in the inner man, that Christ may dwell in your hearts through faith; that you, being rooted and grounded in love, may be able to comprehend with all the saints what *is* the width and length and depth and height — to know the love of Christ which passes knowledge; that you may be filled with all the fullness of God.

Now to Him who is able to do exceedingly abundantly above all that we ask or think, according to the power that works in us.

Philippians 4:6-7
Be anxious for nothing, but in everything by prayer and supplication, with thanksgiving, let your requests be made known to God; and the peace of God, which surpasses all understanding, will guard your hearts and minds through Christ Jesus.

James 5:13-16
Is anyone among you suffering? Let him pray. Is anyone cheerful? Let him sing psalms. Is anyone among you sick? Let him call for the elders of the church, and let them pray over him, anointing him with oil in the name of the Lord. And the prayer of faith will save the sick, and the Lord will raise him up. And if he has committed sins, he will be forgiven. Confess *your* trespasses to one another, and pray for one another, that you may be healed. The effective, fervent prayer of a righteous man avails much.

1 John 5:14-15
Now this is the confidence that we have in Him, that if we ask anything according to His will, He hears us. And if we know that He hears us, whatever we ask, we know that we have the petitions that we have asked of Him.

Prospering in Life:
Joshua 1:8
This Book of the Law shall not depart from your mouth, but you shall meditate in it day and night, that you may observe to do according to all that is written in it. For then you will make your way prosperous, and then you will have good success.

Psalm 1:3
He shall be like a tree planted by the rivers of water, that brings

forth its fruit in its season, whose leaf also shall not wither; and whatever he does shall prosper.

Psalm 35:27
Let them shout for joy and be glad, who favor my righteous cause; and let them say continually, "Let the Lord be magnified, Who has pleasure in the prosperity of His servant."

Proverbs 10:22
The blessing of the Lord makes *one* rich, and He adds no sorrow with it.

Proverbs 11:24-25
There is *one* who scatters, yet increases more; and there is *one* who withholds more than is right, but it *leads* to poverty. The generous soul will be made rich, and he who waters will also be watered himself.

Proverbs 22:9
He who has a generous eye will be blessed, for he gives of his bread to the poor.

Matthew 6:33
But seek first the kingdom of God and His righteousness, and all these things shall be added to you.

Luke 6:38
Give, and it will be given to you: good measure, pressed down, shaken together, and running over will be put into your bosom. For with the same measure that you use, it will be measured back to you.

2 Corinthians 8:9
For you know the grace of our Lord Jesus Christ, that though He was rich, yet for your sakes He became poor, that you through His poverty might become rich.

THERE'S A LIGHT AT THE END OF YOUR TUNNEL

2 Corinthians 9:6-10
But this *I say:* He who sows sparingly will also reap sparingly, and he who sows bountifully will also reap bountifully. *So let* each one *give* as he purposes in his heart, not grudgingly or of necessity; for God loves a cheerful giver. And God *is* able to make all grace abound toward you, that you, always having all sufficiency in all *things,* may have an abundance for every good work. As it is written:
"He has dispersed abroad,
He has given to the poor;
His righteousness endures forever."

Now may He who supplies seed to the sower, and bread for food, supply and multiply the seed you have *sown* and increase the fruits of your righteousness,

Philippians 4:19
And my God shall supply all your need according to His riches in glory by Christ Jesus.

3 John 2
Beloved, I pray that you may prosper in all things and be in health, just as your soul prospers.

Protection:
Psalm 3:3
But You, O Lord, *are* a shield for me, My glory and the One who lifts up my head.

Psalm 4:8
I will both lie down in peace, and sleep; for You alone, O Lord, make me dwell in safety.

Psalm 27:1
The Lord *is* my light and my salvation; whom shall I fear?
The Lord *is* the strength of my life; of whom shall I be afraid?

Psalm 32:7
You *are* my hiding place; You shall preserve me from trouble;
You shall surround me with songs of deliverance. *Selah.*

Psalm 46:1
God *is* our refuge and strength, a very present help in trouble.

Psalm 91:1-10
He who dwells in the secret place of the Most High
Shall abide under the shadow of the Almighty.
I will say of the Lord, "*He is* my refuge and my fortress;
My God, in Him I will trust."

Surely He shall deliver you from the snare of the fowler
And from the perilous pestilence.
He shall cover you with His feathers,
And under His wings you shall take refuge;
His truth *shall be your* shield and buckler.
You shall not be afraid of the terror by night,
Nor of the arrow *that* flies by day,
Nor of the pestilence *that* walks in darkness,
Nor of the destruction *that* lays waste at noonday.

A thousand may fall at your side,
And ten thousand at your right hand;
But it shall not come near you.
Only with your eyes shall you look,
And see the reward of the wicked.

Because you have made the Lord, *who is* my refuge,
Even the Most High, your dwelling place,

No evil shall befall you,
Nor shall any plague come near your dwelling;

Psalm 118:6
The Lord *is* on my side; I will not fear. What can man do to me?

Psalm 121:7-8
The Lord shall preserve you from all evil; He shall preserve your soul.
The Lord shall preserve your going out and your coming in from this time forth, and even forevermore.

Proverbs 18:10
The name of the Lord *is* a strong tower; the righteous run to it and are safe.

Isaiah 54:17
"No weapon formed against you shall prosper, and every tongue *which* rises against you in judgment You shall condemn. This *is* the heritage of the servants of the Lord, and their righteousness *is* from Me," says the Lord.

2 Timothy 4:18
And the Lord will deliver me from every evil work and preserve *me* for His heavenly kingdom. To Him *be* glory forever and ever. Amen!

Strength:
Psalm 27:1
The Lord *is* my light and my salvation; whom shall I fear?
The Lord *is* the strength of my life; of whom shall I be afraid?

Psalm 28:7-8
The Lord *is* my strength and my shield; my heart trusted in Him, and I am helped;
Therefore my heart greatly rejoices, and with my song I will

praise Him. The Lord *is* their strength, and He *is* the saving refuge of His anointed.

Isaiah 40:31
But those who wait on the Lord shall renew *their* strength;
They shall mount up with wings like eagles, they shall run and not be weary,
they shall walk and not faint.

Ephesians 6:10
Finally, my brethren, be strong in the Lord and in the power of His might.

Philippians 4:13
I can do all things through Christ who strengthens me.

Victory:
2 Chronicles 20:15b
And he said, "Listen, all you of Judah and you inhabitants of Jerusalem, and you, King Jehoshaphat! Thus says the Lord to you: 'Do not be afraid nor dismayed because of this great multitude, for the battle *is* not yours, but God's.'"

Psalm 34:19
Many *are* the afflictions of the righteous, but the Lord delivers him out of them all.

Psalm 118:6
The Lord *is* on my side; I will not fear. What can man do to me?

Romans 8:31
What then shall we say to these things? If God *is* for us, who *can be* against us?

THERE'S A LIGHT AT THE END OF YOUR TUNNEL

Romans 8:37
Yet in all these things we are more than conquerors through Him who loved us.

1 Corinthians 15:57
But thanks *be* to God, who gives us the victory through our Lord Jesus Christ.

2 Corinthians 2:14a
Now thanks *be* to God who always leads us in triumph in Christ, and through us diffuses the fragrance of His knowledge in every place.

2 Peter1:2-4
Grace and peace be multiplied to you in the knowledge of God and of Jesus our Lord, as His divine power has given to us all things that *pertain* to life and godliness, through the knowledge of Him who called us by glory and virtue, by which have been given to us exceedingly great and precious promises, that through these you may be partakers of the divine nature, having escaped the corruption *that is* in the world through lust.

1 John 4:4
You are of God, little children, and have overcome them, because He who is in you is greater than he who is in the world.

1 John 5:4
For whatever is born of God overcomes the world. And this is the victory that has overcome the world — our faith.

Waiting:
1 Kings 8:56
Blessed *be* the Lord, who has given rest to His people Israel, according to all that He promised. There has not failed one word of all His good promise, which He promised through His servant Moses.

Psalm 62:5
My soul, wait silently for God alone, for my expectation *is* from Him.

Isaiah 55:11
So shall My word be that goes forth from My mouth; it shall not return to Me void,
But it shall accomplish what I please, and it shall prosper *in the thing* for which I sent it.

Jeremiah 1:12
Then the Lord said to me, "You have seen well, for I am ready to perform My word."

Mark 4:26-29
And He said, "The kingdom of God is as if a man should scatter seed on the ground, and should sleep by night and rise by day, and the seed should sprout and grow, he himself does not know how. For the earth yields crops by itself: first the blade, then the head, after that the full grain in the head. But when the grain ripens, immediately he puts in the sickle, because the harvest has come."

Luke 21:19
By your patience possess your souls.

2 Corinthians 5:7
For we walk by faith, not by sight.

Galatians 6:9
And let us not grow weary while doing good, for in due season we shall reap if we do not lose heart.

Ephesians 3:20
Now to Him who is able to do exceedingly abundantly above all that we ask or think, according to the power that works in us,

THERE'S A LIGHT AT THE END OF YOUR TUNNEL

Hebrews 4:14
Seeing then that we have a great High Priest who has passed through the heavens, Jesus the Son of God, let us hold fast *our* confession.

Hebrews 6:12
That you do not become sluggish, but imitate those who through faith and patience inherit the promises.

Hebrews 10:23
Let us hold fast the confession of *our* hope without wavering, for He who promised *is* faithful.

Hebrews 10:35-36
Therefore do not cast away your confidence, which has great reward. For you have need of endurance, so that after you have done the will of God, you may receive the promise:

Hebrews 12:1-3
Therefore we also, since we are surrounded by so great a cloud of witnesses, let us lay aside every weight, and the sin which so easily ensnares *us,* and let us run with endurance the race that is set before us, looking unto Jesus, the author and finisher of *our* faith, who for the joy that was set before Him endured the cross, despising the shame, and has sat down at the right hand of the throne of God.

For consider Him who endured such hostility from sinners against Himself, lest you become weary and discouraged in your souls.

James 1:2-4
My brethren, count it all joy when you fall into various trials, knowing that the testing of your faith produces patience. But let patience have *its* perfect work, that you may be perfect and complete, lacking nothing.

Who You Are in Christ:
John 1:12
But as many as received Him, to them He gave the right to become children of God, to those who believe in His name:

Romans 3:24
Being justified freely by His grace through the redemption that is in Christ Jesus.

Romans 5:1
Therefore, having been justified by faith, we have peace with God through our Lord Jesus Christ.

Romans 5:9
Much more then, having now been justified by His blood, we shall be saved from wrath through Him.

Romans 8:1
There is therefore now no condemnation to those who are in Christ Jesus, who do not walk according to the flesh, but according to the Spirit.

Romans 8:15
For you did not receive the spirit of bondage again to fear, but you received the Spirit of adoption by whom we cry out, "Abba, Father."

Romans 8:37
Yet in all these things we are more than conquerors through Him who loved us.

1 Corinthians 1:30
But of Him you are in Christ Jesus, who became for us wisdom from God — and righteousness and sanctification and redemption.

THERE'S A LIGHT AT THE END OF YOUR TUNNEL

2 Corinthians 2:14
Now thanks *be* to God who always leads us in triumph in Christ, and through us diffuses the fragrance of His knowledge in every place.

2 Corinthians 5:17
Therefore, if anyone *is* in Christ, *he is* a new creation; old things have passed away; behold, all things have become new.

2 Corinthians 5:21
For He made Him who knew no sin *to be* sin for us, that we might become the righteousness of God in Him.

Galatians 3:28
There is neither Jew nor Greek, there is neither slave nor free, there is neither male nor female; for you are all one in Christ Jesus.

Ephesians 1:3
Blessed *be* the God and Father of our Lord Jesus Christ, who has blessed us with every spiritual blessing in the heavenly *places* in Christ.

Ephesians 2:4-7
But God, who is rich in mercy, because of His great love with which He loved us, even when we were dead in trespasses, made us alive together with Christ (by grace you have been saved), and raised *us* up together, and made *us* sit together in the heavenly *places* in Christ Jesus, that in the ages to come He might show the exceeding riches of His grace in *His* kindness toward us in Christ Jesus.

Colossians 2:9-10
For in Him dwells all the fullness of the Godhead bodily; and you are complete in Him, who is the head of all principality and power.

1 Peter 2:5
You also, as living stones, are being built up a spiritual house, a holy priesthood, to offer up spiritual sacrifices acceptable to God through Jesus Christ.

1 Peter 2:9
But you *are* a chosen generation, a royal priesthood, a holy nation, His own special people, that you may proclaim the praises of Him who called you out of darkness into His marvelous light.

1 John 3:2
Beloved, now we are children of God; and it has not yet been revealed what we shall be, but we know that when He is revealed, we shall be like Him, for we shall see Him as He is.

Revelation 1:5-6
And from Jesus Christ, the faithful witness, the firstborn from the dead, and the ruler over the kings of the earth. To Him who loved us and washed us from our sins in His own blood, and has made us kings and priests to His God and Father, to Him *be* glory and dominion forever and ever. Amen.

Wisdom:
Proverbs 1:7
The fear of the Lord *is* the beginning of knowledge, b*ut* fools despise wisdom and instruction.

Proverbs 3:13-18
Happy *is* the man *who* finds wisdom, and the man *who* gains understanding;
For her proceeds *are* better than the profits of silver, and her gain than fine gold.
She *is* more precious than rubies, and all the things you may desire cannot compare with her. Length of days *is* in her right

hand, in her left hand riches and honor.
Her ways *are* ways of pleasantness, and all her paths *are* peace.
She *is* a tree of life to those who take hold of her, and happy *are all* who retain her.

Proverbs 4:7-8
Wisdom *is* the principal thing; t*herefore* get wisdom.
And in all your getting, get understanding.
Exalt her, and she will promote you; she will bring you honor, when you embrace her.

Proverbs 19:8
He who gets wisdom loves his own soul; he who keeps understanding will find good.

Proverbs 24:3-7
Through wisdom a house is built, and by understanding it is established;
By knowledge the rooms are filled with all precious and pleasant riches.

A wise man *is* strong, yes, a man of knowledge increases strength; For by wise counsel you will wage your own war, and in a multitude of counselors *there is* safety.

Wisdom *is* too lofty for a fool; he does not open his mouth in the gate.

Matthew 7:24
Therefore whoever hears these sayings of Mine, and does them, I will liken him to a wise man who built his house on the rock.

James 1:5
If any of you lacks wisdom, let him ask of God, who gives to all liberally and without reproach, and it will be given to him.

James 3:17
But the wisdom that is from above is first pure, then peaceable, gentle, willing to yield, full of mercy and good fruits, without partiality and without hypocrisy.

THE PRAYER OF SALVATION

A holy, righteous, and just God looked upon the sin of man and saw that it was only worthy of the judgement reserved for such sin — Hell and the Lake of Fire — eternal separation from God. Because of this sin we were all headed to that destination. Yet it was the *love* of God toward you and me that prompted Him to do His part what you and I couldn't do on our own — make a payment to satisfy what holy, righteous judgement required. His love for you and me sent Jesus to live as a man, face life as you and I do, and die on a cross as a replacement and payment for our sin. This loving God didn't send people to Hell — He made a way for them not to end up there.

In doing this He has made a way for us to be free of that punishment. He gives us the opportunity to receive this gift from Him:

> *For God so loved the world that He gave His only begotten Son, that whoever believes in Him should not perish but have everlasting life. For God did not send His Son into the world to condemn the world, but that the world through Him might be saved. He who believes in Him is not condemned; but he who does not believe is condemned already, because he has not believed in the name of the only begotten Son of God.*
> — John 3:16-18

You can receive God's gift of forgiveness right now, right where you are. We are promised in Romans 10:9-10:

> *If you confess with your mouth the Lord Jesus and believe in your heart that God has raised Him from the dead, you will be saved. For with the heart one believes unto righteousness, and with the mouth confession is made unto salvation.*

To receive God's salvation for you, repeat this prayer:

Heavenly Father, I come to You in the Name of Jesus. I believe that Jesus is your Son, that He paid the price on the Cross for my sins, and that He rose from the dead for my justification. I ask you to forgive me of my sins. Jesus, I ask you to become my Savior and the Lord of my life. From this day forward, I pledge myself to follow after you and ask for Your presence to be with me and guide me as I seek to become more and more like You. Thank you for saving me, and for being my Lord. Amen.

If you've prayed this prayer from your heart, you can rest in the knowledge that God heard you, forgave you of your sins, and took you in as His child. You are now part of the family of God!

If you would like to go further in God and have all He has for you, I encourage you to go to the next page and learn how you can receive the baptism in the Holy Spirit.

PRAYER FOR THE BAPTISM IN THE HOLY SPIRIT

If you would like to receive the baptism in the Holy Spirit, you can receive it right now, right where you are. God wants you to have the presence of the Holy Spirit living inside you AND the power of the Holy Spirit empowering you to live victoriously as a witness for Him to the world around you.

Repeat the prayer below and expect Jesus to baptize you in the Holy Spirit — just as He said He would do:

Jesus, I believe you are the Son of God and that you died for my sins. I believe You are faithful to Your word, and I come asking you to baptize me in the Holy Spirit.

After repeating this prayer, keep speaking out loud, thanking God for His faithfulness, praising Him for His goodness. You may experience new words coming up from inside you and out of your mouth as you speak. This is not something to be afraid of — it is the Holy Spirit speaking with and through you — a gift from God to every believer! It is often called "tongues," and it is scriptural. Allow it to flow out of you, understanding that it is the evidence of being baptized or filled with the Spirit. (*See* Acts 2:4; 10:45-46; 19:5.)

This praying in the Spirit, or praying in tongues, is more than just an initial experience. It is meant to empower you in your relationship with God on a daily basis. As you pray in the spirit, you will find it does the following:

IT WILL HELP YOU PRAY ACCORDING TO GOD'S WILL

Likewise the Spirit also helps in our weaknesses. For we do not know what we should pray for as we ought, but the Spirit Himself makes intercession for us with groanings which cannot be uttered. Now He who searches the hearts knows what the mind of the Spirit is, because He makes intercession for the saints according to the will of God.
— Romans 8:26-27

IT WILL STRENGTHEN YOUR FAITH

But you, beloved, building yourselves up on your most holy faith, praying in the Holy Spirit....
— Jude 20

YOU WILL SPEAK DIRECTLY TO GOD

For he who speaks in a tongue does not speak to men but to God, for no one understands him; however, in the spirit he speaks mysteries.
— 1 Corinthians 14:2

Make prayer a regular part of your life, both in your known tongue and praying in the spirit. It will revolutionize your relationship with God, and you will see Him move in amazing ways!

ENDNOTES

[1] Seifert, Bill. "Bridge and Tunnel Management." U.S. Department of Energy, December 11, 2020. https://www.directives.doe.gov/terms_definitions/tunnel-pedestrian.

[2] Spurgeon, Charles. "Profit and Loss." C. H. Spurgeon: Spurgeon's Sermons Vol. 02: 1856. https://ccel.org/ccel/spurgeon/sermons02/sermons02.xxxviii.html.

[3] Giles, Lionel, trans. "The Internet Classics Archive: The Art of War by Sun Tzu." The Internet Classics Archive | The Art of War by Sun Tzu. https://classics.mit.edu/Tzu/artwar.html.

[4] Easton, M.G. "Cubit." Easton's Bible Dictionary Online. https://www.biblestudytools.com/dictionaries/eastons-bible-dictionary/cubit.html.

[5] "Hope." Merriam-Webster. Accessed February 9, 2025. https://www.merriam-webster.com/dictionary/hope.

[6] "Wish ." Merriam-Webster. Accessed February 9, 2025. https://www.merriam-webster.com/dictionary/wish.

[7] "No Man's Land." Wikipedia. Accessed February 9, 2025. https://en.wikipedia.org/wiki/No_man%27s_land#:~:text=No%20man's%20land%20is%20waste,ground%20for%20refuse%20between%20fiefdoms.

WHEN GOD CHOSE A FATHER

When God chose a man to raise His Son, He looked for a man who would model His ways. In choosing Joseph, God committed Himself to helping him accomplish what was asked of him. Joseph was not alone, and neither are you. God desires to be intimately involved in your life and is ready to be all that you need Him to be. He created you for a purpose, and His love for you is great. Just as Joseph was chosen with a calling in mind, you have been called as well.

"When God Chose a Father" follows the unique perspective of Joseph, the earthly father of Jesus, using his story and anecdotes from Michael's own life to illustrate the detail that God desires to take as He is involved in our lives. Through the lens of what God looked for in the man to raise His own Son the reader is introduced to the realities of the situation Joseph faced, and the godly character traits found in him that qualified him in God's eyes. God's presence and provision are displayed in the life of the man that needed them dearly, with an emphasis on Joseph's trust in and reliance on God to help him be the man God had called him to be. Most of all, you will find that God has that same desire to be intimately involved in your life as well.

Available on Amazon, Barnes and Noble, and michaelclarkministries.org

www.ingramcontent.com/pod-product-compliance
Lightning Source LLC
Chambersburg PA
CBHW071953070526
44583CB00015B/1175